M&A

A Practical Guide to
Doing the Deal

Wiley Frontiers in Finance

M&A

A Practical Guide to
Doing the Deal

Jeffrey C. Hooke

John Wiley & Sons, Inc.

New York • Chichester • Brisbane • Toronto • Singapore • Weinheim

Copyright © 1997 by Jeffrey C. Hooke.
Published by John Wiley & Sons, Inc.

Library of Congress Cataloging-in-Publication Data:

Hooke, Jeffrey C.
      M&A : a practical guide to doing the deal /
Jeffrey C. Hooke
          p.   cm. — (Wiley frontiers in finance)
      Includes index.
      ISBN 0-471-14462-2 (cloth : alk. paper)
          1. Consolidation and merger of corporations—Finance.   I. Title.
      II. Series.
      HG4028.M4H66   1997
      658.1'6—dc20   96-10547

Printed in the United States of America

10   9   8   7   6

To Patty, for her love and understanding

PREFACE

Mergers and acquisitions occupy a strong position in American business and 1995 was a record year. The value of all announced deals exceeded $400 billion in 1995, including such blockbuster transactions as Disney's $19 billion acquisition of Capital Cities and Chemical Bank's $10 billion merger with Chase Manhattan. This surge in activity spread across all industry lines and encompassed corporations both large and small. While there was no guarantee that this wave of corporate combinations resulted in stronger operations and higher profits, many companies increasingly viewed buying others as a dynamic means of fostering growth.

In this charged environment, a modern manager understands the factors driving merger mania and considers acquisitions as one element of a broad corporate development plan. To do otherwise is to ignore a major source of corporate investment opportunities. After all, no one company has all the answers, or all the resources, and joining forces is sometimes the best way. Today's executive acknowledges this possibility, realizing that if a company isn't a buyer, then it might be a seller. For alert businesspeople, the proper response to this predicament is to learn more about doing deals and to prepare their company to be the hunter, rather than the hunted.

This book provides corporate executives and business students with a primer on merger and acquisitions. Items covered are the motives behind mergers, the pricing of transactions and the related negotiations, as well as key topics such as finding a deal and conducting due diligence. We will compare textbook theories with current practice and consider numerical examples against real-life illustrations.

Most of what you will read in this book refers to my experiences in investment banking. Other material consists of brief distillations of textbook theories I used as an adjunct professor at the business schools of the University of Maryland, Georgetown University, and George Washington University. The combination of real-world ideas with academic views is unique. It should make the book interesting to practitioners and students alike.

Most books surveying mergers and acquisitions fall into two categories: (1) academic textbooks and (2) practitioner-oriented handbooks. Both fail to give the reader a succinct, comprehensive, and practical review of the subject. Academic textbooks present lengthy theoretical overviews of the history and motives for corporate combinations, but shed little light on how real-world participants size up individual transactions. Furthermore, textbooks don't provide information on how to look for an acquisition, price a business, or negotiate a deal. The practitioner-oriented handbooks endeavor to supply guidance on these three subjects, but they emphasize one or two at the expense of the other. Handbooks compound this weakness by presenting the data in mind-numbing detail. They confront the reader with hundreds of pages on the manner of valuing companies or on the legal aspects of the merger process. Precious little time is devoted to rounding out the reader's knowledge of the totality of doing mergers. The forest is lost on account of the trees.

It is not surprising, therefore, that many students and businesspeople do not understand the dynamics behind the merger business, and may retain the mass media's preoccupation with the field as a "get rich quick" scheme achieved through hostile takeovers and merciless employee downsizing.

Why should a corporation pursue an acquisition program, instead of building up a business from within? There are grandly conceived reasons such as technology access, market share gain or product line extension, but what is the cost of carrying out these objectives for shareholders? This book contains an analytical method to evaluate acquisition strategies applicable to either the large or small company considering the purchase of a business.

The singular objective of any merger or acquisition should be to increase or maintain shareholder value. While this goal can be stated simply, the means of achieving it through mergers and acquisitions are many and varied. A key part of any corporate acquisition strategy is narrowing the management's focus to those transactions which fit the acquirer's operating skills, the acquirer's financial capabilities, and its shareholders' risk-taking profile. While certain elements of the strategy may be financially driven (e.g., the company may be only able to raise a certain amount of financing), a lot of consideration needs to be paid early on to a corporate self-examination regarding the reason for undertaking a merger. The book begins with a discussion of this topic, which is then followed by chapters reviewing each step of the acquisition process, from finding a possible opportunity and analyzing it, to closing a transaction. Distinct chapters are devoted to studying the motives of financial buyers, or management buyout firms, which represent a significant portion of acquisition activity. The final part of the book considers the process of selling a business, an important step for large corporations as well as family-run companies that are contemplating the sale of all, or a portion, of a business.

For convenience, the pronoun "he" has been used throughout this book to refer nonspecifically to buyers and sellers; the material herein will be equally useful to both men and women who are doing deals in the "real world."

Finally, a word of caution for potential practitioners. This book's objective is to provide a practical, well-rounded overview of the mergers and acquisitions business, but no book can substitute for skilled and experienced advisers in the fields of investment banking, law, and accounting—areas of expertise that are critical to carrying out a transaction properly. While the adviser's participation can usually be delayed until the buyer is contemplating a bid, the high cost of acquisitions, the individualized nature of each transaction, and the number of arcane details involved call for experienced professionals to play an active role in at least these three specialties, not to mention additional experts in fields such as labor relations, employee benefits, and taxes.

JEFFREY C. HOOKE

Chevy Chase, Maryland
September 1996

CONTENTS

1 CORPORATE GROWTH STRATEGIES

Sustained growth of sales and earnings is vital to the survival of the firm. This growth is also critical for evaluating and compensating management. Mergers can be a tool to foster growth alongside alternative strategies such as start-ups, joint ventures, marketing affiliations, licensing, and franchising.

CORPORATE VERSUS BUSINESS UNIT STRATEGY

Corporate strategy is an outgrowth of the long-term evaluation of a business. A company typically starts out as a one-product-line business, a status that then changes as it expands into areas related to the original product focus, enters new product lines, and extends its reach into new markets. Multiple-industry activities are now the norm for the Fortune 500 companies, which are often active in several businesses that may seem entirely unrelated to one another. General Electric Corporation, for example, has gone far afield of its roots. From originally manufacturing electric lights, it now segments its diversified business units among 12 divisional groupings, including industries as different as aircraft engines, broadcasting, and appliances.

As large corporations have evolved into groupings of disparate businesses, senior managers have increasingly sought to distinguish between "corporate strategy" and "business unit strategy."

Business unit strategy is easy to define for managers because it is expressed in terms of the competitive environment for a single business; the discussion is thus limited to a select group of products and markets. What will be the business unit's strategy to increase market share, to roll out new products, to respond to competitor innovations? These questions are answered in a three- to five-year planning framework that incorporates management's views on likely changes in the relevant industry. Imagine this same process for a diversified corporation like General Electric. Integration of the business plans of its many businesses into some grand, unified "corporate strategy" is a tall order.

Long-term considerations extend past the scope of the five-year business plan, and they involve an ephemeral kind of study as the planners realize the futility of predicting the distant future. Common long-term strategic plans catalog the business unit's internal strengths and weaknesses, and how these attributes present future market opportunities. To wit, a U.S. cereal company believes it has demonstrated strengths in producing and marketing cereal in the United States and Mexico. A long-term strategic option is to extend the company's market penetration into Brazil and Argentina, two large Latin markets that are heavily influenced by Mexican and U.S. consumer trends.

For years, McKinsey & Company, the management consulting firm, directed the development of competitive strategies with its popular SWOT analysis.

S	Strengths
W	Weaknesses
O	Opportunities
T	Threats

The SWOT acronym appears constantly in business magazines and business school publications. The SWOT framework offers managers a clear-cut outline on weighing units' strengths and weaknesses, seeking new growth opportunities within this evaluation, and protecting base businesses against encroachment from competitors. SWOT and similar strategic modes of thinking enable managers to address key issues of business growth and survival, in a simple and appealing framework.

EXHIBIT 1-1   Typical holding company structure

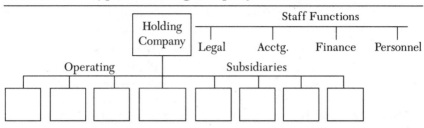

Consider the typical, Fortune 500 corporation (see Exhibit 1-1). It is organized as holding company, and its primary assets are the common shares of various companies. These many subsidiary firms are the business units which actually make the products or provide the services that are sold to customers.

While SWOT is helpful at the single business unit level, it has less relevance for larger companies. Too many variables need to be plugged into the SWOT framework for the big holding company. How can GE integrate its Gas Turbine SWOT with its Financial Services SWOT in a sensible way? The end result is a "garbage in, garbage out" collage of corporate SWOT for the diversified enterprise. How does a rational person then develop a coherent strategy for the holding company, remembering that each operating business is constantly refining its own competitive strategy?

This question has perplexed business school professors and high-level executives alike. To date, their ruminations on corporate strategy have been hopelessly intertwined with business unit competitive strategies. The nebulous result has been an articulation of corporate strategy that is neither understandable nor satisfying.

CORE COMPETENCIES

One widely accepted principle is that the holding company strategy should be to nurture and preserve a group of "core competencies" in the corporation. These competencies can be shared within the corporation, and also extended to entirely new businesses or acquisitions entering the holding company fold. From this sharing principle, the concept of "synergy" is easily drawn, implying as it does, that a holding company's resources can improve the operational performance of a start-up business, medium-stage venture, or new acquisition.

The "core competence" strategic discipline would make sense if companies exchanged skills and resources in a seamless fashion, but such an ideal operating environment would require a strong senior management that is in constant control. The logical theory thus encounters problems in the everyday world of corporate life. Most multidivisional corporations are highly decentralized. Operating managers are reasonably autonomous. In return for this independence, they are expected to meet clearly established numerical targets in such statistical categories as sales, earnings, and return on assets. These managers have little incentive to contribute to "core competence" sharing. Preoccupied with their own subsidiary objectives, they have even less incentive to attend theoretical corporate strategy sessions that don't affect them directly. Large corporations are not "big, happy families." Competition within corporations is fierce and division executives have little desire to share competencies.

PORTFOLIO APPROACH

Recognizing the limitations of sharing competencies, a popular competing strategic framework for the large holding company is the "portfolio approach." For example, Hanson Industries describes its operations as a portfolio. It participates in six different industry segments: Aggregates, Chemicals, Coal, Construction, Forest Products, and Tobacco. Under this discipline, the disparate operating businesses of a large corporation are nothing more than a collection of assets. Any business units having similar operational characteristics are combined, leaving little substantive operating synergy between the divisions, which act more or less independently. The holding company acts as the repository of excess cash generated at the divisional level, and it dispenses finance, legal advice, personnel regulations, and accounting services to the divisions. In most cases, the holding company is the divisional bank, and the division managers must apply to the bank to obtain new capital. New business ideas are appraised by the bank, which considers whether the divisional applicant has researched its request properly and whether the divisional applicant has the skills necessary to put the capital to efficient use.

The "portfolio strategy" approach became widely accepted in the 1960s as "beta" and "portfolio" theory reached their zenith. Companies sought to acquire a portfolio of nonrelated assets to reduce their perceived business risk. Investors, they reasoned, would pay more for low-risk stocks. Since then, the portfolio approach has evolved and deviated from its equity investment roots. Operating managers now place less importance on reducing beta and risk. Instead, they focus on finding, growing, and harvesting a collection of businesses. This revised corporate strategy is summarized by the famous Boston Consulting Group (BCG) growth/share matrix (see Exhibit 1-2).

The growth/share matrix enables holding company managers to classify each "division," each "business," or each "asset" into a quadrant. The manager then considers whether to implement the recommended strategy for assets falling into that respective quadrant. According to the strategy, the cash thrown off by divisions with strong market shares in low-growth markets (cash cows) is reinvested in "stars" to support their growth and market share objectives. Alternatively, the cash is siphoned off to "question marks" to assist in their push to become stars. "Dogs" (mature divisions with small market shares in low-growth markets) receive little capital, even if they are profitable; they are candidates for divestiture, as a means to generate more cash for the question marks and stars. Like SWOT, the BCG framework is simple, but effective, and it has influenced a generation of managers.

EXHIBIT 1-2   How to define an operating division by the BCG Growth/Share Matrix

Market Growth Rate	10%		
		Star	Question Mark
	5%		
		Cash Cow	Dog
	0%		
		×2.0	×1.0 ×0.5

Divisional Market Share Relative to Largest Competitor

VALUE-BASED STRATEGY

Over time, many investors have realized that neither the "core competency" nor the "portfolio assets" strategy works properly. Multidivisional holding companies offer neither dramatic operating synergies nor reduced business risk. Instead, these companies often present investors with an eclectic collection of businesses overloaded with expensive corporate overhead and ill-defined strategy. Matters reached a head in the 1980s when many conglomerate businesses were acquired, either through corporate takeovers or leveraged buyouts. The slices of the "corporate pie" were then sold off to the highest bidder. Rising from the ashes of these early restructurings was a strategic framework based on "creating value." Like the portfolio of assets theme, value-based thinking emphasizes maximizing shareholder value over the near term. Essentially, if the stock market values a holding company below the sum of its individual divisional values, value-based strategy advocates separating the divisions to overcome the price discount. A holding company could sell an individual division for cash, spin off a portion of a division's shares to existing shareholders, or simply liquidate itself by selling off all its component parts. To follow this strategy, each division, as part of the holding company, must contribute positively to stock market value.

The growing acceptance of this value-based strategy has caused holding company directors to look far more closely at proposed acquisitions that don't clearly contribute to "total corporate value." The obvious offenders are "diversification-type" acquisitions, which don't bring complementary core competencies to the corporation.

Professional managers and business school professors continuously struggle with the concept of a unified strategy for a diversified enterprise. Financial objectives, such as EPS growth are easy to define, and can be expressed in comparative terms. Business objectives are less quantifiable. Most strategists suggest beginning a corporate strategy by defining the corporation and its goals. Often times this effort fails, and the vision statement deteriorates into simplistic statements that offer executives considerable latitude. A cable TV executive can say, "We're not in the cable TV business; we're in the entertainment business," thereby justifying entries into all kinds of entertainment businesses ranging from movie studios to amusement parks. Ted

Turner is a good example of this mentality. A software executive can say, "We want to be the IBM of the software business," without mentioning more specifics. Consider the remarks of Tom Johnston, a Hallmark Cards vice president who was appointed the new president of Sutton Place Gourmet, a Maryland-based gourmet food chain. How to establish the link between greeting cards and foods? "I've been in the occasion-celebration business for 18 years . . . and food is one of the key ways to celebrate an occasion."

Value-based management encourages a close examination of growth alternatives which are cheaper than acquisitions. The obvious alternative is internal growth but reasonably-priced external measures may include:

- Joint ventures.
- Investment in outside start-ups.
- Marketing and distribution alliances.
- Franchising.
- Licensing.

Each of these five alternative strategies involves a third party. For the corporation, this means a reduced degree of control and ownership relative to an acquisition. Each alternative also carries the risk of the third party copying the corporation's product or technology in anticipation of the eventual termination of the arrangement.

2 WHY ACQUIRE A BUSINESS?

Mergers and acquisitions have promoted corporate growth for over a century. The most pronounced results of the earliest efforts were the huge corporate combinations that produced the Standard Oil Trust, U.S. Steel, and General Motors. Economies of scale and market share gains were key development goals of these companies, which sought to expand within their base businesses. While this type of acquisition activity has been a consistent theme, it has been supplemented at various times with different objectives. In the 1960s, a sharp increase in mergers was sparked by a conglomeration craze, as firms such as ITT and RCA attempted to reduce their business risk through diversification. Accordingly, many firms purchased businesses that had operations that were far afield of the buyer's base business. The 1970s saw many companies preferring to "buy" rather than "build" as stock prices for businesses failed to reflect the inflation-induced increase in the value of their underlying assets. In the 1980s, financial buyers created a merger boom, in part backed up by the lending community's willingness to provide large sums to highly leveraged companies, which in turn predicted ever-rising earnings levels. Whatever the format turns out to be for 1996 and beyond, it is clear that mergers and acquisitions have become a staple of the American business scene. Indeed, thousands of transactions have been completed already in the 1990s.

Nevertheless, despite the continuing popularity of mergers, many acquisitions lose money for the buyers after considering the cost of financing. In fact, even with positive cash flow many transactions become significant drains on the acquirer's management resources, which, in turn, lowers the perception of the buyer's market value. With these apparent pitfalls, why do mergers and acquisitions continue? Because history shows that acquisitions are one of the surest ways of accomplishing ambitious corporate growth targets with acceptable returns.

Buying a business can be favorably compared with expanding an existing line of products, starting up an entirely new venture, or entering into a halfway arrangement such as a joint venture, passive investment, or marketing alliance. Compared with these alternatives, buying an established business can be a preferable development strategy for four key reasons:

1. *Less Risk*. Established businesses that are acquired have a developed customer base, a verifiable financial track record and a demonstrated product line. The prospective acquisition has long ago passed its most risky phase of corporate life, the start-up.

2. *Infrastructure for Growth*. The acquired company's plant, technology, reputation, and employee base provide the buyer with a ready-made infrastructure. The potential for growth is significantly enhanced if the buyer uses this infrastructure more effectively than the prior owner.

3. *Conservation of Capital Investment*. Most extensions of existing product lines require significant operating capital beyond an initial investment. In contrast, as a stand-alone investment, many acquisitions produce income and positive cash flow immediately. Financing corporate growth can be easier via acquisition because lenders and outside investors see the acquisition itself as predictably contributing funds to pay debt service and provide shareholder returns, respectively.

4. *Control*. Alternatives to an acquisition—joint ventures, passive equity investments in third parties, and marketing/distribution alliances—require less capital, but offer reduced control. The potential

acquirer's return on its investment would depend on someone outside of the corporate umbrella.

An acquisition may be a low-risk alternative to internal expansion or a new venture, but buying businesses in itself holds no guarantee of higher shareholder value. Whatever value is to be obtained from an acquisition must be derived from a formal strategy that is carefully implemented. Knowledge of when to pay the right price is an important element of this strategy. The opportunities are there, but true wealth creation through acquisition often eludes even the most capable businesspeople. Thus, a deliberate plan of action is critical for the potential acquirer.

Perhaps the first question before corporate management is: Which of the numerous M&A strategies should be followed in the pursuit of profits? Successful programs have included the following:

- Purchasing businesses that compete with the buyer's products to gain market share.
- Buying companies with products that flow through the same distribution system as the buyer's.
- Acquiring companies that represent product line extensions of the buyer.
- "Breaking up" businesses to realize hidden asset values.
- "Bottom fishing" for distressed companies.
- Management buyouts.

For each strategy, one finds numerous corporations, investment groups, or wealthy individuals who have turned that strategy to their own advantage. Yet among these successful investment professionals runs a consistent theme: a disciplined approach to the business of mergers and acquisitions.

3 DISCIPLINE IN ACQUIRING COMPANIES

Successful acquisitions depend not only on the strategy a person selects but also on the discipline with which the strategy is implemented. The corporate world is littered with hundreds of companies suffering from the ill effects of an excessive leverage incurred from buying a business entirely with debt, an overpayment for an acquisition that diluted earnings per share, or an ill-planned attempt at diversification. In many of these cases, management may have evinced a clear-cut set of goals for its acquisition strategy, but when faced with a sizable and immediate opportunity, rationalized the disciplined goals away, to claim a visible prize. AT&T's 1990 takeover of NCR for $7.5 billion was supposed to be the start of a global computer network. Postintegration problems, cultural differences, and the high price conspired to hurt AT&T's operating results for years.

INSTANT SUCCESS IS RARE

Many poor acquisitions are the result of the "Let's Do Something" corporate mentality, which equates patience or inaction in the M&A field with passiveness. The ensuing rush to do a deal can be harmful, particularly when the buyer gets into a protracted auction for an acquisition target and ends up paying a much higher price than originally anticipated. Immediate success is rare in any field and acquisitions are no exception. Potential buyers must exercise discipline in purchasing businesses. Caution and patience are essential. The books written by chest-beating practitioners such as Donald Trump would have you believe the opposite. Many magazine and newspaper articles echo similar sentiments, often describing only wildly profitable transactions such as where a leveraged buyout firm made ten times its money over a three-year period, or where a conglomerate restructured an acquired firm and sold it for five times the original price.

Academic textbooks and practitioner-oriented handbooks do little to dispel these notions. Even the most complete handbook spends very little time explaining the need for discipline in evaluating acquisitions, and most make short shrift of the analytical process that would narrow the reader's focus. Acquisition textbooks invariably emphasize the history of mergers, their strategic rationale, and the financial modeling that accompanies a proposed deal. Practitioner guidebooks provide either a lengthy elaboration of the step-by-step process needed to close a transaction, or a sterile, quantitative explanation of how to value a potential acquisition. Nowhere do the authors mention the difficulty in locating the right business or the disappointments and frustrations encountered along the way. The importance of developing a disciplined strategy and sticking to it is usually lost in the thicket of development theories and financial calculations.

In fact, successful acquirers look very hard to find acceptable transactions. Many firms employ executives who work full time, constantly screening acquisition proposals brought to them, or developing leads from their contacts in the business and financial communities. They may review hundreds of opportunities per year and visit 20 to 30 prospects annually before they feel comfortable enough to bid on an acceptable transaction. Even then, the deal may be lost to a competitor, or the owner of the business may simply decide not to sell.

An acquisition search can be long and tedious, stretching over months and years and requiring the intense effort of numerous professionals. At any given time, there are usually thousands of prospects. For every business that is openly being advertised by investment bankers or business brokers, there are dozens whose owners will quietly consider unsolicited offers. The vast majority of these companies are not good investments under any acquisition strategy. The primary reason for their unsuitability is that the owner is asking for a price that prevents an acquirer from making a reasonable return on investment. The rare opportunity that meets the criteria of a given acquisition strategy *and* is fairly priced must be gleaned from hundreds of unsuitable candidates.

Once a deal is done, however, its effects on corporate growth can be substantial. In one transaction, a discount department store chain increased the number of its stores by 40% by acquiring for $25 million an underperforming chain adjacent to its market area. Negotiating and closing the transaction took over two years. Within six months of the signing, the buyer remodeled the stores, stocked them with fresh inventory, and reduced overhead. By employing a classic "bottom fishing" or "buy cheap, fix it up" strategy, which it had used once before on a smaller deal, the acquirer was able to turn a break-even operation into a division earning more than $8 million annually in less than 10 months. As a result of the transaction and its follow-up, the acquirer's earnings per share doubled over the period and propelled its share price to new highs. The stockholders enjoyed an increase in the value of their shares that far exceeded the $25 million purchase price. The company could not have grown as quickly or as successfully by adding to its store base through new construction. An acquisition was the key to growth.

That particular buyer was constantly looking for acquisition candidates that fit its "buy cheap, fix it up" strategy. Even after the decision was made to undertake the described transaction, the investigation, analysis, and closing process was arduous, complicated, and frustrating. The completion of the transaction took slightly over two years, and the buyer's upfront due diligence and legal costs easily exceeded a half million dollars.

THE LONG SEARCH PROCESS

Notwithstanding the braggadocio of various self-styled acquisition gurus, truly good deals are difficult to find. No matter which strategy a company chooses to pursue, the inevitable result is a long, tedious march through the morass of investment bankers, business brokers, financial advisers, reluctant sellers, target company executives, corporate lawyers, independent accountants, tax experts, pension consultants, and environmental experts. The search is destined to be long for three reasons: (1) The strategy selected is bound to limit the criteria through which candidates are selected; (2) the owners of many candidates have unrealistic price expectations and frequently refuse to acknowledge the shortcomings of their respective businesses; and (3) a potential buyer faces competition from others in the same business, some of which are not exercising the same price discipline.

Although active acquirers need to look for acceptable acquisitions, the *perfect* deal is almost impossible to find—perhaps one among a thousand candidates. There are those corporate development officers, investment groups, or entrepreneurs who insist on purchasing businesses that meet all their respective strategic criteria. Such participants labor under illusions about the realities of the merger and acquisition field and they represent the field's more nettlesome players—the "Window Shoppers." They seek something that tends to exist only in the imagination of most deal makers: a quality business at a dirt-cheap price.

Nevertheless, Window Shoppers routinely try to see every property crossing the market and continually request to the various purveyors of transactions that they be permitted to examine the merchandise. A smart buyer, on the other hand, has a sensible goal in mind—to get the good value. The prime acquisition candidate may not be top-ranked in every category set by the buyer's strategic goals, but the deal has a price that can yield an acceptable return on investment.

Many a potential acquirer abandons a disciplined search in exchange for an immediate result. Impatience arises as deal after deal is found wanting, or its bids are superseded by eager competitors. In other cases, the sellers may pull out at the last minute for unexplained reasons, or the deals may be held up by arcane legal problems or environmental issues. The livelihoods of many development executives depend on closing transactions rather than increasing long-term shareholder value. Thus, they are motivated to compromise on their employer's acquisition criteria by nailing down businesses that raise the buyer's sales volume, without a realistic chance for a corresponding increase in earnings. If top management is aware of the possibility of this charade and refuses to go along, the appropriate top-level response to the line executive's frustrations has to be either "Don't worry, just keep trying," or "Let's consider a change in our criteria, or an alteration in our strategy."

The seller's financial adviser frequently adds to the pressure on the buyer. This adviser, usually an executive of an investment bank, a commercial bank or a business brokerage, minimizes every flaw in his client's business and point out its "tremendous prospects for the future." He might point out the unique synergies in a proposed combination, or the "understated" asset values on the seller's balance sheet. The arguments strongly justify his client's price objectives. The buyer's executives should not be seduced by these relentless sales pitches.

Whenever an ideal acquisition appears, the frustrated buyer may disregard its acquisition criteria and justify a high purchase price. This situation becomes particularly acute when well-financed competitors bid for a large, well-managed public company. When anxiety threatens to overwhelm the application of reason, the potential buyer should step back and examine the implications of buying the wrong business or paying too much. The 1988 bidding for RJR Nabisco, for example, started at $75 and ended at $109 per share. Before the auction, the stock traded at $45 per share. In many cases, the price required to purchase the public company is excessive, but the potential buyer, having already invested thousands of dollars and hours in investigating the transaction, is reluctant to let the deal slip away. In such a circumstance, walking away from the deal is difficult, but it is probably the best decision. The alternative is to analyze the transaction through rose-colored glasses, either by inflating the acquisition's asset values or by subjecting its cash flow projections to superoptimistic assumptions.

Deluding oneself to get a deal done is quite common. Perhaps in no other time were the excesses more apparent than with leveraged buyout firms in the late 1980s. An LBO firm paid over 20 times earnings for a cyclical manufacturing business in a 1989 auction. The financial projections provided to the firm's lenders group and investors showed a steady 8 percent growth in sales over the 10-year projected period, with gradual increases in operating margins. The plan ignored probable interruptions of sales growth and profit margins due to an economic recession, despite a preponderance of evidence indicating these risks. Recessionary price reductions and unit volume declines hurt the LBO's financial performance in 1991, eventually causing the company to file for bankruptcy.

SUMMARY

The search for good acquisition candidates is long and tedious. Most of the candidates that meet a defined set of criteria will be unsuitable because of an unreasonably high asking price. Months of studying potential prospects, visiting companies, and bidding on possible transactions may result in frustration and a temptation to close a transaction that results in unsatisfactory returns. The key for success is maintaining a discipline throughout the process by keeping a rigorous balance between value and price.

4 THE MERITS OF GROWTH THROUGH ACQUISITION

Most companies do not start out looking to grow through acquisition. Buyers decide to search for other businesses when they realize that their core operations are not providing sufficient opportunities for growth or adequate investment returns. Expanding the existing product line would appear to be the most sensible growth tactic, but the company's traditional products may have low margins or tough competitive prospects that discourage making additional commitments. A totally new business sector might be an appealing alternative, but starting up a new venture is problematic for most established corporations. Many companies can afford initiating a new business, yet they lack the entrepreneurial drive to succeed. Also, the chance of failure is quite high in a new venture and therefore too risky for most modern-day corporate managers, who are expected to provide corporate lenders and shareholders with a steady stream of quarterly earnings per share increases. A write-off from a losing new business idea can damage these earnings trends.

TYPICAL ALTERNATIVE GROWTH STRATEGIES FALLING SHORT OF AN ACQUISITION

Common half measures that fall in between "building" (establishing a new venture from the ground up) and "buying" (acquiring an existing business "lock, stock, and barrel") include joint ventures, minority shareholdings in alliances, franchising, and licensing. Each of these growth strategies entails less management and monetary commitment than a full-scale acquisition. A lower commitment level has a distinct appeal for a company that may be unsure of a new product or market, or one that doesn't want to risk the capital that growth requires. These half measures permit the would-be acquirer to "get its feet wet" in a new business; the main drawback is a lack of control, a critical obstacle for many managers. These arrangements employ separate management groups that are less than 100% beholden to the company that is seeking growth in its own financial results. Summary advantages and disadvantages of key growth strategies are presented in Exhibit 4-1.

While many corporate managers are attracted to strategies that offer more corporate growth with reduced capital investment, they dislike the poor control features that accompany extensive third-party participation, such as in Strategies 3–7 (see Exhibit 4-1). They know that they are accountable for overall corporate performance, which includes the results of joint ventures, marketing alliances and licensing arrangements, so why place a lot of resources where management control is less than complete?

CONTROLLING EARNINGS PERFORMANCE

The avoidance of third-party alliances by some firms seems a narrow view but it is logical. Large corporate managers are expected to show a continuous increase in sales and earnings. Unforeseen earnings "hiccups" can be one outcome of a strategy that is dependent on operations administered outside the corporate control umbrella. Repeated deviation from a predictable pattern of growth sounds a death knell for a company's share price, and while a chief executive can delay his own ouster for years, the possibility of third parties advancing the event through a takeover increases if a public company underperforms. Control thus continues to be a key managerial consideration.

EXHIBIT 4-1   Key corporate growth strategies that fall short of an acquisition

Strategy	Primary Advantages	Primary Disadvantages
1. Expansion or extension of existing product lines	Logical progression of core competencies Probably less expensive Reduced risk	Not accessing new markets
2. In-house new venture	100% control Provide complete technology and customer access	High failure rate Large companies are not entrepreneurial
3. Joint venture	Share expenses Learning experience Partner may have complementary core competencies not owned by company	Share control and profits Theft of core competencies
4. Passive minority shareholding in an unaffiliated company	Little management commitment Outside start-ups may welcome the interest Liquid investment in the case of publicly traded firms	Poor control elements Unknown endgame in most cases No enhancement of corporate competencies
5. Marketing and distribution alliances	Capital investment needs reduced in comparison to alternatives Cheap means of accessing new markets Often cancelable with few penalties	Limited control ability Risk of third-party theft of product knowledge or technology
6. Franchising	Capital usually provided by franchisee Rapid expansion potential	Application limited to a few industries (restaurants, retailing, some services) Limited control over franchises
7. Licenses	Near zero capital investment Extend brand to new products Cheap means of accessing new markets	Very poor control elements

THE KEY MERIT OF ACQUISITIONS: REDUCED RISK

The element of risk in a new business start-up cannot be understated. Even the most skillful venture capital firm accepts that 7 of 10 new businesses are going to fail. Of the remaining three investments, two are likely to be break-even or marginally profitable propositions. One out of 10 start-ups is successful, perhaps wildly so. In fact, returns of 40 to 1 are not unheard of in the venture capital industry. For every "home run" investment, however, venture capitalists experience dozens of strikeouts. While venture capitalists can commiserate with their colleagues over their low success rate, the large corporation faces a public shareholder constituency. Public shareholders are less forgiving of failure and have less understanding of risk than the venture capital community. To satisfy shareholders, the large company has to strike a fine balance between return and risk. It emphasizes investments that for the most part, promise reasonable returns in exchange for moderate risks. The majority of acquisitions fit into this characterization.

Reduced operating risk and complete control are the primary virtues of growing through acquisition. Two other factors promote transactions: *leverage potential* and *value enhancement*.

Virtues of Acquisitions
- *Reduced Operating Risk.* The buyer avoids start-up problems.
- *Complete Control.* The buyer owns 100 percent of the business.
- *Leverage Potential.* The buyer can borrow part of the acquisition price.
- *Value Enhancement.* The buyer can improve the acquisition's earnings.

LEVERAGE

Because they often generate their own cash flow, most acquisitions provide the buyer with additional borrowing power. Internal start-up businesses, in contrast, are more dependent on the sponsoring corporation providing the cash for working capital, preoperating costs, and capital investment. The acquired cash flow increases the buyer's earnings before the effect of acquisition debt service, and many times earnings are higher after debt service. The buyer's total asset values also increase, by including the acquired assets on the buyer's balance sheet. Lenders like lending against asset values so more assets usually translate into more leverage availability. The purchaser, therefore, need only finance a portion of the acquisition price from its own capital. The remainder is obtained from a bank loan, institutional debt placement, or bond sale. Debt financing limits the need for equity funding, reducing ownership dilution resulting from an acquisition.

Acquisition leverage reached its zenith during the LBO craze of the 1980s. Financial investors frequently purchased large operating businesses with an equity investment as low as 10% of the purchase price. Ninety percent leverage increased the equity investor's potential rate of return.

Assume an investor has the choice of buying a $20 million business with either a 50% cash down payment or a 10% cash down payment:

Safe Alternative— 50% Down Payment	LBO Alternative— 10% Down Payment
Debt: $10 Million	Debt: $18 Million
Equity: $10 Million	Equity: $2 Million
$20 Million Purchase Price	$20 Million Purchase Price

Over the five-year holding period, the investor anticipates $1 million per year in dividends under the Safe Alternative. By year 5, he hopes to sell the company, net of debt, for $30 million. The rate of return on this investment is 23%. Exhibit 4-2 summarizes the investor's cash flow on a pretax basis.

The LBO Alternative (Exhibit 4-3) has higher debt service, so the same investor receives no dividends over the period. Indeed, the lenders prohibit the payment of cash dividends with such high leverage. The LBO Alternative's 50% internal rate of return, nevertheless, is far superior; it is two times higher than that of the conservative Safe Alternative.

The LBO Alternative carries more risk. A downward movement in the acquisition's earnings from a recession or competitive price war would damage the debt-servicing capability. One missed interest

EXHIBIT 4-2　Safe Alternative—50% down payment (US$ millions)

	Year					
	0	**1**	**2**	**3**	**4**	**5**
Equity investment	(10.0)	—	—	—	—	—
Dividends	—	1.0	1.0	1.0	1.0	1.0
Sale of company	—	—	—	—	—	30.0
Repayment of debt	—	—	—	—	—	(10.0)
Cash (outflow) inflow, net	(10.0)	1.0	1.0	1.0	1.0	21.0

payment can throw the business into the hands of its lenders, wiping out the owner's equity values. A moderately leveraged business, in contrast, has breathing room when cash flow difficulties occur.

LBO investors routinely use high leverage. Knowing the risks, they evaluate risk/return parameters in a venture-capitalist-like framework. Recessions, price wars and other business problems occur routinely, so they figure 10% to 20% of their transactions will be wildly successful, 20% to 30% moderately profitable to break-even, and 50% to 60% money losers or bankruptcies. The average result provides a satisfactory investment return. One study by two University of Chicago professors backed up this view of risk. It concluded that one-third of the LBOs completed between 1985 and 1989 defaulted on their debts. Other LBOs avoided defaults by restructuring obligations and diluting their owners' equity interests in favor of the creditors.

EXHIBIT 4-3　LBO Alternative—10% down payment (US$ millions)

	Year					
	0	**1**	**2**	**3**	**4**	**5**
Purchase of company	(2.0)	—	—	—	—	—
Cash dividends	—	—	—	—	—	1.0
Sale of company	—	—	—	—	—	30.0
Repayment of debt	—	—	—	—	—	(18.0)
Cash (Outflow) inflow, net	(2.0)	—	—	—	—	13.0

Financially oriented acquirers and many established companies speculate when granted access to substantial amounts of leverage. "Speculation" means that investors spend a little of their own money (and a lot of their lenders') for companies with purchase prices that are out of line with future prospects. The primary opportunity for profit is another optimistic buyer down the road, the "greater sucker theory." One firsthand example of leverage's excesses occurred in 1986, when I was advising a $60 million (sales) consumer products company. Having received two bids of US $30 million from industry players, I was surprised when a respected LBO firm offered 50% more, or $45 million. The firm insisted on going to contract before seeing the operation, interviewing the owner, or visiting the management!

LEVERAGE AND ACQUISITION SPECULATION

By the late 1980s, high prices turned many corporate acquisitions into speculative investments. Financial buyers no longer appraised a company on its ability to generate cash flow so as to provide a long-term return to its new shareholders. Instead, buyers were drawn to the acquisition market solely on the basis of the laws of probability. With only a 10% down payment in each deal, LBO investors could achieve acceptable rates of return with only three or four successes in every ten deals. The bankrupt transactions meant losses of 100%, but the successful deals provided returns of 400% to 500%. Predicted losses were covered by the prospective gains. As a consequence, the demand for an acquisition that could support leverage, even if fanciful projections were needed, exceeded the supply. Large and small companies alike received multiple LBO inquiries.

The optimistic views of anxious lenders and frenzied equity investors fueled the price spiral. Established companies reliant on acquisition growth contributed to the mania. Both sets of buyers used imaginative financing schemes to attract lenders. Toward the end of the LBO craze, normally conservative bond investors were handing over hard cash for payment-in-kind (PIK) debt securities. Issued by companies hard-pressed to make cash interest payments, PIK securities didn't pay cash interest because the LBO was simply too strapped by the need to allocate cash to senior bank lenders. Upon seeing the first publicly traded PIK issue, a senior investment banker, who had seen it all over a 30-year career, handed me the prospectus and re-marked, "When bonds don't pay cash interest, it's a whole new world."

ENHANCING THE VALUE OF THE DEAL: $2 = $3

Besides additional leverage capacity, a buyer receives another important benefit from an acquisition: the possibility of enhancing the target's value. Once the transaction is complete, the buyer's management can make over the new operation. Duplicative costs are reduced and unnecessary overhead is eliminated. Perhaps the sales of the acquired business can be increased by integrating its marketing efforts with those of the buyer. This was the thinking of Quaker Oats management when it bought Snapple for $1.7 billion in 1994; it wanted to integrate Snapple into its Gatorade marketing and distribution systems. In certain cases, a clever buyer sells off nonessential assets to decrease the deal's effective price. Buyers enhance acquisition values in any number of ways, and many gladly pay "$2" for a business, confident that they can transform it into a "$3" value. One deal-making skill is the ability to envision the full potential of a company's assets.

The "$2 equals $3" rationale takes many forms. One common justification is "undermanagement," an implication that the target firm's management is either incompetent, poorly motivated, or just not performing up to potential. A senior corporate development executive at ITT Corporation, a conglomerate that used to buy 40 to 50 businesses a year, told me that undermanagement was the motivating factor in 80% of ITT's deals. A second "$2 equals $3" approach results from complementary resources among buyers and sellers. A firm may be very weak in one area such as marketing; and consequently, a merger with a company that has a strong marketing department can lead to improved sales. Pillsbury's purchase of Haagan Dazs is a good example of this kind of synergistic merger, since Pillsbury used its marketing strengths to expand Haagan Dazs nationally. Selling a company to obtain marketing or other skills is a drastic step; hiring a few marketing professionals may be preferable to auctioning off the entire business.

SYNERGY: $2 + $2 = $5

In larger corporate combinations, the value enhancement sometimes spills over to the buyer's operations. Combining the buyer's business with the acquired business brings the potential for better performance in both operations. The resulting "2 + 2 = 5" effect is referred to as "synergy." While operating synergies do occur, many buyers abuse the term to justify high-priced deals.

A popular 2 + 2 = 5 rationale lies in the economies of scale that exist in an industry in which the buyer and seller are active. One or both of the companies may not be operating at a level high enough to achieve these economies of scale. Chrysler's acquisition of the much smaller American Motors in 1987 was a good example of an acquisition prompted in large part by the need for American Motors to achieve economies of scale. At the time, auto industry experts acknowledged that survival in the U.S. auto industry required annual volume of one million cars. American Motor's annual production levels were then hovering around 400,000. Chrysler was a distant third in the U.S. auto industry and needed more cars to put through its distribution system. The combination of Chrysler and American Motors provided mutual economies of scale. It demonstrated the 2 + 2 = 5 rationale.

While economies of scale are one rationale, the 2 + 2 = 5 argument finds its most frequent use in three other kinds of transactions: buying the competition, strategic deals, and leveraged buyouts.

2 + 2 = 5 Deals

- *Economies of Scale.* The economies promote efficiencies for both parties.
- *Buying the Competition.* The combination brings efficiencies and less competition for both parties.
- *Strategic Deals.* Two different businesses can exchange skills and resources.
- *Leveraged Buyouts.* Management incentives motivate performance.

"*Buying the competition*" can increase the buyer's economic value after factoring in the acquisition's cost. This is particularly true if the higher concentration resulting from one less industry participant leads to monopolistic pricing behavior. Operating synergies become secondary. In one such transaction, a national drug distributor with a 35% market share in northern Florida purchased a local competitor with a 20% share. The combined 55% market share ensured pricing stability and presented a strong barrier to potential market entrants.

The Justice Department reviews mergers that increase industry concentration because the federal government considers most oligopolies to be undesirable from a public policy standpoint. The Justice Department has the ability to thwart a proposed merger on antitrust grounds, as it did in 1995 when it derailed the proposed Microsoft/Intuit merger. This deal would have severely reduced competition in certain segments of the software industry.

A *"strategic deal"* describes a transaction in which a company is buying an unrelated business. On the surface, entering a new industry may seem illogical, but the buyer maintains that the acquisition is part of a scientific corporate plan designed to achieve some defined end. The "end" is the assumption that the combination enhances the value of both firms, or, in other words, a "2 + 2 = 5" deal. Some examples are instructive. After American Express Corporation announced that its goal was to be a leader in financial services, it implemented a broad acquisition plan that diversified its travel business into the financial services industry. Over a 10-year period, American Express acquired a money management firm (The Boston Company), a property and casualty insurance company (Fireman's Fund), and several brokerage firms (Shearson Lehman Brothers, Robinson Humphrey, and E. F. Hutton). Philip Morris fulfilled its strategic goal of becoming a major consumer products company when it acquired Kraft Foods and Miller Brewing Company. Both Amex and Philip Morris claimed that these diversifications were strategic realignments necessitated by changing environments.

American Express was caught up in the fashionable "financial superstore" concept. This idea attracted Sears (Allstate, Dean Witter, Coldwell Banker) and Xerox (Crum & Foster, Furman & Selz, and VMS, a municipal bond firm) among other major corporations. The financial superstore premise suggested that the typical consumer's financial needs—car loans, mortgage loans, credit cards, personal loans, mutual funds, etc.—were going to be serviced by one provider. Any financial service business not supplying a panoply of products was headed for extinction. Forward-looking service providers thus combined with others.

At the time of its acquisition binge, Philip Morris faced serious questions over the tobacco industry's prospects and its stock price suffered from the tobacco "image problem." Accordingly, the company's foray into the food and beverage business diminished the negative tobacco image, thereby lifting Philip Morris's fortunes on Wall Street. Also, Philip Morris's massive distribution, marketing, and financial resources provided a boost to both Kraft and Miller Brewing.

One megamerger idea justified by strategic considerations was the $23 billion proposed Bell Atlantic takeover of Telecommunications Inc., the largest cable television concern. Bell Atlantic maintained that the combination was imperative to prepare it for the future "electronic information superhighway," a path on which the services of cable TV, computer data, and telecommunications would be transmitted over the same electronic systems. A Bell Atlantic/Telecommunications combination, therefore, would increase both companies' business opportunities and fortify their competitive strengths.

EARNINGS DILUTION: $2 + $2 = $3

The Bell Atlantic/Telecommunications deal, like many strategic combinations, would have resulted in substantial earnings per share (EPS) dilution for the Bell Atlantic's shareholders. Earnings per share are diluted when the buyer's pro forma EPS, (pro forma means EPS calculated "as if" the deal had occurred already) are less than its actual EPS before the deal. The calculation of pro forma or as-if EPS is always done as soon as a deal is announced. Market observers add the acquirer's sales and earnings to the seller's results. At the same time, they include the pro forma interest and amortization charges resulting from the new acquisition debt and any associated asset write-ups. Furthermore, if the acquirer's stock is used as a currency to pay for the deal, the analysts add the new shares in calculating pro forma EPS.

In dilutive deals, the buyer's management "pooh poohs" EPS dilution. Inevitably, the executives insist that there is a higher EPS growth rate set into place by the acquisition. This added growth overcomes cover the dilution in a couple of years, leaving shareholders in a better position than that which they occupied previously. Moreover, the higher EPS growth rate means a higher price-earnings ratio (P/E) for the buyer's stock. If investors follow this way of thinking, an acquirer's stock price increases even after a dilutive deal is announced, because the investment community attaches a higher P/E ratio to the now smaller EPS. Consider the following: Tiger Company's EPS is $2.00 per share and its P/E is 10. Tiger's stock price is, therefore, $20 (10 P/E × $2.00). When Tiger buys Lion Company, the pro forma EPS for 1994 is $1.90, a 5% reduction from actual EPS. Without a P/E ratio adjustment, Tiger's shares drop to $19 (10 P/E × $1.90), a 5% decrease from the $20 price. Suppose that the investment community reaches the following consensus: the combined Tiger/Lion Company will grow faster than Tiger on a stand-alone basis. As shown in Exhibit 4-4, with this "high growth" image, the P/E of the combined Tiger/Lion Company climbs to 12×, giving the shareholders of Tiger/Lion stock a value of $22.80 per share (the new 12 P/E times the $1.90 pro forma EPS).

Just before a possible Telecommunications takeover was announced, analysts estimated Bell Atlantic's 1993 EPS at $2.30, and its stock sold for $34.50 per share, a 14× P/E ratio. Investors assigned this low P/E because the company was perceived as a boring, slow-growth telephone utility. Most investors bought the shares for their high dividend yield, not for growth. After the impending transaction became public, analysts calculated Bell Atlantic's pro forma EPS to be $1.88, a 17% dilution from $2.30. Nevertheless, Bell Atlantic's stock price increased. The $1.88 of pro forma EPS were valued at a 23× P/E, providing a $43.24 stock price, a 26% gain. Overnight, the "new" Bell Atlantic was perceived as a growth business in tune with the coming information age. The 2 + 2 = 5 hypothesis turned out to be true temporarily, but

EXHIBIT 4-4   Overcoming EPS dilution with a higher P/E ratio

	Tiger Stand-Alone	Tiger/Lion Combined	Adjusted Tiger/Lion Combined
P/E ratio	10×	10×	12×
Growth perception	Moderate	Moderate	High
EPS	2.00	1.90	1.90
Share price	$20.00	$19.00	$22.80

the long-term effects of the acquisition will never be known, since federal regulatory problems killed the deal.

Strategic acquisitions have a mixed record in enhancing shareholder values. In part, the competitive market for acquisitions implies that the acquirers are paying full price, leaving them with little room for error in integrating the new additions. Indeed, buyer managements can jeopardize their base businesses by devoting an inordinate amount of attention to absorbing acquisitions. This means that the base business runs on autopilot while management irons out the day-to-day merger difficulties. Second, acquirers emphasize sizable operating synergies to justify expensive strategic transactions. Exaggerations take place during the crucial preacquisition phase, when lenders and shareholders alike need convincing. After the buyer has closed the deal and is in the post transaction phase, the unfortunate "hangover" of the deal is that "2 + 2" does not equal "5" as promised. Instead "2 + 2" equals "4." For those acquisitions in which the buyer overpaid, 2 + 2 equals only 3, as the buyer's economic value suffers under the weight of a heavy purchase price.

The frequency with which corporate America dismisses acquisition risks gave rise to the "hubris" theory developed by Richard Roll. Sometimes called the "winner's curse" phenomenon, this theory states that exuberant managers, driven by machismo, commit errors of overoptimism in corporate auctions by submitting bids based on inflated projections of postmerger performance. The winner of the target, therefore, is actually the loser, since it will never be able to recoup the purchase price from the target's own cash flows or those extra cash flows derived from synergies. My experience gives considerable credence to Roll's hypothesis, which was tested and proven repeatedly in the 1980s. Interestingly, management buyouts were among the most prominent examples of the hubris theory, for many went bankrupt. This in itself is a surprising fact. After all, a management team buying its own company should have a high degree of accuracy in projecting financial results.

MANAGEMENT BUYOUTS

Management buyouts, which are interchangeable with the term "leveraged buyouts" here, are a variation on the 2 + 2 = 5 school of value enhancement. In addition to the higher expected returns from the use of leverage, LBO investors aim for additional returns from managerial efficiencies. The idea is that the existing management will squeeze more profits out of the same asset base. Why? The source of this new motivation is the significant equity participation reserved for the LBO's operating management. By allowing executives to participate directly in corporate profits, the buyout concept resolves the inherent conflict of many big-time corporate managers. According to their job descriptions, they are supposed to maximize corporate values, but their ownership in the corporation is often minimal. Their real interests lie in preserving their prestigious jobs, high salaries, and generous perquisites.

TAX DEALS

A separate category of value-enhancement merger is the tax-oriented transaction. When a company with prior tax losses acquires a company with taxable profits, the latter can be shielded from income tax levies by the buyer's tax losses. The federal government has instituted numerous restrictions governing tax-loss mergers and their popularity has declined. Tax-loss transactions add value to both seller and buyer if structured properly, since surviving shareholders receive cash that otherwise would go to the federal government in the form of income taxes.

SUMMARY

Acquisitions often provide the buyer with additional leverage capability. The acquisition's assets and earnings are combined on a pro forma basis with the buyer's, providing lenders with the ability to extend more funds. Start-up ventures, in contrast, must be funded completely from the sponsoring company's balance sheet.

The value of a specific acquisition, or the value of the combined company, can be enhanced in many ways. Part of the skill in acquiring businesses is the ability to envision an acquisition's full potential, either as a stand-alone business or as part of a larger entity. Basic rationales for "buying" rather than "building" include "2 = 3" and "2 + 2 equals 5."

Acquisitions have been viewed as good corporate investments for three key reasons:

1. Acquisitions are less risky than start-up ventures.
2. Acquisitions can be self-financing.
3. The value of an acquisition, and that of the acquirer, can be enhanced through improved management techniques, changed market perceptions, and operating synergies.

5 THE IMPORTANCE OF A BUSINESS PLAN

If the merger and acquisition business were like the images portrayed in movies such as *Wall Street*, every M&A deal would be finished in two weeks. The buyer's executives would read only a few pieces of paper before making a decision, and the negotiations would take place in richly appointed, oak-paneled conference rooms studded with well-coifed, expensively tailored advisers. The discussions would involve hundreds of millions of dollars, and toward the end of the process the requisite legal documents would be drawn up in a jiffy, just waiting for the signatures of the respective representatives of buyer and seller. This glamorous ideal, unfortunately, is far from the truth. The Hollywood portrayal represents only a few snapshots of the efforts needed to engineer a successful transaction.

To synthesize an entire deal on film would bore most viewers and discourage even the most intrepid corporate strategist from entering the arena. The extended search process, the analytical study of the targets, the frustrating negotiations with hardheaded sellers, and the complex legal documents are all fraught with details and arcane minutiae. Nevertheless, the rewards of such toil-filled efforts are substantial.

Not surprisingly, the merger business has attracted some of the sharpest minds on the American business scene.

The field of mergers and acquisitions can be properly called a "business." One can say "I'm in the M&A business," in the same sense as saying "I'm in the computer software business." Thousands of transactions are completed every year and the value of the companies changing hands exceeds hundreds of billions of dollars. A veritable army of professionals conducts the large volume of transactions, consisting of thousands of corporate executives, investment bankers, business brokers, lawyers, accountants, tax advisers, asset appraisers, commercial bankers, leasing and personnel experts, management, pension and labor consultants, investment fund managers, and risk arbitrageurs.

This list of functional specialists illustrates the vast number of individuals who make their living from merger transactions, and the breadth of skills that come into play. The primary mover behind a deal—the buyer—needs at its disposal the proper mix of skills to work effectively in this environment. Spearheading the buyer's in-house efforts should be a well-rounded businessperson, but actually buying a company involves specialized skills beyond the resources of many businesses. Knowledge in accounting, finances, negotiations, marketing, business analysis, law, taxes and the related paperwork is critical. The average buyer hires and supervises several of the experts specialized in these fields.

At any point along the way, a potential buyer has the option of hiring outside talent to find, evaluate, and close a transaction. Experienced buyers typically use outside advice when entering into the final stages of an acquisition. During the initial stages of the process, external expertise is poorly motivated. Outside advisers realize that the chances of closing a prospective deal are small. Since they make most of their money on successful transactions, outside advisers are motivated and play a constructive role only as a buyer gets close to finalizing a deal.

The most efficient way of screening candidates, making preliminary evaluations, and developing purchase prices is to do it in-house. An in-house executive is far more cost-efficient than outside advisers in the early stages and has a far better sense of how a potential target "fits" with his employer. The executive's job continuity is also a plus, since the person has less incentive to oversell a transaction merely to earn kudos from doing "something." Many advisers and consultants have ulterior motives for advancing transactions, no matter whether the adviser is paid by the hour or by the deal.

The first reward for a company that has just closed an acquisition is the opportunity to review more acquisitions. As the word gets around that "so and so" is a "player," intermediaries representing sellers or offering acquisition ideas will contact the new player. As a result, the buyer's previously ad hoc or part-time acquisition function can evolve into a full-time job if the inquiries are answered properly. As the buyer's activities grow, its relationships with investment bankers, business brokers, attorneys, accountants, and other professionals, built up over the course of a few transactions, solidify and bring mutual understandings. This means that the deals themselves move faster and smoother, freeing time for reviewing even more opportunities. Following the completion of a few transactions, the in-house executive can look forward to a dynamic corporate development operation.

AN ACTIVE APPROACH

Potential buyers cannot count on intermediaries to bring in all the potential candidates. Any effective development effort is proactive. As a matter of tactics, the would-be acquirer makes the effort to approach potential targets and intermediaries directly. While investment banks, commercial banks, and business brokers discuss their "deal inventory" freely with respectable buyers, corporations that are not openly for sale are harder to find. The buyer must approach them on a proactive basis, either by phone, letter, or personal contact. The contacts are frustrating since owners/managers often turn their backs on takeover invitations. This reaction is natural, given the disruption that the rumor of a sellout gives to the candidate's employees. As rejections pile up from the proactive approach, the buyer's managers should not be discouraged. The odds are in their favor. About 1 in 10 businesses are open to offers, and perhaps another 2 in 10 are "silent sellers," who will talk with a persistent buyer.

Maintaining an aggressive, proactive approach in the acquisition search requires a definite plan that will allow the potential buyer to conserve its human resources. Just through intermediaries, the buyer can see dozens of opportunities each week. Most are too small to merit the buyer's interest, too far from the buyer's product line to represent a good "fit," or too expensive to be a good financial investment. Nevertheless, the buyer must review the candidates before making these determinations. To reduce the time spent reviewing inappropriate deals, it sends intermediaries the guidelines that the buyer follows in proactive contacts.

THE ACQUISITION PLAN

The acquisition plan has four components. The first is an executive assessment: Is management prepared to acquire another business and take on the added responsibilities? The second component is financial: How large a deal can the company afford? How much added leverage? What earnings per share dilution are the shareholders willing to risk? The third element of the acquisition plan narrows down the number of target industries: Is the corporate strategy to extend the product line, to diversify into related businesses or to integrate vertically? The final part of the plan is tactical: Does the company work through advisers or take the direct approach?

The Acquisition Plan
- Management Readiness.
- Financial Capability.
- Target Industry.
- Tactics.

EXECUTIVE ASSESSMENT

A corporation contemplating a productive acquisition campaign should devote at least one executive full-time to this effort. If this minimal commitment is impossible, the company should abandon any hope of realizing long-term benefits from acquisitions. Assuming this decision is made, the would-be acquirer must accurately gauge the managerial capability required to add new businesses to the existing asset portfolio.

Many companies err on the side of optimism when evaluating the risks of integrating one business into another. Potential problems are underestimated, and the synergies forecast at the start of the deal can go up in smoke. Two companies, a hotel operator and a retail chain, told me that their first acquisitions almost bankrupted them. They had underestimated the required time commitment of senior management. With valuable resources being drained into fixing the acquisitions, the core businesses were left to fend for themselves with near-disastrous results.

Beside examining human resources in this regard, top management should determine what type of acquisition is most suitable for the corporation. All companies have character traits that govern how various groups perceive them. One company's character might be called staid and conservative. Another might be referred to as dynamic and entrepreneurial. We all know how organizations inevitably build reputations that seem to have human qualities. These cultural and character factors have to be probed before a company selects what type of business to pursue. Many companies find it helpful to employ consulting firms in completing this self-examination.

SUMMARY

An acquiring company wastes time in surveying inappropriate acquisition opportunities. A business plan assists the company in defining its objectives and limiting its survey costs.

6 TYPICAL BUYER CATEGORIES

Corporate business plans result in unique acquisition strategies, but most buyers fall into five distinct modes of behavior. It is important that corporate managers recognize how the practitioners synthesize their strategies. Knowing the market vernacular helps prospective buyers in their search for deals, since they understand the marketplace better. This understanding is critical for successful interaction with the sellers' intermediaries.

Nearly all corporations interested in acquisitions fall into one of the following categories:

- *Window Shopper.* Likes to look, but rarely buys.
- *Bottom Fisher.* Constantly hunting for bargains. Active buyer.
- *Market Share/Product Line Extender.* Most common buyer category, because fewer operating risks are involved.
- *Strategic Buyer.* Seeking to diversify and redeploy assets.
- *Leveraged Buyout.* Very active sector. Financially oriented buyers.

Each of these investor types is pursuing acquisitions for the same reason—profit. And while there are a number of secondary rationales, such as a CEO's desire to build an empire, profit is still the prime motivation.

THE WINDOW SHOPPER

The Window Shopper represents the most tiresome phone call for intermediaries. Window Shoppers are large companies that insist on looking at any deal with a relevance to their businesses. Because of their size, Window Shoppers generate instant respect from intermediaries such as investment banks, which typically are seeking to cross-sell them financial products and services. Showing a Window Shopper a deal is one way of building a banking relationship. Once in a great while a Window Shopper closes an acquisition. In the years between transactions, however, the Window Shopper's executives use their search process to review dozens of related firms, even their competitors in some instances.

The primary motivation of the Window Shopper is to study other businesses. It uses the knowledge gained in this fashion in its strategic planning and intelligence processes. Over time, the Window Shopper sees a "perfect" deal, and its cautious management finally takes the plunge. Many Window Shoppers use proactive tactics in approaching other companies in their ostensible search for an acquisition candidate. When contacted by a larger corporation in this regard, a potential target should give out information only after receiving the strongest evidence of serious intentions on the Window Shopper's part. The best proof is a long history of successfully closed transactions, which the Window Shopper lacks.

THE BOTTOM FISHER

There are many Bottom Fishers in the merger business. They are equated by their fellow professionals with what the average person might call a "cheapskate." A Bottom Fisher constantly complains about the asking prices attached to potential acquisitions. Unlike the individual cheapskate, however, a Bottom Fisher spends liberally if it sees exceptional value for its money. Before closing a deal, a Bottom Fisher needs to believe it is getting something for nothing, like paying 50 cents to buy a $1 bill. This quest for value means the Bottom Fisher tends to purchase profitable companies carrying low P/E ratios and low Price/Book ratios. These statistics are the marks of an out-of-favor industry, deeply cyclical company, or turnaround candidate. Most often, other possible buyers have considered the acquisition and passed on it. In these "wallflower" businesses, the Bottom Fisher sees an asset that can be rehabilitated and upgraded with aggressive management. Bottom Fishers study balance sheets more than most acquirers; and, as a result, they are not reluctant to buy money-losing enterprises if the asset liquidation values exceed the purchase price. In this sense, Bottom Fishers take on substantial operating risk, but incur less financial risk, particularly when their purchase prices are compared with the Price/Earnings or Price/Book ratios paid by buyers for more popular companies.

It is difficult for widely held, publicly traded companies to purchase distressed firms because of the high level of operating risk. Consider the following two gambles: (1) Bet $10 to win $0 or $35; or (2) bet $10 to win $12 or $15. The first bet has an expected value of $17.50; the second, $13.50. Most large, publicly held corporations would take the second bet, even though it has a far lower expected value, because management can't bear the risk of receiving zero in the first bet. Institutional shareholders demand steady quarterly earnings for public companies and not surprisingly, corporate managers do not want to disappoint them with an erratic operating performance. The hallmark of a turnaround is, however, an unpredictable return, which runs against the grain of institutional shareholders. As a result of this reluctance, the best bottom fishing is done by closely held firms. These organizations have higher levels of operating flexibility compared with publicly held firms. They are neither constrained by quarterly performance targets nor obligated to consult institutional shareholders. Also, their ability to structure acquisitions on a deal-by-deal basis sets them apart from widely held companies. "Deal-specific financing" shields the "mother firm" from problems located in its risky corporate relations.

As a business, bottom fishing is not for faint-hearted investors who like steady earnings gains. Fixing up a substandard business entails significant management effort and opens the door to follow up capital investment. For many mediocre properties, a turnaround attempt becomes futile, or far too costly to make economic sense, and the temptation to throw good money after bad is a constant threat. The Bottom Fisher must prepare for the occasional misstep when buying on the cheap. In difficult economic times, debt financing is unavailable, meaning the profitability of the strategy falls considerably because of reduced leverage. These complications are part of the Bottom Fisher's hazardous environment, and while formidable, they have been successfully negotiated by many notable financiers. Good examples are Irwin Jacobs, Sam Zell, and Victor Posner. Irwin Jacobs ("Irv the Liquidator") made his first big money by buying assets out of bankruptcies. Sam Zell (the "Gravedancer") has long been a contrarian, investing in out-of-favor industries; he now runs a $1 billion "vulture" fund that buys foreclosed real estate. Victor Posner made his first millions as a slumlord, buying rundown buildings in poor areas and milking them for cash flow; he eventually developed a similar tactic for the corporate world.

Nowadays, a lot of bottom fishing occurs in the defaulted bond market, as shrewd investors scoop up major positions in bankrupt corporate obligations. They hope to secure a major equity participation in the surviving business pursuant to the Chapter 11 reorganization. Many such investments, such as the investments of Dickstein's Partners in Zale bonds and Fidelity's investment in Macy's bonds, were quite profitable. Notwithstanding these successes, bottom fishing is a tough business; it requires a thick skin and a strong stomach.

MARKET SHARE/PRODUCT LINE EXTENDER

The Market Share/Product Line Extender purchases businesses that (1) expand the market for its products or (2) extend its product line. Market Share/Product Line Extender deals are the most common transaction for one reason: they are more logical than starting a new product or entering a new market from scratch. Not surprisingly, many companies choose these two kinds of deals when starting an acquisition program. Not only is the underlying business of the potential target understandable, since its operations are similar to the buyer's, but the asking price is easy to justify since the buyer can look to its own valuation as a starting point. The integration risk is less for extension deals than other acquisition categories because the target is comparable to the buyer and thus has a good chance of being absorbed smoothly. In such transactions, there is not much new information for the buyer to learn; both companies speak the same language in terms of markets, customers, and operations. Because of the practicality of these deals, many firms refuse to consider any acquisition that doesn't fit into either the "market share" or "product line" extender categories.

Companies differ in how they define their market or their product line. One branded food company that worked with me considered any branded food to be a product line extension. A similar firm ruled out branded foods that required special handling or refrigeration. One blanket manufacturer believed its business interests encompassed numerous home furnishings, including curtains, rugs, pillows, towels, and bathroom accessories. A similar firm limited its acquisition scope to those woven products that went into the bedroom. Market definitions are also individualistic. A regional department chain only reviewed acquisitions in, or adjacent to, its existing geographic area. Management believed its merchandising and presentation skills were highly adapted to this area, concentrated in the Deep South. A regional music retailer viewed its market quite differently. With headquarters in the Northeast, where a good portion of its stores were located, the company defined its market as any music consumer who patronized a suburban mall. Any U.S. recorded music chain that serviced these consumers was fair game.

Even in the same industry, strategists give a variety of interpretations to the words "market" and "product." The flexibility in definitions provides corporate managers, consultants and financial advisers with considerable scope in the market/product line extender search, particularly if frustration sets in after the first few bids or approaches are rejected.

This latitude gives managers of large American companies the justification to enter many fields. The diversified nature of large American firms means that many acquisition candidates are bound to fit as "market expansions" or "product line extensions" for a variety of big corporations. This fact, and the inherent attractiveness of buying versus building, ensures that spirited bidding takes place for all profitable firms put up for sale in the United States. The competition is intense when the target participates in a fashionable industry, for this brings out the strategic buyers that look beyond economics in pricing a deal.

Fashionable industries, like women's hemlines, vary with the times. A regular occurrence in U.S. industry is corporate America streaming herdlike into a sector that suddenly has great urgency. Remember the purchase of energy companies in the 1970s, the frenzy over entertainment businesses in the late 1980s and the keen interest in communications in the early 1990s. Exploiting these fashions will be addressed in a later chapter, but for now it suffices to say that being a seller in these instances is usually more profitable than being a buyer.

It stands to reason that certain industries fall out of favor from time to time. During such periods, industry participants refuse to entertain acquisition opportunities that expand their market coverages or their product lines. Management seeks to limit its exposure to the downtrodden industry in question, not to increase it. Sellers in these out-of favor sectors have a problem because the logical buyers, meaning those companies in the same business, are taking a back seat. Sellers who find themselves in this position of trying divest an unfashionable business should try to delay their transaction in the hope that the fashion cycle turns around. If the "wait and see" alternative is not available to the prospective seller because of estate problems, liquidity needs, or other reasons, the transaction in the out-of-fashion industry is a candidate for the bottom fisher or leveraged buyout specialist. Both of these buyer categories are habitual employers of the contrarian approach.

"Buying the competition" is the favorite deal of the Market Share/Product Line Extender and it deserves a special mention. Such transactions keep a tight lid on the buyer's operating risk and have many potential synergies. Unlike acquisitions which merely complement the buyer's business, such as when a ketchup manufacturer buys a mustard producer, the purchase of a competitor can have the immediate beneficial impact of (1) reducing the pricing pressure on the buyer's product line; and (2) decreasing the need for certain nonproduction/distribution related costs, such as advertising, sales promotions, and salespeople. If the deal causes a sufficiently high level of concentration in the buyer's industry, the buyer might be able to take advantage of an oligopolistic pricing policy for its products, increasing its returns on both the existing core business and the new acquisition.

American business history is full of transactions structured to achieve these goals. The Standard Oil Trust, General Motors, and U.S. Steel were three early examples of corporate combinations put together to reduce competition and to improve economies of scale. The Kimberly-Clark 1995 takeover of Scott Paper for $6.8 billion is a recent example. After the deal, the combined company had a 55% market share in facial tissues and a 57% market share in baby wipes.

One of the chief tenets of capitalism is that open competition is the most productive economic system, but the evidence indicates that profit-driven companies are motivated to acquire their competitors. The Market Share/Product Line Extender can be counted on to pursue this objective within the confines of antitrust laws.

THE STRATEGIC BUYER

The Strategic Buyer wants to enter industries through acquisition. The rationale for such acquisitions has been discussed in numerous books and articles, but it suffices to say that the Strategic Buyer either doesn't like the prospects of its base business, or simply can't find enough attractive investments there to absorb excess cash flow. Consequently, the Strategic Buyer has two options: (1) It can remit excess cash to its shareholders through higher dividends or share buybacks, or (2) it can invest in diversifications. Noncore acquisitions are then clothed in the mantle of a cerebral "corporate strategy" that is typically unintelligible to the average shareholder, who understandably complains about diversification. After all, if a shareholder wants to diversify out of the steel business into the oil industry, he can easily sell his U.S. Steel shares and purchase Exxon shares. He does not need U.S. Steel to buy Marathon Oil Company for $5 billion, as was the case in 1986. Furthermore, the lone shareholder need not pay a stiff premium over the market price for his diversification, as U.S. Steel did for Marathon Oil. Rather, the investor can buy oil shares on the stock exchange at market. The corporate strategic buyer, on the other hand, seeks control over its target. Otherwise, there's no opportunity for operating synergies between the two companies. This means that a price substantially in excess of market must be offered to the target's owners (i.e., a "control premium"), resulting in a dilution of the buyer's earnings per share. Not surprisingly, following the announcement of a strategic bid, the buyer's share price often declines, while the target's stock price skyrockets. The buyer's share price decline shows two fundamental valuation factors at work: (1) the acquirer's stockholders are concerned about EPS dilution, and (2) they are worried about the setbacks that arise in combining two different businesses.

The Xerox acquisition of Crum & Foster for $5.6 billion in 1983 was a strategic acquisition. The copier business of Xerox was flattening out. Market penetration was already high and competitors were entering copier markets with better technology. Faced with a stagnant future for its base business, which was nonetheless generating huge amounts of cash each year, Xerox looked at a variety of diversifications. At the time, the financial service industry was a "hot" area, and numerous mainstream U.S. companies were entering financial services through acquisition. Like many equipment manufacturers, Xerox had started a leasing subsidiary, Xerox Financial Services, which offered long-term rental contracts for Xerox copiers. While a growing business, Xerox Financial Services was a small effort, and the proposed Crum & Foster deal was a major diversification for Xerox. Upon announcing the acquisition, Xerox management confronted a skeptical investment community, obviously worried about Xerox's lack of experience in financial services and the shortage of synergies between the two companies. Xerox management's support of the deal centered around the following points: Both companies served a similar client base and could, therefore, cross-sell products and share customer contacts. More importantly, Crum & Foster represented a strategic leap into financial services; it was going to represent the core (along with Xerox Financial Services) of a new financial services group. Over the next five years, Xerox purchased a number of other financial services companies. Later, it curtailed its expansion in the area and sold many of the acquisitions.

Every year sees blockbuster strategic deals. Big transactions of the 1980s that fit into this category included Kodak's $3 billion purchase of Sterling Drug, Exxon's $2 billion takeover of Reliance Electric, and General Motors' $5 billion acquisition of EDS. The success of these transactions has been mixed. Examined under the cold hard light of rational analysis, the related investment returns were dismal for shareholders compared with the alternatives of common stock repurchases and higher dividends. Unfortunately, publicly listed acquirers don't provide the data needed to perform an exact post facto deal analysis. The Security and Exchange Commission (SEC) regulations do require extensive disclosure on a listed company's business, but it is generally not enough to assess a specific acquisition's returns.

Strategic transactions came into their own with the acceptance of the "portfolio theory" promoted successfully by the Boston Consulting Group (Exhibit 6-1). As noted earlier, the theory's foundation places

EXHIBIT 6-1   Corporate definition matrix

		2.0×	1.0×	0.5×
Market Growth Rate	10%	2 Star	1 Question Mark	
	5%	3 Cash Cow	4 Dog	
	0%			

Market Share Relative to Largest Competitor

most corporate businesses into one of four groups. Each group is fitted into a grid with dual axis of growth rate and market share. The grid represents a pictorial summary of the corporate "life cycle" theory. Companies begin life as small, entrepreneurial organizations with a high revenue potential, but only a few survive. Heavy start-up capital needs and working capital requirements dictate negative cash flows even as revenue growth accelerates (Box 1 in the matrix). As the company's market develops and its financial situation stabilizes, the business reaches its peak earnings growth phase (Box 2). The third part of the life cycle (Box 3) occurs when the market for a company's products matures and competition accelerates. The final phase, Box 4, illustrates the declining demand for the company's products, the vestiges of a competitive struggle for market share in a shrinking market, and the resultant loss of cash flow.

Strategic management consulting firms suggest that slow-growth, cash-rich companies falling into Box 3 consider buying fast-growth, cash-poor businesses occupying Box 1. The marriage is one of convenience. The potential acquisition (Box 1) needs cash for growth, whereas the buyer (Box 3) has few growth prospects and lots of cash flow. By making the deal, the buyer gains growth potential from the cash-hungry target. Other matters such as return on investment, corporate culture, and stockholder desires are important follow-up considerations in the BCG model, which has been a staple of business school courses and management seminars for years.

The poor track record of many strategic deals should serve to discourage the consultants who trumpet such transactions as a cure-all for poor growth prospects. At the very least, corporate directors should exercise caution in evaluating any strategic transaction. Anecdotes abound about public company executives promoting far-reaching strategic acquisitions, while paying scant attention to the long-term interests of their own shareholders. The latter are often dispersed and unorganized, and therefore powerless to stop management from implementing its deals. This situation is particularly apparent in cash tender offers, where the buyer's shareholders don't have a vote.

The limited attention given by some managements to shareholder concerns seems odd, but in corporate America there are executives who have a limited interest in the opinions of the shareholders of their corporate employer. The importance attached to shareholder returns by these managers is often outweighed by the large salaries, prerequisites (such as limousines, private planes, and large entertainment budgets), personal powers, and social positions that come with the job. The fragmented ownership of many large public companies strengthens the hands of these executives because public shareholders have serious logistical problems in trying to band together. Finally, because executive benefits tend to expand as a company grows in size, corporate managers naturally want to enlarge their employers through acquisitions, even if the economics of such deals are found wanting.

Recognizing the checkered history of strategic deals, corporate boards are more circumspect about approving "pure diversification" acquisitions. Nowadays, when a potential acquisition means a new business entry, managers increasingly look for ways in which the new addition can assist the corporation in improving the existing core group of businesses. For example, as cable TV technology advances to interactive communications services, telephone companies have become interested in cable TV companies. When Merck Corporation, a large pharmaceutical manufacturer saw prescription drugs being sold through mail-order companies and managed-care providers, it purchased, for $5.5 billion, Medco Containment Services, the leading distributor of prescription drugs through these two channels. With acquisitions of this type, the Strategic Buyer is not seeking to diversify out of its basic business, nor is it trying to reduce its basic business there. Rather, the acquisition is an attempt by management to augment the Strategic Buyer's present capabilities. This approach is a reminder of earlier discussions on the Market Share/Product Line Extender.

THE LEVERAGED BUYOUT BUYER

Leveraged buyout buyers are seeking acquisitions in which a small equity down payment is required. During the height of the 1980s LBO boom, these investors were extremely active, accounting for 40% to 50% of merger volume. At that time, leveraged buyouts were accomplished with equity contributions of 5% to 10% of the purchase price. Banks and other institutional lenders were cooperative because the performance record of earlier LBOs was good. Buoyed by past results, lenders loaned the buyers 90% to 95% of the acquisition cost. This aggressive leverage and the 1990–1992 recession led to numerous defaults on LBO loans in the 1990s. The resultant losses tempered the lenders' eagerness, and a typical LBO now begins with an equity investment of 20% to 25% of the purchase price.

The fundamental premise behind the leveraged buyout is simple: Buying corporate shares using *borrowed* funds is a profitable strategy in the long run. The use of margin, or leverage, magnifies investment returns, either up or down. For example, suppose an individual is confronted with two investment alternatives. The first is an opportunity to buy 1,000 shares of Athens Corporation stock at $50 per share, for a total cash investment of $50,000. The second is to purchase 5,000 Athens shares, paying for the larger $250,000 investment by putting up the same $50,000 in cash, and borrowing the remaining $200,000. During times of rising stock prices, the second investment strategy, employing 80% leverage, does much better than the all-equity alternative. In Exhibit 6-2, Athens stock increased 10% over the first year following the initial investment. The 14% annual return from the all-equity investment is satisfactory to most investors, yet the 42% return provided by the leveraged alternative is outstanding. It illustrates the benefits of leverage in times of rising stock prices.

The use of leverage has a negative side, as value declines are magnified. Suppose the aforementioned Athens stock dropped 10% in price over the one-year period, instead of rising. Exhibit 6-3 shows the downside of borrowing money to finance the purchase of an asset.

When the Athens stock price declines, the advantages of the two strategies are reversed. Losses are far less in the all-cash alternative (minus 6%), compared with the leveraged buyout (minus 58%). In the

EXHIBIT 6-2 Comparable returns

	Initial Athens share price	= $50
	Final Athens share price	= $55
	Interest on borrowing	= 7% per year
	Cash dividend per share	= $2 per year

	All Equity Pay 100% Cash	LBO Pay 20% Cash, 80% Borrowing
Initial Purchase		
Initial cash investment	$50,000	$ 50,000
Borrowing	0	200,000
Value of Athens stock	$50,000	$250,000
Number of shares	1,000	5,000
Sale after One Year		
Number of shares sold	1,000	5,000
Sale price per share	$55	$55
Calculation of Net Proceeds		
Sale proceeds	$55,000	$275,000
Less, interest costs on borrowing	0	(14,000)
Add, cash dividends	2,000	10,000
Less, repayment of borrowings	0	200,000
Net proceeds	$57,000	$ 71,000
One year return on $50,000 investment	14%	42%

LBO alternative, the investors' initial $50,000 capital is almost wiped out, dropping from an initial value of $50,000 to a value of $21,000 in one year. In fact, with any price decline exceeding 15%, the leveraged investor loses the total investment. Not only does such a price decrease eat through the investor's $50,000 in capital, it also results in the lender losing money, as net sale proceeds are less than the $200,000 in outstanding debt. This calculation assumes that the loan is nonrecourse, meaning the lender can only seek repayment from the share collateral, not from the investor's other assets.

By the same token, returns are increasingly magnified for the leveraged investor as the higher price movements occur. Exhibit 6-4 provides a simple illustration that points out the basic advantage of

EXHIBIT 6-3   Comparable returns

	Initial Athens share price	= $50
	Final Athens share price	= $45
	Interest on borrowing	= 7% per year
	Cash dividend per share	= $2 per year

	All Equity Pay 100% Cash	LBO Pay 20% Cash, 80% Borrowing
Initial Purchase		
Initial cash investment	$50,000	$ 50,000
Borrowing	0	200,000
Value of Athens stock	$50,000	$250,000
Number of shares	1,000	5,000
Sale after One Year		
Number of shares sold	1,000	5,000
Sale price per share	$45	$45
Calculation of Net Proceeds		
Sale proceeds	$45,000	$225,000
Less, interest costs on borrowing	0	(14,000)
Add, cash dividends	2,000	10,000
Less, repayment of borrowings	0	200,000
Net proceeds	$47,000	$ 21,000
One year return on $50,000 investment	Minus 6%	Minus 58%

leverage. Whatever happens to the price of the Athens stock, the leveraged investor's losses are limited to $50,000. His profit potential, in contrast, is generally higher than the all-equity alternative. This advantage belies the motives of the Leveraged Buyout Buyer, who wishes to use as much leverage as is available.

LBO equity investors include an LBO specialist firm that arranges the deal and the related debt financing, and the acquired company's top management, which has the job of running the business. The top operating managers typically receive a 10% to 15% ownership of the business on attractive "no money down" terms. Usually, this setup provides the executives with their first meaningful equity interest in their employer. Freed from the bureaucracy of a large parent

EXHIBIT 6-4 Superior gains with leverage

Price Change in Athens stock	Profit on $50,000 Equity Investment with $200,000 Borrowing						
	−100%	**−50%**	**−10%**	**0%**	**+10%**	**+50%**	**+100%**
Profit in dollars	(50,000)	(50,000)	(21,000)	(4,000)	21,000	121,000	246,000
Annual percentage return to investor	−100%	−100%	−58%	−8%	42%	242%	492%

	Profit on $50,000 Equity Investment with No Borrowings						
Profit in dollars	(48,000)	(23,000)	(3,000)	2,000	7,000	27,000	52,000
Annual percentage return to investor	−98%	−46%	−6%	2%	14%	54%	104%

company, the mercurial management style of a family business, or the constraints of being a public company, the executives gain a new entrepreneurial spirit and develop a corporate culture directed solely at making money. In many cases, LBOs have transformed salaried corporate executives into multi-millionaires. These vast material rewards stand in sharp contrast to the generous, but less valuable, perks available in normal corporate jobs.

The LBO specialist firm provides the equity in the deal but it does not guarantee the acquisition loans. As a result, the specialist firm targets companies that can support the debt needed to finance their own purchase prices. Having found such a candidate, the firm's secondary goal is convincing lending sources to put up 70% to 80% of the purchase price. Compared with the heady days of the 1980s, lender recruitment is now more difficult for the LBO specialist firms. Many lenders suffered heavy losses in LBO loans and these memories are still fresh. Banks and insurance companies discovered too late in the game that corporate values fluctuate far more widely than, say, home values. The painful experience taught a general rule: Corporate acquisitions don't merit the same 80% to 90% loan-to-value ratios of home purchases.

To facilitate their deals, LBO Buyers search for transactions with characteristics that appeal to large institutional lenders. These lenders have a fondness for LBOs involving manufacturing companies with (1) a large tangible asset base, and (2) a small purchase-price-to-tangible-assets ratio.

Tangible assets, such as buildings, machinery, and equipment, represent good collateral. Intangible assets, such as brand names and patents, have demonstrable worth, but they have uncertain values. The prospective LBO's balance sheet should have little or no debt, and the income statement must show a record of steady earnings. A solid asset base and reasonable operating record make the prospective lenders confident that the LBO will pay future debt service. Finally, its growth outlook must be positive, indicating that the new owners can sell the LBO within a five-year holding period, thereby realizing additional cash to repay the lenders.

In practice, the supply of reasonably priced manufacturing firms has declined below the demand, and many LBO transactions involve service, distribution, and retail companies. Yet the two basic principles of LBO investment remain the same. First, the acquisition has enough positive attributes to induce lenders to put up the bulk of its purchase price. Second, the acquisition, as a stand-alone business, has good growth prospects; and, thus, both the buyer and its lenders are convinced that the company can be sold at a high price in three to five years, enabling the buyer to repay the acquisition debt and reap a capital gain.

REVIEW OF BUYERS

Each of the buyer types profiled in this chapter—the Window Shopper, Bottom Fisher, Market Share/Product Line Extender, Strategic Buyer, or Leveraged Buyout—is driven by a different view on what it takes to be successful. For many participants, the merger business requires that they combine elements of one or more of these profiles. Few opportunities fit one category perfectly and acquisitive companies take on the attributes of more than one buyer category to justify purchasing businesses that are not ideal candidates. With the exception of firms headed by ego-driven CEOs, most companies realize the purpose of an acquisition is to make money for shareholders. Confining an acquisition search to one mode of thinking is helpful because it sets up screening criteria, but realistic investors modify their tactics as circumstances warrant. That is the real world. Strategic Buyers sometimes make Product Line Extensions and Leveraged Buyout firms sometimes make Strategic Acquisitions.

SUMMARY

This chapter has reviewed the five most common buyer categories in the merger and acquisition field:

- Window Shopper.
- Bottom Fisher.
- Market Share/Product Line Extender.
- Strategic Buyer.
- Leveraged Buyout.

Which category matches your organization? The answer to this question is important because it establishes a framework for how your company conducts an acquisition search. It also indicates how your organization will be perceived by the practitioner community.

A prospective buyer completes a dual assessment of its acquisition strategy: an internal review and a practitioner's summary. A few businesses appear to be promising acquisitions, but more preparatory steps are ahead. Next, the would-be buyer determines the amount of risk it is willing to undertake in pursuit of its goals. Three primary risks are evaluated: operating risk, overpayment risk, and financial risk.

7 KEY RISKS

Three primary risks face corporate acquirers: operating risk, overpayment risk, and financial risk:

1. *Operating Risk.* The acquired business doesn't perform as well as expected after the integration.
2. *Overpayment* Risk. Although the acquisition's operations are sound, the high purchase price eliminates the possibility of receiving a satisfactory investment return.
3. *Financial Risk.* The acquisition was financed with debt, which strains the buyer's ability to fund its operations and service its debt at the same time.

OPERATING RISK

Operating risk refers to the buyer's specific ability to manage the business of the acquired company. External business risks such as product obsolescence and new competition fall in a separate category. Where the buyer and the acquisition's businesses are closely allied, a true merger takes place, with product lines combined, assets rearranged, and the acquisition's personnel allocated among the buyer's various departments. The obvious operating risk here is a melding process that goes badly. Where a functional combination is not appropriate, the acquisition stands as an independent unit, drawing on the buyer for capital, managerial expertise, and other resources, while perhaps providing the buyer with a new product line, technology, or market. In this situation, many of the acquisition's employees stay in their original jobs. Motivating these employees, while cultivating the acquisition's new image as part of a larger organization, is a challenging process that involves operating risk. So many deals are justified by the buyer's promise to cut the acquisition's costs—a common euphemism for reducing headcount—that the target's workforce is naturally suspicious of the buyer's motives. An uncooperative workforce disrupts the operations, perhaps by focusing on job searches instead of the buyer's objectives.

The buyer has less operating risk when it purchases a competitor, extends its product line, or widens its market share. With such deals, the buyer is working in familiar territory. The greater operating risk is found in bottom fishing, strategic, or LBO transactions. Here the buyer may have only a superficial knowledge of the target's business and this inexperience can result in poor management decisions early on. Experienced buyers tend to foresee problems by preparing extensive integration plans.

When Shearson Lehman Brothers acquired E.F. Hutton, for example, the postclosing integration plan comprised a 900-page booklet. The plan tried to cover every conceivable element of the transition and it represented the years of Shearson's experience in carrying out previous mergers.

Transition plans have a hard time gauging the one operating risk that is always downplayed on numbers-obsessed Wall Street: culture clash. Organizations, like people, have their own personalities. Cultural differences can wreck the postmerger environment just as easily as the buyer's limited industry experience. Eli Lilly's acquisition of Hybritech was one such example. In 1986, Eli Lilly, a pharmaceutical giant, paid $300 million for Hybritech in order to enter the biotechnology business, but the authoritarian Lilly managers had difficulty working with the entrepreneurial Hybritech executives, many of whom left the firm to join other biotech companies. Lilly sold Hybritech in 1995 for $10 million, less than 5% of the original purchase price.

Buyers study potential operating problems in a transaction. Appropriate contingency plans are developed to resolve these issues, but there is no substitute for extensive postclosing preparation.

OVERPAYMENT RISK

A second key risk is overpayment. If the acquisition's cost is large compared with the buyer's value, the aftereffects of paying too much can last for years, and the buyer's earnings per share and balance sheet may never recover. Assume that a would-be buyer decides to make an offer at a "fair" price. How does this price impact the buyer's value?

Evaluating a deal's effect on a buyer's future results is an interesting numbers game. Rightly or wrongly, publicly traded buyers place a heavy emphasis on the pro forma effect of the deal on the buyer's earnings per share for the coming year. Reduced buyer earnings per share are bad; increased buyer EPS is good. Deals involving a high level of dilution in the following year are usually discarded for one reason: Wall Street's negative perception of dilution.

Despite arguments of future synergies, a transaction involving high EPS dilution usually punishes the buyer's share value, as investors cynically question the buyer's ability to recoup the lost EPS over a reasonable period. Acquirers thus focus on deals with little or no dilution. A "little" is a reduction in the buyer's EPS of 6% or less. In this range, the buyer has a reasonable assurance of no immediate and substantial drop in its stock price. Further analysis of the acquisition can then proceed.

Assuming the would-be buyer settles the question of the coming year's EPS dilution, it considers the deal's influence on future years' earnings per share, along with the impact on operating financial risk levels. In-house analysts project financial statement data for various operating scenarios with, and without, the potential acquisition. Given this data, the buyer (and perhaps its investment banker) gauge the long-term benefits of implementing the transaction by focusing on the probable increases in buyer's share price. At the same time, they consider the stock market's likely reaction to the deal, since Wall

Street's perception of the future is as important as the buyer's in setting posttransition share values. If the "Street" develops a negative image of an acquisition proposal, no amount of optimistic projections is going to deter a drop in the buyer's share price.

Rosy EPS estimates carry some weight with investors, but after having seen many deals "go up in smoke," investors now realize that skilled investment bankers and corporate development personnel can use forecasts to rationalize any acquisition. Equity investors, as a result, do their own analysis and evaluate carefully the assumptions implicit in any pro forma financial data. (Since SEC regulations prohibit the public release of projections, investment bankers and corporate executives typically leak information.) The primary weaknesses of these forecasts are overoptimistic assumptions regarding the acquisition's sales growth, cost cuts, or margin increases. Achieving these objectives is not only a function of the target's operations, but also the amount of earnings that actually accrue to the buyer's preacquisition shareholders. Many merged companies enjoy successful operations, but the benefits never reach the buyer's shareholders. Why? The EPS and dividends available to these shareholders are dependent on the purchase price paid and the related financing. An expensive acquisition results in either a greater debt load, a higher number of shares outstanding or a lower amount of remaining cash reserves. Even with the acquisitions earnings contribution, the effect of these changes reduces the buyer's EPS.

OVERPAYMENT AND REDUCED EPS

The use of leverage magnifies investment returns, both good and bad. Sometimes buyers use leverage to mask the EPS dilution of a costly acquisition. The Zorba Corporation/Euclid Inc. merger shown in Exhibit 7-1 illustrates that debt-financed deals can enhance EPS growth relative to an all-equity transaction. In this example, higher leverage means less dilution, but the debt financing creates more financial risks. Note how Zorba's estimated 1990 EPS are $1.24 under the all-debt scenario, compared with $1.17 with all-equity. Consider the following two Zorba acquisitions of Euclid. The purchase prices are identical, but different financing methods are utilized.

EXHIBIT 7-1   Zorba Corporation purchase of Euclid Inc.

Pretransaction Data

Zorba stock price	$15.00
Earnings per share	$ 1.00
P/E ratio	15×
Number of shares outstanding	100 million
Total market value	$1.5 billion
Euclid stock price after Zorba purchase announcement	$38.00
Earnings per share	$ 2.00
P/E ratio	19×
Number of shares outstanding	10 million
Total market value	$380 million

Transaction—All Debt

Zorba purchases Euclid shares for $38 per share in cash, representing a $380 million acquisition price.

Transaction—All Equity

Zorba exchanges 25 million Zorba shares for all Euclid shares, representing a $380 million acquisition price. To start the analysis, review the stand-alone data of each firm (Exhibit 7-2) and then the posttransaction Zorba EPS (Exhibit 7-3).

The acquisition contributes to higher Zorba EPS under both the equity and debt finance alternatives. Without the deal, Zorba's 1998

EXHIBIT 7-2   Projections of Zorba and Euclid (US$ millions)

	Pretransaction			
	Actual	Projected		
	1995	1996	1997	1998
Zorba net income	$100	$108 ·	$117	$125
Euclid net income	20	23	27	32
Zorba EPS	1.00	1.08	1.17	1.25
Euclid EPS	2.00	2.30	2.70	3.20

EXHIBIT 7-3   Posttransaction pro forma calculations[1]

	1995	1996	1997	1998
Old Zorba EPS	$1.00	$1.08	$1.17	$1.25
Merger Financed with 25 Million Zorba Shares				
New Zorba EPS	0.96	1.05	1.15	1.27
Merger Financed with 10.5%, $380 Million, Zorba Debt				
New Zorba EPS	0.96	1.07	1.20	1.33
EPS Benefits of Using Debt vs. Equity				
EPS differential	—	0.02	0.05	0.06

[1] Before purchase accounting adjustments and synergies.

EPS are forecast at $1.25, versus $1.27 and $1.33, respectively. Some initial dilution occurs in 1996, but the company recovers by 1997 in the debt alternative and by 1998 in the equity scenario. The time period is shortened if one assumes that Zorba reduces Euclid's annual costs by $5 million. This cost synergy reduces the recovery period from three years to two years in the equity alternative and from one year to six months in the debt scenario.

Eager buyers use synergies, like overoptimistic projections, to minimize dilution forecasts. Synergies justify transactions that might otherwise require the buyer's stockholders to acknowledge too much EPS dilution. Dilution is immediate and obvious, while promises of synergy and expanded growth are inherently uncertain. Investors react accordingly. Corporate managements place limits on the EPS dilution that they tolerate in deals. The uppermost limit is around 6%, which restricts potential overpayment issues.

FINANCIAL RISK

In addition to operating and overpayment risks, buyers consider the amount of additional financial risk that a deal presents. The determinants of this financial risk are (1) the amount of debt used to finance the acquisition, and (2) the amount of the target's debt assumed by the buyer. The Zorba/Euclid merger illustrated that debt-financed deals can enhance EPS growth relative to all-equity transactions, but debt financing has a downside. It is more risky than equity since debt increases earnings volatility.

In Exhibit 7-4, note how the debt produces a large EPS drop in recessionary conditions. Earnings per share fall 27% under the debt alternative, from $1.07 to $0.78, compared with 14%, from $1.05 to $0.91, under the equity alternative. Exhibit 7-4 shows that the expected EPS have a far wider range under the debt financing, $0.78 to $1.23, compared with the $0.91 to $1.18 range under equity financing.

Zorba faces risk/return tradeoffs in merger financing. How much leverage? Should the use of debt be consistent with corporate policy?

EXHIBIT 7-4   Pro forma earnings per share calculations of Zorba Corporation, three scenarios in 1996 (US$ millions)

	Recession	Moderate Economy	Growth Economy
Probability	0.2	0.5	0.3
Operating Results			
Zorba EBIT[1]—Alone	$160	$180	$200
Euclid EBIT—Alone	30	38	45
Combined EBIT	$190	$218	$245
Financing with Debt			
Combined EBIT	$190	$218	$245
Adjustments[2]	—	—	—
Less: New interest	40	40	40
Earnings before taxes	130	178	205
Less: Income taxes	52	71	82
Net income	$78	$107	$123
EPS on 100MM shares	$0.78	$1.07	$1.23
Financing with Equity			
Combined EBIT	$190	$218	$245
Adjustments[2]	—	—	—
Less: New interest	—	—	—
Earnings before taxes	190	218	245
Less: Income taxes	76	87	98
Net income	$114	$131	$147
EPS on 125MM shares	$0.91	$1.05	$1.18

[1] EBIT means Earnings Before Interest and Taxes.
[2] The analysis excludes purchase accounting and synergy adjustments.

Should Zorba change the policy to fit the combined entity? The answers to these questions depend on Zorba's confidence in its projections, its attitude toward risk and the stock market's perspective of the combined entity's debt servicing ability. Pessimists and risk-avoiders would prefer that Zorba issue common stock to finance the deals, while the optimists and those less averse to risk would favor leverage.

SUMMARY

Disagreements over financing policy are not unusual, but internal corporate discussions over the use of acquisition leverage should be sensitive to market perceptions about general business conditions, industry trends, and the combined business "fit." The stock market is one of the few areas in American business where perception can become reality. If investors begin to think that an acquisition is overpriced, represents a poor operating fit, or overleverages the buyer, the buyer's share price is going to decline, notwithstanding the confidence the buyer may have in the detailed studies which it prepared in considering the transaction. If a buyer decides to use leverage to reduce EPS dilution, it should balance carefully the negative effects of more debt against the positive effects of better earnings growth.

Acquisitions are not risk-free investments. Revenues can be lower than expected. Expenses can be higher. The melding of the target into the buyer can present operating problems. Asset sale values can be lower than anticipated. This is part of the merger business. Successful acquirers evaluate the attendant risks of doing a deal and decide if the risk/reward profile is appropriate for their respective organizations.

A cautious and deliberate consideration of an acquisition opportunity need not inhibit the buying process. Rather, it should provide the

EXHIBIT 7-5   Zorba earnings per share ($)

	Actual	Projected		
	1995	1996	1997	1998
EPS	1.00	1.08	1.17	1.25
% growth	—	8%	8%	7%

**EXHIBIT 7-6   Postacquisition Zorba earnings
per share ($)**

	Pro Forma	Projected		
	1995	1996	1997	1998
EPS	0.96	1.07	1.20	1.33
% growth	—	11%	12%	11%

buyer and its shareholders with sufficient confidence to make an offer. With publicly traded deals, a hard fact of life is that acquirers pay a large premium over the market price to acquire a business. In the private arena, medium-size to large private companies also carry premium prices when compared with the public valuation statistics, such as P/E and Price/Book ratios. The cost of an acquisition can drag down the buyer's earnings per share. As a rule of thumb, this dilution shouldn't last more than two years, after which time the buyer should have earned its way out of the dilution by virtue of its higher growth rate. Assuming an increase in the buyer's P/E ratio as a result of the deal, shareholders should be better off with the deal than without it.

The Zorba/Euclid deal illustrates this point: Before the acquisition, Zorba's shares were trading at $15 per share, based on the EPS estimates shown in Exhibit 7-5.

After Zorba buys Euclid for $380 million, and finances the transaction entirely with debt, the revised estimates are as shown in Exhibit 7-6. The transaction enhances EPS, so an increase in Zorba's P/E ratio seems warranted. Offsetting a portion of this upward adjustment is a downward P/E bias due to financial risk concerns. Controlling these market adjustments to the P/E ratio is Zorba's balancing act. Any acquisitive management has the same concern.

8 HOW LARGE A DEAL?

A company decides to consider entering the acquisition market. How large a deal should it consider?

At a minimum, the transaction should be large enough to warrant the close attention of the executives responsible for appraising, closing, and transitioning the deal. Small acquisitions, representing only 1% or 2% of the buyer's business, are frequently as time consuming and headache-prone as larger transactions; and thus, a small deal isn't worth the management effort, unless, for example, it represents a purchase of special technology. The management time and institutional distraction that are an inevitable deal cost should be expended on a sufficiently large prize. Since most acquisition evaluations result in fruitless negotiations and suitor rejections, the time and expense consumed in these failed efforts is added to the cost of the closed deals. Taken together, these items make the processing expense of a small deal very high in relation to its purchase price. A rule of thumb is that a minimum deal size should be around 5% to 10% of the buyer's market value. Using this maxim, a company with a $200 million market value would limit its acquisition search to companies with a minimum $10 to $20 million purchase price.

Large deals impact significantly on the buyer's financial results and its market valuation. What should be the maximum deal size to consider?

A proper response begins with a caveat. The acquisition market is opportunistic. Transactions which fit well with a buyer may only come along every few years. Any size guidelines may be discarded in favor of the buyer "seizing the moment." A buyer should consider opportunism as a "wild card" in evaluating the three key size parameters: affordability, management experience, and corporate risk tolerance.

Maximum Deal Size Guidelines

1. *Affordability.* What the buyer can pay without upsetting its share price and capital structure.
2. *Management Experience.* Integrating a large deal requires related management experience.
3. *Corporate Risk Tolerance.* Larger deals mean bigger risks. Is the company ready for a high-risk profile?

AFFORDABILITY

Affordability is difficult to pinpoint. Merger professionals begin with an estimate of how much a buyer can afford if it uses only debt to finance a deal. Since any new debt is supported by both the buyer and its new acquisition, this calculation is deal-specific.

EXHIBIT 8-1   Tiger Bread acquisition of Lion Roll, income statement data (in millions)

	Tiger Bread	Lion Roll	Adjustments[1]	Pro Forma Combined
EBIT	$20.0	$5.0	$ —	$25.0
Interest	0.0	0.0	4.0[2]	4.0
Pretax income	$20.0	$5.0	$(4.0)	$21.0
Taxes (40%)	8.0	2.0	(2.0)	8.0
Net income	$12.0	$3.0	$ 2.0	$13.0
Interest coverage ratio	—	—	—	6.3×

[1] Before any purchase adjustments or synergy effects.
[2] Annual cost of $50 million borrowing at 8% interest.

EXHIBIT 8-2   Tiger Bread acquisition of Lion Roll, balance sheet data (in millions)

	Tiger Bread	Lion Roll	Adjustments	Pro Forma Combined
Current assets	$ 40	$10	$—	$ 50
Fixed assets	60	15	30[1]	105
Total assets	$100	$25	$ 30	$155
Current liabilities	20	5	—	25
Long-term debt	—	—	50[2]	50
Stockholders' equity	80	20	(20)[3]	80
	$100	$25	$ 30	$155

Adjustments

[1] Write-up of Lion Roll assets by $30 million ($50 million purchase price less $20 million equity book value). This write-up doesn't necessarily correspond to the economic value of the assets. It is an accounting convention.

[2] Addition of $50 million debt to finance the acquisition.

[3] Elimination of Lion Roll's equity book value.

As an example, if Tiger Bread Corporation, with annual earnings before interest and taxes (EBIT) of $20 million, bought Lion Roll Corporation, with EBIT of $5 million, the combined entities' $25 million EBIT would be available to support the repayment of acquisition debt. If Tiger Bread bought Lion Roll for $50 million and borrowed the entire $50 million purchase, Lion Roll's earnings would contribute to covering the related debt service (see Exhibit 8-1).

Likewise, the companies' combined balance sheet would give Tiger Bread a greater asset base, thereby augmenting its ability to incur debt. Tiger Bread's assets increase by 55% after the acquisition as shown in Exhibit 8-2.

THE ROLE OF LENDERS IN DETERMINING AFFORDABILITY

The demonstrated earnings power of a viable acquisition, its recognized asset value, and the buyer's own financial history make an attractive credit package for lenders. Not surprisingly, acquisition financing is a favorite pastime for money center banks, yet most of these same lenders would be reluctant to lend substantial sums to their clients if the monies were targeted for new business start-ups. Despite the safety of a given acquisition loan, banks and other lending institutions restrict the combined company from exceeding certain credit ratios, designed specifically for its combined business, industry sector, and financial record. Typically, the following credit ratios must be maintained by industrial borrowers on a pro forma basis:

- Current ratio must be larger than 1.3.
- Total debt divided by total debt plus equity must be less than 0.65.
- EBIT divided by interest expense must be larger than 1.5.

Note that the Tiger Bread/Lion Roll combination has a 2.0 Current Ratio, a Total Debt/Total Debt plus Equity Ratio of 0.43, and an EBIT/Interest Ratio of 6.3. The deal easily passes the first round of banker credit guidelines.

The banking industry has dozens of guidelines for lending to industrial mergers. The exact criteria used for a specific deal depend on a multitude of variables beyond the scope of this book. Key credit aspects that banks consider in setting credit standards include the historical operating records of buyer and seller; possible synergistic effects of the combination; total pro forma leverage; projected interest coverage and liquidity ratios; industry prospects; respective competitive positions; and the value of any security or third-party guarantees offered to the lenders.

Credit guidelines vary by industry, and lenders tailor loans to the individual requirements of each transaction. Many deals appear similar, but invariably each transaction has unique characteristics that demand an individualized financing package. The terms of similar loans are used as road maps by lenders, but there are few absolutes in structuring acquisition financings.

JUNK BONDS AND AFFORDABILITY

For deals that fall outside bank guidelines, the "junk bond" market is an option. Although considered the province of leveraged buyout investors and takeover artists, the junk bond market serves many companies contemplating transactions that are unsuitable for 100% bank financing. The junk bond market encompasses large billion-dollar public bond issues as well as privately placed deals that are as small as $5 million. Junk bond lenders often fill the financing "gap" between the debt provided by banks and the total amount of debt needed to close the deal.

In the next example, Tiger Bread decides to make a $300 million bid for a conglomerate's Cookie Division. With the same size as Tiger Bread, this Division represents a substantial acquisition opportunity. Because of internal credit guidelines, Tiger Bread's banks can provide only $150 million toward the $300 million purchase price. As shown in Exhibit 8-3, Tiger Bread solicits another $150 million from the junk bond market, but the price is steep, a 12% interest rate. Tiger Bread's EBIT/interest coverage ratio of 1.3× is typical for a junk bond issuer. The same ratio for an investment-grade company is 3.0 or higher. Summary pro forma balance sheet data appear in Exhibit 8-4.

The pro forma long-term debt ($300 million) to long-term debt plus equity ($380 million) ratio of 79% (300/380) reaches LBO levels in this scenario, and represents the upper limit for most industrial companies. But Tiger Bread is unable to borrow $300 million on its own. It needs the assets and earnings power of the Cookie Division. By combining the companies, Tiger Bread can afford a business equal in size to itself.

EXHIBIT 8-3 Tiger Bread acquisition of Cookie Division, income statement data (in millions)

	Tiger Bread	Cookie Division	Adjustments[1]	Pro Forma Combined
EBIT	$20	$20	—	$40
Interest—Bank loan	—	—	12[2]	12
Interest—Junk bonds	—	—	18[2]	18
Pretax income	$20	$20	$(30)	$10
Taxes	8	8	(12)	4
Net income	$12	$12	$(18)	$ 6
Interest coverage ratio	—	—	—	1.3×

[1] Before purchase accounting adjustments or synergy effects.
[2] Annualized cost of bank loans and junk bonds.

EXHIBIT 8-4   Tiger Bread acquisition of Cookie Division, balance sheet data (in millions)

	Tiger Bread	Cookie Division	Adjustments	Pro Forma Combined
Current assets	$ 40	$ 40	$ —	$ 80
Fixed assets	60	60	60[1]	180
Goodwill	—	—	160[2]	160
Total assets	$100	$100	$220	$420
Current liabilities	$ 20	$ 20	$ —	$ 40
Long-term debt	—	—	300[3]	300
Stockholders' equity	80	80	(80)[4]	80
	$100	$100	$220	$420

Adjustments

[1] Write-up of Cookie Division's fixed assets.

[2] Set up goodwill account to reflect excess of purchase price over asset write-ups and Division's equity values.

[3] Addition of $300 million of debt to finance the acquisition.

[4] Elimination of Cookie Division's equity value.

Junk bond type leverage is risky. Problems merging buyer and seller, operating setbacks in the buyer's base business, and industry-wide downturns can lead to earnings shortfalls that scare lenders and panic shareholders. The mere rumor, not to mention the actual threat, of debt service difficulties can lead to a sharp decline in the market's perception of the buyer's equity value, and a commensurate drop in its stock price. Over a two-month period in late 1995, for example, Kmart's share price dropped 50% on unsubstantiated bankruptcy rumors despite management's intense efforts to counteract them.

The vast majority of corporate executives prefer to avoid these risks, so a "bet the ranch" strategy, like Tiger Bread's $300 million all-debt acquisition of the Cookie Division, is too dangerous. Corporate managers are more comfortable reviewing deals in the range of 10% to 40% of their employer's market value. For a company with a $250 million market capitalization, this involves searches for a $25 million to $100 million business. A $50 million company looks at $5 million to $20 million deals. This range guarantees management attention to the transaction, without presenting the looming risks accompanying the purchase of a larger firm.

AFFORDABILITY AND EQUITY FINANCING

What if Tiger Bread Corporation wants a large deal, but is reluctant to take additional debt? Suppose that bank and junk lenders are unwilling to loan the company sufficient cash to cover the purchase price? Tiger Bread then considers issuing equity to finance a portion of the acquisition cost.

Equity investors, like lenders, impose certain quantitative and qualitative criteria on the deals they finance. It follows that a firm cannot obtain an unlimited amount of equity, even though it may have an immediate need to take advantage of an acquisition opportunity. The additional shares can result in EPS dilution, and shareholders tolerate only a limited amount of dilution before protesting.

AFFORDABILITY AND EPS DILUTION

Most institutional shareholders criticize deals in which the acquirer experiences EPS dilution of more than 6%. Using publicly available data (which in a share exchange must include pro forma EPS calculations prepared by an independent accounting firm), institutional shareholders predict how much a potential transaction dilutes the earnings power of their investment. In the pro forma calculation, all new financing is included, along with the appropriate accounting adjustments. Common adjustments in the pro forma data include additional depreciation and goodwill amortization expenses reflecting the write-up of the target's assets. This increase in asset values corresponds to the difference between historical book value and the purchase price (where the purchase price is below book value, there is an asset write-down). In many public transactions, the acquirer discloses expected synergies, necessitating additional adjustments to the pro forma calculations.

Exhibits 8-5 and 8-6 set forth summary financial results on the $50 million Tiger Bread/Lion Roll acquisition. This time, the data includes pro forma income statement adjustments. Increased depreciation is factored into the cost of goods sold. Overhead savings appear as SG&A (selling, general, and administration expenses) reductions. The EPS dilution with the adjustments is calculated at 5%, the difference

EXHIBIT 8-5   Tiger Bread acquisition of Lion Roll, income statement data (in millions)

	Tiger Bread Corp.	Lion Roll Corp.	Adjustments	Pro Forma Combined
Sales	$100.0	$25.0	$ —	$125.0
Cost of goods sold	50.0	12.0	3.0[1]	65.0
Gross profit	50.0	13.0	3.0	60.0
Selling, general & adm. expenses	30.0	8.0	(1.0)[2]	37.0
Operating income	20.0	5.0	(2.0)	23.0
Interest expense	—	—	4.0[3]	4.0
Pretax income	20.0	5.0	(6.0)	19.0
Income taxes	8.0	2.0	(2.4)	7.6
Net income	$ 12.0	$ 3.0	$(3.6)	$ 11.4
Earnings per share	$ 1.00	$0.30	—	$ 0.95
Shares outs. (000)	12,000	10,000	(10,000)[4]	12,000

Adjustments

[1] $30.0 million fixed asset write-up amortized over 10 years.
[2] $1.0 million reduction of redundant corporate overhead at Lion Roll.
[3] 8% interest on 100% debt financing of $50 million purchase price.
[4] Cancellation of (Lion Roll's) shares.

EXHIBIT 8-6   Tiger Bread acquisition of Lion Roll, balance sheet data (in millions)

	Tiger Bread	Lion Roll	Adjustments	Pro Forma Combined
Current assets	$ 40	$10	$ —	$ 50
Fixed assets	60	15	30[1]	105
Goodwill	—	—	—	—
Total assets	$100	$25	$ 30	$155
Current liabilities	$ 20	$ 5	$ —	$ 25
Long-term debt	—	—	50[2]	50
Stockholders' equity	80	20	(80)[3]	80
Total liabilities & stockholders' equity	$100	$25	$ 30	$155

Adjustments

[1] $30.0 million fixed asset write-up.
[2] Addition of $50.0 million acquisition debt.
[3] Cancellation of Lion Roll's equity.

between Tiger Bread's $1.00 EPS before the deal and its $0.95 EPS afterward.

In preparing their data, investors realize that Tiger Bread has some latitude in determining where to allocate the asset write-ups. Fixed assets, goodwill, leaseholds, and customer lists are a few of the eligible possibilities. Most acquirers have some flexibility in assigning the depreciable lives of these "written-up" assets. Longer lives lead to higher EPS results.

Investors also consider management's ability to cut costs before adjusting the combined income statement.

Equity investors forecast combined results 5 or 10 years into the future. If the deal contributes to EPS growth while keeping risks at tolerable levels, the acquirer has a good chance of selling stock to finance the deal.

SUMMARY

Acquisition leverage concerns shareholders. As noted earlier, one way for management to reduce EPS dilution and inflate EPS growth is to use more leverage. Many chief executives succumb to this temptation. Debt invariably heightens the financial risk of the combined company, compared with the "predeal" buyer. In the end, the new financial risk can outweigh the benefits of growth, and the attractiveness of the "postdeal" buyer's stock actually declines, no matter how rosy the projections. As shareholders start selling their stock in light of the perceived risk, the potential for a sustained price decline in the acquirer's shares becomes apparent.

Lenders are eager to finance acquisitions. The most "bankable" deals involve two successful businesses, each of which has an established track record of profitability.

Buyers find resistance from their shareholders for deals encompassing more than 6% EPS dilution. Shareholders also dislike transactions involving substantial changes in the buyer's financial risk level. These concerns affect the range of "doable deal" sizes. Knowing these limits is an important element in determining a buyer's acquisition budget.

9 AN EQUITY VALUATION PRIMER

The stock market's addiction to fashion, its herdlike mentality, and its instinctual drive for profit are key factors influencing the values of companies. Within the chaotic and emotional framework of the day-to-day buying and selling of securities, there is an underlying current of discipline governing share prices. This discipline is founded primarily in two valuation approaches: "intrinsic value" and "relative value." Corporate sellers and buyers can both benefit from an understanding of these two valuation techniques.

VALUATION APPROACHES

The analysis and valuation of common stocks is far from the quasi-scientific discipline extolled in business school textbooks. Of the four broad approaches to common stock valuation, only two lend themselves to the scientific approach—the intrinsic value approach and the relative value approach. Both forecast stock prices on the basis of historical economic, capital market, industry, and company statistics, which are then used to establish predictive trends for corporate operating results. The principal decision variables are earnings and dividend projections. Under the intrinsic value method, future dividends are discounted to the present, thereby establishing a "present value" for the stock. If the stock is trading at a price lower than this value, it is a "buy"; if the market price is higher than this value, the stock is a "sell." The relative value approach considers intrinsic values too difficult to establish, owing to the arguments over hard-to-make projections and controversial discount rates. Instead, various valuation parameters of a publicly traded stock, such as its P/E, Price/Book, or Price/Sales ratios are compared with the stocks of companies in the same industry. If the P/E ratio of the stock being evaluated is substantially lower than its peer group, and if there is no justifiable reason for the discrepancy, the relative value approach views the stock as a "buy."

The third and fourth approaches are called "market anticipation" and "technical analysis," respectively. The market anticipation approach acknowledges that most stocks are fairly valued by the many security analysts using the intrinsic and relative value methods. The market anticipation approach suggests that at some future point the consensus view on any given stock's earnings power or business risk will change, providing impetus to a higher (or lower) stock price. A typical pronouncement from a market anticipation analyst might be, "The Starbucks shares will increase in value as the market realizes the reduced volatility of the company's earning stream." Such conclusions carry little analytical weight and are most effective when repeated loudly and continually, thus echoing "The squeaky wheel gets the grease" tactic used by promoters in any business. Such repetition can be quite useful in questionable merger transactions where the promoter can dismiss critics as "not understanding" a deal's impact on future earnings. Technical analysis is the fourth approach. It is concerned with the price and volume trading patterns of a stock. This valuation technique does not consider a company's operating history, its earning potential, or other microeconomic factors as relevant to the valuation process. Rather, the technician believes that trading patterns reflect all logical and emotional forces affecting a stock price. An analysis of these patterns, usually in conjunction with various industry and market trading indicators, provides predictive trends that enable the technician to forecast stock prices.

Academics have tested various technical theories and concluded that there is no evidence to support the claim of technicians. Nevertheless, Wall Street is one place where perception easily becomes reality. Since thousands of investors believe in technical analysis, market participants must be sensitive to technical opinions in evaluating stock prices. Likewise, even the most rigorous disciples of intrinsic or relative value investing are cognizant of the sometimes relentless drumbeating of "market anticipation" investors, who are trying desperately to influence the consensus decision on a stock's value. Their influence has been strong in certain cases and has been observed in the rise and fall of numerous "high flyer" stocks, the peak prices of which defy rational explanation. How else does one explain the rocketlike rise of Scoreboard, Inc. from $5 per share to $19 in nine months in 1993, or the lightning "round trip" of Applied Magnetics shares, from $14 in March 1993, to $2½ in December 1994, and then its return to favor at $14 in November 1995?

Four Valuation Approaches

1. *Intrinsic Value.* A business equals the net present value of its dividends.
2. *Relative Value.* Determine value by comparing similar companies' values.
3. *Market Anticipation.* Valuation parameters change precipitously among industries and companies.
4. *Technical.* Share prices can be divined from prior trading patterns.

STARTING WITH INTRINSIC VALUE

Acquisitions are designed to increase the share value of the buyer. As a first step, I consider them in the context of the intrinsic value framework: A company's value is the present value of the stream of future dividends.

An acquisition, like any other corporate investment, should contribute toward increasing projected per share dividends or lowering the rate at which future cash flows are discounted. This section reviews key financial concepts underlying the valuation of a company.

The fundamental value of a common share can be equated to future dividends by various formulas. The best known formula is the

**EXHIBIT 9-1   Discounted cash dividend valuation approach,
constant growth model**

$$P = \frac{D_1}{k - g}$$

where P = current stock price.

D_1 = next year's cash dividend.

k = annual rate of return required by shareholders.

g = expected annual growth rate of dividends.

dividend discount model, which is best applied to the shares of firms that are assumed to have a constant rate of growth. This formula is shown in Exhibit 9-1.

For companies that are not expected to have anything approaching a constant growth rate, such as a cyclical business, a start-up venture, or a firm with a history of special dividends and spin-offs, the formula is modified for different dividend patterns. The practice is to predict dividends for a 5- or 10-year period, after which time the company under study is assumed to pay out dividends in a constant fashion. A 10-year time horizon is used in the next formula, shown in Exhibit 9-2.

In the two-step model, g_1 is the growth rate of the dividend in year one, g_2 in year two, and so on until year 11 when the model becomes steady state. Alternative dividend models value companies that

**EXHIBIT 9-2   Discounted cash dividend valuation approach,
two-step growth model**

$$P = \frac{D_0\,(1 + g_1)}{(1 + k)} + \frac{D_1\,(1 + g_2)}{(1 + k)^2} + \ldots + \frac{D_9\,(1 + g_{10})}{(1 + k)^{10}}$$

$$+ \; \frac{\dfrac{D_{10}\,(1 + g_{11})}{k - g_{11}}}{(1 + k)^{10}}$$

EXHIBIT 9-3   Mountain Electric Company (MEC) common stock

Compound annual dividend growth	8.0%
Next year's dividend	$1.50
Expected constant dividend growth rate ("g")	8.0%
Dividend payout ratio	50.0%
Earnings per share	$3.00
Compound annual earnings per share growth	8.0%
MEC stockholder's required annual rate of return ("k"), given a choice of alternative investments	11.0%

don't pay dividends and consider situations involving short-term holding periods.

The inability of businesspeople to predict accurately the future growth rates of a company's dividend, and the lack of a market consensus on the appropriate discount rate for almost any stock, combine to generate an enormous amount of equity trading activity based simply on differing views regarding these two fundamental aspects of a stock's worth. Even if there appears to be an underlying consensus on future dividends and on what an equity holder's expected return should be, minuscule differences in the P, g, and k estimates provide a broad band of trading values.

Consider the analysis of the fictitious Mountain Electric Company's common stock shown in Exhibit 9-3. An MEC stockholder seeks an 11.0% annual rate of return because alternative investments with less risk provide expected annual returns not far below 11%. Exhibit 9-4 lists sample alternative investments. It shows that MEC stock (and almost any corporate stock) is a riskier investment than a U.S. government bond or a high-quality corporate bond. For this reason, MEC offers its shareholders the potential for a superior return.

EXHIBIT 9-4   Sample alternative investments' expected rates of return

U.S. government bonds	6.0%
"AA" rated corporate bonds	7.0%
"BBB" rated bonds	9.0%
MEC stock	11.0%

Using information on MEC's common stock, an analyst can use the dividend discount valuation formula to derive a $50 share value:

$$\text{MEC Price} = \frac{D_1}{k - g}$$

$$\text{MEC Price} = \frac{\$1.50}{.11 - .08}$$

$$\text{MEC Price} = \$50.00$$

An investor who disagrees just slightly with the 11% k and 8% g estimates has a substantially different MEC stock value. For example, if he concludes that MEC's growth rate will be 7.5% annually (vs. 8%) because of an economic slowdown in MEC's service area, this small 0.5% *deviation* causes him to price MEC shares at $43, a 14% difference with the $50 value. If the shares are trading at $50, he is a seller.

Since small differences in investor opinions on k and g move a stock price up or down, public companies pay critical attention to how dividend growth rates and required returns are perceived by shareholders. Even a minor decline in the consensus growth rate of a company's dividend is very damaging. A small increase in k, the investor's desired rate of return (i.e., the "discount rate") produces a similar result (increase k from 11% to 11.5% and the MEC's stock price drops to $43). Thus, in addition to implementing strategies that actually achieve higher dividends, companies must foster an image of predictable growth. This image of constancy is quite valuable because investors view the company's shares in a less risky light. They award a lower discount rate to the company's cash flows, resulting in a bigger present value.

This portrait of stability is in obvious contrast to the volatile environment that is endemic to a market economy. Nevertheless, in an effort to defy economic gravity, public companies avoid cutting dividends, notwithstanding earnings declines, and seek to "smooth out" or "manage" their natural variability in annual income by timing revenue recognition, incurring special charges, or taking one-time gains. The feigned stability provides confidence to investors, who then consider the stock as having a lower risk profile.

In this valuation framework, it is clear why large acquisitions demand so much attention from security analysts and equity investors.

Their size, immediate balance sheet impact, frequent diversification aspects, and earnings growth implications influence dramatically the key variables that compose the price equations,

$$P = \frac{D}{k - g} \text{ or } P = \frac{D_1}{(1 + k)} + \frac{D_2}{1 + k^2} + \cdots \frac{\dfrac{D_{n+1}}{k - g}}{(1 + k)^n}$$

A large deal causes security analysts to revise the buyer's earnings projections and to consider the company's dividend growth prospects in light of their findings. After the analysts complete pro forma projections of income statements, balance sheets, and sources and uses of funds, they look to the quality of the dividend stream being forecast. Did the buyer finance the deal entirely with debt? If so, the combined company's leverage may indicate that future dividends are subject to greater volatility, thereby mandating a higher required rate of return than before the deal. Likewise, a diversification acquisition might lead to another k downgrade by altering the buyer's industry risk.

For example, if a volatile high-tech firm purchased a stable food business, investors would consider the combined earnings stream as less risky than the high-tech business on a stand-alone basis, assuming no change in leverage ratios. This sentiment of "less risk" would result in a lower k for the surviving company. The opposite would happen if a gas distribution utility purchased a biotech firm, since the latter would probably have a greater risk profile.

The use of k and g as individual company statistics independent of the broader market is a key tenet of the "intrinsic value" crowd, but the sheer difficulty in forecasting corporate dividends and determining the appropriate discount rate spawns many arguments. Discussions among intrinsic value investors typically involve comments such as: "How can you assign an 11% growth rate to the stock's dividends when its historical growth rate is 14%?" "Other firms in the industry are growing at 12%; why is your projected growth rate only 8%?" "Your 18% discount rate is too high; if we drop it to 16%, we can justify buying the stock." "Our estimates of $g = 12\%$ and $k = 17\%$ can't be correct; they indicate a $14 stock price when the market price is $24. Our numbers must be wrong!"

RELATIVE VALUE APPROACH

K and *g* are still popular subjects in business schools, but the inability of investors and analysts to agree on exact estimates of *k* and *g* for individual stocks, and the huge differences in prices that only small differences in these statistics make, reduce their relevance in the "real world." While believing that the intrinsic value concept is intuitively correct, a large portion of the investment community abandons it as unworkable from a practical point of view. In its stead has risen the "relative value" concept, which uses comparisons as the basis for establishing value. The theory is simple enough: If companies participate in the same industry, those with comparable track records and balance sheets should have comparable valuation yardsticks. Since *k* and *g* statistics are indeterminate, the relative value school adopts substitute measures, the most popular being the P/E ratio.

Relative value adherents can be spotted when they are saying something like, "Safeway's stock is undervalued at a 14 P/E ratio because it is growing as fast as Giant Food, which has a 17 P/E ratio," or "Long's Drug Stores is overvalued because its 22 P/E ratio is 47% higher than the industry's 14 P/E ratio, but its projected earnings growth is only 30% higher than the industry's."

Relative value investors employ many other financial statistics. Ratios such as the Share Price to Book Value and Share Price to Sales per Share Ratio are popular. Many industry-specific ratios exist. For example, retail store analysts use Share Price to Number of Stores per Share Ratio as one barometer of relative value. Cable TV analysts use the Share Price to Number of Connected Homes per Share Ratio: cement companies, Tons of Production Capacity per Share Ratio and so on. The P/E ratio, however, remains the most popular relative valuation statistic.

THE P/E RATIO

Wall Street synthesizes the *k* and *g* variables of the dividend discount model into one statistic, the price/earnings ratio. Many acquirers fail to anticipate stock price movements resulting from a change in the market's perception of their postacquisition *k*. The main reason for this oversight is that the vast majority of news stories on transactions emphasize the buyer's added EPS growth or added dilution. Rarely does the media analyze the effect of the acquisition on the investor's risk, even when the buyer is confronting significant leverage or diversifying its business.

Business publications constantly print statements such as "Philip Morris is trading at a 16 P/E ratio, 10% over the market average." "Dow Chemical looks cheap at a 15 P/E ratio," or "Apple Computer is overpriced at a 22 P/E ratio." Individual P/E ratios are often expressed in relative terms. When a company's P/E ratio exceeds the P/E ratio of the stock market as a whole, that company is considered to have earnings growth potential exceeding the growth prospects of the average listed company. Conversely, a relatively low P/E indicates a growth profile that is below average. Analysts extend these comparisons to a company's peers.

For either a "high growth" company or a "low growth" company, the P/E ratio is a function of two perceptions: (1) What is the company's future growth rate; and (2) How much of a return should this stock provide relative to other investments? The same questions must be asked by investors in evaluating an acquisition's impact on the acquirer's P/E. Consider the interrelationships involved in the following two formulas:

Dividend Discount Model	*Price Earnings Multiple*
$$P = \dfrac{D_1}{k - g}$$	$$\text{P/E Multiple} = \dfrac{P}{EPS}$$

$$P = \text{Current stock price}$$
$$D_1 = \text{Expected dividend rate}$$
$$k = \text{Investors' required rate of return}$$
$$g = \text{Expected growth rate in dividends}$$
$$EPS = \text{Current earnings per share}$$
$$\text{P/E Multiple} = \text{Price/Earnings ratio}$$

For every publicly traded stock, its price, dividend rate, and earnings per share are known facts, which cannot be disputed. These statistics are available in various business newspapers. The variables open to interpretation and educated guesswork are k and g; these

EXHIBIT 9-5   Mountain Electric Company P/E calculation using intrinsic value variables

$$P/E = \frac{\dfrac{D_1}{k - g}}{EPS}$$

$$= \frac{\dfrac{\$1.50}{11.0\% - 8.0\%}}{\$3.00}$$

$$= \frac{\$50.00}{\$3.00}$$

$$= 16.7\times$$

same publications only provide estimates of these statistics. Changes in the market's perception of a stock's risk or growth characteristics alter the P/E ratio. This is illustrated in Exhibit 9-5 by substituting $D_1/k - $ "g" for "P" in the Price/Earnings Multiple calculation.

Consider the situation in which MEC announces a major acquisition. If investors decide that the deal increases MEC's growth rate, the P/E ratio goes up considerably. Suppose MEC's growth rate increases to 10.0% from 8.0%. The stock price then reaches $150 and the P/E ratio climbs to 50.0× (Exhibit 9-6).

If the P/E Multiple stayed at only 16.7× after the completion of the proposed transaction, the investors would consider MEC a "BUY."

EXHIBIT 9-6   Mountain Electric Company adjusted P/E calculation for acquisition

$$P/E \text{ Multiple} = \frac{\dfrac{\$1.50}{11.0\% - 10.0\%}}{\$3.00}$$

$$P/E \text{ Multiple} = \frac{\$150.00}{\$3.00}$$

$$P/E \text{ Multiple} = 50.0\times$$

EXHIBIT 9-7   Mountain Electric Company adjusted P/E calculation for acquisition and new debt

$$\text{P/E Multiple} = \frac{\$1.50}{\dfrac{13.0\% - 10.0\%}{\$3.00}}$$

$$\text{P/E Multiple} = \frac{\$50.00}{\$3.00}$$

$$\text{P/E Multiple} = 16.7\times$$

Assume MEC incurs substantial acquisition debt in the deal. The investors' new perception is one of increased earnings volatility. They demand a higher rate of return, thereby reducing the 50.0× multiple to a number more down to earth. Exhibit 9-7 shows the impact of a 13% required return instead of the earlier 11% return. In this case, the acquisition doesn't improve MEC's P/E ratio.

The P/E ratio is a statistic that incorporates the *growth* and *risk* aspects of a stock. The P/E ratio climbs when investors assign an increase to a stock's indicated growth rate. Likewise, the P/E ratio increases or decreases with changes in the market's perception of the stock's risk characteristics. This having been said, Wall Street analysts mostly analyze acquisition-derived changes in the buyer's perceived growth rate. This investigation far outweighs the emphasis given to the perceived movement in k.

THE PRICE OF RISK

The determination of the required rate of return of a stock is based on a relative analysis of the returns being offered by competing investments, taking into account the respective risks involved. Investments perceived as "risky" because of checkered track records or questionable prospects should provide investors with a high expected rate of return. Exhibit 9-8 illustrates a risk/return matrix for competing investments.

The notion that the risks of competing investments can be (1) measured; and then (2) priced, is derived from the capital asset

EXHIBIT 9-8   Risks and returns,
November 1995

Investment	Annual Expected Return
U.S. Government bonds	6.00%
"A" rated corporate bonds	6.50
Utility stock mutual fund	12.50
Industrial stock mutual fund	13.00
Biotech company common stock	20.00
Leveraged buyouts	30.00

pricing model (CAPM), a theoretical financial concept refined in the 1960s. The principal measure of risk under CAPM is beta (β), which is a statistic that measures the historical volatility of a given investment's rate of return with the historical return of the U.S. stock market. The β (beta) of an individual stock is calculated empirically and there are many data services that sell statistical calculations of betas.

The logic of the CAPM is simple. Unpredictability and volatility in investment returns are bad. Stability and assurance of returns are good. The required return of any stock should be equal to the rate of return on a relatively riskless investment, such as a U.S. government bond, plus a premium for the added risk incurred by the investor for holding a non-government-guaranteed investment. The premium is obtained in a two-step process. First, the government bond rate is subtracted from the expected return of the stock market. Second, the result of this subtraction, which is defined as the "market premium" for risk, is multiplied by the stock's beta to determine the applicable risk premium. If government bonds yield 6% and people believe the stock market has an expected rate of return (i.e., dividends plus capital gains) of 13%, the "market premium" can be estimated at 7% (13% minus 6%). If the relevant beta for an individual stock is 1.50, this means that its risk premium should be 1.50 times the 7% market premium, or $1.50 \times 7\% = 10.5\%$. The calculation appears in Exhibit 9-9.

Based on the preceding information, a rational investor would only purchase the stock when he believed he could achieve a 16.5% return from the investment. Projected cash returns from the stock would be discounted at 16.5% and the resultant present value of these cash flows would then be compared with the stock price. If the present value is higher than the price, the stock is a "BUY."

EXHIBIT 9-9 Sample calculation of risk premium for an individual stock with 1.5 beta

(1) Market Premium × Beta = Individual Stock Risk Premium

(2) Expected Return − Yield on × Beta = Individual Stock
on Stock Market Government Bond Risk Premium (ISRP)

(3) (13% − 6%) 1.5 = ISRP

(4) 10.5% = ISRP

Once the individual stock risk premium has been calculated, k can be derived by adding the government bond yield to the previous calculation:

(1) k = Government Bond Yield + Individual Stock Risk Premium

(2) k = 6% + 10.5%

(3) k = 16.5%

Suppose a rational investor forecast the following cash flows from a Troy Corporation share, which has a 1.5 beta and is currently trading at $30 per share (see Exhibit 9-10). Are Troy Corporation shares a "BUY"? The answer is no. The present value of the positive cash flows only equals $27.64, which is below the share's trading price of $30.00 (see Exhibit 9-11).

BETA

The beta statistic premium is, by itself, a mathematical calculation involving a comparison of the stock's historical returns to the market's. The beta of the broad stock market indices is defined as 1.0. A common stock that has returns identical to the market would have a 1.0 beta. If the stock market was forecast to provide investors with capital gains

EXHIBIT 9-10 Troy Corporation shares, sample investor's dividend and sale price estimates

	1995	1996	1997	1998
Purchase cost	$ 30.00	—	—	—
Cash dividends	—	$2.00	$2.20	$ 2.42
Sale of shares	—	—	—	36.00
	$(30.00)	$2.00	$2.20	$38.42

EXHIBIT 9-11   Calculation of present value of cash flows

Year	Cash Flow ($)		Discount Factor (k)		($)
1996	2.00	÷	1.165	=	1.72
1997	2.20	÷	$1.36 \ (1.165)^2$	=	1.62
1998	(2.42 + 36.00)	÷	$1.58 \ (1.165)^3$	=	24.30
			Present value of cash flows		27.64

and dividend income equivalent to a 10% rate of return, the 1.0 beta stock would have an expected rate of return of 10%. Should the market return forecast drop to negative 5%, the prognosticators would say that the stock's forecast mirrors the −5% market return. A stock with a beta of 1.5, on the other hand, is forecast to move one and one-half times the movement of the broad stock market. So if the equity market is projected to return 10% in the next year, the 1.5 beta stock would have an estimated 15% return. Likewise, a −5% market return would lead a −7.5% return estimate for the 1.5 beta stock. Because more volatility in investment returns is bad, investors require higher returns for the risk of a 1.5 beta stock, as compared to the assumed return for a 1.0 beta stock.

A stock's beta is only a measure of its *past* sensitivity to market moves. For any one stock, beta's applicability as a predictor of future price sympathy with the market is limited. While all stock prices have a tendency to go up and down with the market, individual share prices are heavily influenced by factors peculiar to that one company; a management change, a new product and so on. An investor's portfolio can largely eliminate firm-specific risks by combining 20 or more stocks into a portfolio. The diversification achieved thereby tends to bring the portfolio's expected returns more into line with what its weighted-average beta would predict, as aberrant individual stock returns cancel each other out.

Designed and nurtured by the academic community in the 1950s and 1960s, beta and the CAPM achieved wide acceptance with equity portfolio managers by the 1970s. Indeed, the CAPM makes common sense: Corporate investments should yield more than U.S. government bonds, and risky industries should offer investors higher prospective returns than conservative businesses. Today, the CAPM offers distinct advantages for M&A practitioners, who need a logical risk framework in which to compare and contrast deals. The CAPM allows them to grade the risk of competing investments and to discount the relevant cash flows accordingly. More importantly, the CAPM is widely accepted in the institutional investment community, the primary source of acquisition financing.

Besides enjoying the benefits of a wide acceptance, the CAPM has another advantage: Its primary elements are easy to find. The government bond rate is available from daily newspapers. The expected return on the stock market is arguable, but over long periods it has yielded 6 to 8 percentage points more per annum than government bonds; when I consider appropriate corporate discount rates I use the Expected Market Return as the 10-year government bond rate plus 7%, the average of the additional return provided by the market. I then look up relevant betas in business publications to develop a reasonable discount rate. While this shorthand method is not accurate from an academic point of view, the result is acceptable for most corporate valuation purposes. Exhibit 9-12 shows calculations for Ford Motor and Hewlett Packard.

These two k calculations involve prominent publicly traded companies, but many times executives work on acquisitions of closely held concerns that don't have betas. For these firms, the beta of a similar publicly traded company is a good proxy. If a close match cannot be found, the average beta of a group of similar public companies is a substitute. To illustrate, a moderately leveraged, privately owned drugstore chain should have a 0.9 beta estimate, given the seven-company average derived in Exhibit 9-13.

EXHIBIT 9-12   Sample k calculations, November 1995

Corporate Dividend Discount Rate	$= k =$	Government Bond Rate	$+$ Beta	$\left[\vphantom{\begin{array}{c}E\\M\\R\end{array}}\right.$ Expected Market Return	$-$	Government Bond Rate $\left.\vphantom{\begin{array}{c}E\\M\\R\end{array}}\right]$

Ford Motor (1.15 Beta)
    $k = 6\% + 1.15\,(13\% - 6\%)$
    $k = 14.1\%$

Hewlett Packard (1.35 Beta)
    $k = 6\% + 1.35\,(13\% - 6\%)$
    $k = 15.5\%$

Where:
10-Year Government Bond Rate $= 6\%$
Expected Market Return $= 13\%$

EXHIBIT 9-13   Beta of publicly traded drugstore companies summary information at July 1995

Company	Beta	Sales (Millions)	Net Income (Millions)	Debt/ Equity	P/E Ratio[1]
		Latest Fiscal Year			
Arbor Drugs	0.8	619	20	0.2	15.5
Big B	0.8	668	15	0.7	14.7
Fay's	0.9	1,038	13	0.8	12.7
Genovese	0.9	570	9	0.5	12.9
Long's Drug	0.8	2,558	49	0.0	14.5
Rite Aid	0.9	4,534	141	0.8	14.8
Walgreen	1.1	9,235	282	0.0	19.2
Average	0.9				

[1] P/E based on forward year's EPS estimate.

RETURNING TO INTRINSIC VALUE

Under the "intrinsic value" framework, a company's equity value is the present value of its dividends. Projections of dividends are calculated, and then discounted using a factor (k) incorporating the CAPM. Potential acquirers should incorporate this notion in considering the appropriate purchase price of an acquisition. The same concepts should then be used in evaluating the impact of the acquisition on the buyer's share price. Pro forma projected dividends can then be discounted by a pro forma k. A "go" or "no go" decision can thus be made within a numerical system, as we will discuss later on.

RETURNING TO THE RELATIVE VALUE APPROACH

The reliance of the intrinsic value school on uncertain projections and arguable discount rates limits its usefulness in the real world. Practitioners have increasingly turned to relative values to price companies. Instead of an intrinsic value estimate based on discounted cash flows, professional investors use relative value analysis, where the positive and negative aspects of a stock are evaluated against those characteristics of similar stocks falling in the same industry category. The stocks' valuation parameters are then compared and contrasted, resulting in statements such as "Kroger shares are undervalued relative to Safeway's shares. Kroger's growth rate is higher, yet its P/E ratio is lower." In addition to the P/E ratio, other popular relative value comparators include the Price/Book, Price/Sales, Price/Cash Flow, and (Price + Debt)/EBIT ratios.

Investment bankers and business brokers generally refer to corporate values in these shorthand terms. In fact, intrinsic value is rarely discussed. Inevitably, the asking price of a business is characterized as "Six times EBIT" or "Twenty times earnings" or "Three times the book value." When either the business owner or bankers are asked how they derived these prices, the response typically is, "Well, the last acquisition in the industry had a value of 'six times EBIT,' 'twenty times earnings,' or 'three times book value.'" If the asking price is higher than the most recent transaction's value multiples, the potential buyer asks the obvious question, "Why is the price higher than the last deal?" He is likely to hear a recitation of the acquisition's positive attributes, such as that it has a better track record than previous deals, better growth prospects, or a solid balance sheet. These and other value-defining characteristics are important elements of the relative value process.

Historical track record is the easiest way to differentiate the value multiples of different companies. Usually, companies with growth-oriented performance records have higher valuation ratios. An examination of the drugstore chains mentioned earlier is instructive (see Exhibit 9-14). Note how the companies with the best historical growth rates, Arbor Drugs and Walgreen, score best in the valuation multiple categories. Their P/E, Price/Book, and Price + Debt/EBIT ratios are the highest in the group. While past performance is no guarantee of future results, investors rely heavily on the historical data in determining appropriate valuation multiples.

The P/E and Price + Debt/EBIT ratios are the best barometers of value for companies with steady records of growth. Inconsistency adds complexity to the analysis. Exhibit 9-15 summarizes the performance of three companies, all operating in the casual dining industry. The three firms have similar growth rates and leverage characteristics, but only Luby's Cafeterias shows *consistent* increases in sales and earnings. NPC International and Ryan's Family Steak House, in contrast,

EXHIBIT 9-14   Key valuation data of publicly traded drugstore companies, July 1995

Company	Compound 5-Year Annual Growth in EPS	Valuation Multiples		
		P/E[1]	Price/ Book	Enterprise Value/ EBIT[3]
Arbor Drugs	13.2%	15.5	2.7	12.8
Big B	N.A.[2]	14.7	1.7	10.8
Fay's	(1.3)	12.7	1.4	8.2
Genovese	8.7	12.9	1.6	7.5
Long's Drug	1.9	14.5	1.4	9.3
Rite Aid	7.7	14.8	2.0	9.9
Walgreen	12.9	19.2	3.5	13.7

[1] Based on forward year's EPS estimate.
[2] Big B's EPS were negative in 1990.
[3] Enterprise value equals (i) market value of the company's equity, minus (ii) outstanding debt, plus (iii) cash on hand.

EXHIBIT 9-15   Casual dining company track records (in millions except for per share data and ratios), September 1995

	1990	1991	1992	1993	1994	1995 (E)	5-Year Compound Growth Rate	P/E Ratio
Luby's								
Sales	311	328	346	367	391	420	6.2%	
								13.2×
EPS	1.17	1.18	1.19	1.31	1.45	1.55	5.8%	
Yr. to Yr. EPS Change	Up	Up	Up	Up	Up	Up		
NPC								
Sales	286	299	285	337	316	330	2.9%	
								11.2×
EPS	0.54	0.50	0.36	0.45	0.44	0.65	3.8%	
Yr. to Yr. EPS Change	Up	Down	Down	Up	Down	Up		
Ryan's								
Sales	273	299	352	396	449	505	13.1%	
								12.0×
EPS	0.46	0.44	0.56	0.53	0.57	0.62	6.2%	
Yr. to Yr. EPS Change	Up	Down	Up	Down	Up	Up		

exhibited *erratic* performance with earnings moving up unevenly. The P/E ratio is most relevant in establishing Luby's value in relation to other *consistent* casual dining chains. When the comparison is between Luby and NPC, or Luby's and Ryan's, the P/E ratio has less significance.

A constant earnings stream implies less risk, so steady earnings are awarded a higher value multiplier. A spotty record carries the connotation of reduced predictability and thus more risk, which means a lower multiplier. In this example, the inconsistency of NPC and Ryan's stands in stark contrast to the steadiness of Luby's. All things being equal, Luby has to be given a higher P/E ratio. But, the relationship between the P/E ratios and the earnings growth records is not linear because other "relative value" comparisons often play a role. M&A professionals look at Price/Sales, Price/Book Value, Price/Number of Restaurants and other multiples in determining whether a casual dining chain is fairly valued.

A few calculations are presented in the Exhibit 9-16. The three additional ratios provided on the right-hand side of the chart indicate that Luby's book value, sales, EBIT, and restaurants were valued relatively more in September 1995 than the less consistent companies, NPC and Ryan's. And while many factors besides growth statistics play a role in comparable valuation analysis, it is clear that the market was penalizing the latter two firms for their erratic behavior.

One complication arising from the use of the P/E multiple in corporate valuation is the variation in leverage found among companies

EXHIBIT 9-16   Alternative valuation ratios casual dining companies, September 1995

	Share Price Divided By		Enterprise Value Divided By		
	EPS[1]	Book Value	Sales	EBIT	Number of Restaurants[2]
Luby's	13.2	2.2	1.3	8.8	$3,030,000
NPC	11.2	1.8	0.8	7.8	840,000
Ryan's	12.0	1.4	1.1	8.2	2,170,000

[1] Based on forward year's EPS estimate.
[2] Luby's restaurants are larger, justifying in part a larger value per restaurant.

operating in the same industry. How does an analyst compare the P/E ratio of a risky, highly leveraged business to the P/E ratio of a safer, debt-free company? On the one hand, a highly leveraged company should merit a lower P/E multiple because of its higher risk. On the other hand, the potential for dramatic EPS growth is enhanced through higher leverage, providing a justification for a higher P/E ratio.

The components of the

$$\frac{\text{Price}}{\text{Earnings}} = \frac{\dfrac{D_1}{k - g}}{\text{EPS}}$$

formula can be tinkered with, so almost any price can be rationalized by crafty analysts, but the real arguments are played out in the stock market for each industry on a daily basis. Many times, higher leverage does result in a P/E penalty. In August 1995, debt appears to have contributed to H.J. Heinz's lower P/E multiple relative to a more conservatively financed Kellogg, which had a lower growth rate (see Exhibit 9-17).

In the mature food business, historical growth rates strongly influence P/E multiples, yet Heinz had a much lower P/E ratio despite

EXHIBIT 9-17 Value comparison of similar firms with different leverage

Company	1995 Estimated Results	1991–1995 Annual Growth Rates		August 1995 P/E Ratio[1]
H. J. Heinz Co.				
Producer of brand-name food products	$9.0 billion sales	Sales	8.1%	16.7×
	$665 million profit	EBIT	9.9%	
	$2.65 EPS	EPS	9.4%	
Kellogg Co.				
Producer of brand-name cereals and other food products	$7.2 billion sales	Sales	5.4%	20.0×
	$700 million profit	EBIT	6.2%	
	$3.50 EPS	EPS	8.7%	

[1] Based on forward years EPS estimate.

its higher growth statistics. The significant difference in debt ratios between the two firms was meaningful in this comparison:

June 30, 1995
Debt/Equity

Heinz	48:52
Kellogg	28:72

RELATIVE EBIT RATIOS

To reduce the effect of leverage on the two firms' valuations, practitioners concentrate on valuing the companies on the basis of two key statistics: Earnings before Interest and Taxes (EBIT) and Earnings before Interest, Taxes, Depreciation, and Amortization (EBITDA). Correspondingly, corporate value is defined as the sum of Equity Value plus Net Debt (i.e., "enterprise value"). This "grosses up" corporate values for the addition of interest expense in the denominator. Thus, Kellogg's equity value is $16 billion, while its enterprise value is $17 billion. Enterprise value is the numerator for the commonly used EBIT ratio:

$$\frac{\text{EBIT}}{\text{Ratio}} = \frac{\text{Market value of company's equity} + \text{Net outstanding debt}}{\text{Earnings before interest and taxes}}$$

or

$$\frac{\text{EBIT}}{\text{Ratio}} = \frac{\text{Enterprise value}}{\text{Earnings before interest and taxes}}$$

where Net Debt equals Total Debt less Cash-on-Hand.

The EBIT ratio is used by practitioners more frequently than the P/E ratio. The real world accepted a long time ago the need to compare companies without the impact of leverage, since a buyer can always change the seller's capital structure after a takeover. The EBIT and EBITDA ratios of the two companies are calculated in Exhibit 9-18. On an EBIT and EBITD multiple basis, the market still valued Heinz less than Kellogg, despite the latter's slower growth record.

EXHIBIT 9-18   Calculation of EBIT and EBITDA ratios

	Heinz	Kellogg
EBIT Ratio	10.0×	13.0×
EBITDA Ratio	8.0×	10.4×

In many other valuations, the EBIT and EBITDA ratios are helpful. Often, when an executive is seeking to determine the worth of a corporate division or a holding company subsidiary, he faces a business that does not report a true net income, since its capitalization structure is artificial or nonexistent. The business unit, however, will report an operating earnings figure, which is equivalent to an EBIT of a publicly traded firm. He thus has an indicator from which to begin a valuation.

Most large corporations use a holding company to segment their various lines of business for legal and financial purposes. Each business line is encapsuled in a subsidiary, a separate legal corporation that receives its permanent capital in the form of equity (and sometimes debt) from the "mother" company. While the subsidiaries own inventory, receivables, plant, and equipment, the mother company's primary assets are the common shares of these subsidiaries. Its primary liabilities are the debt it issues to finance subsidiary operating activities (i.e., the subsidiaries actually make the product or provide a service that is sold to an outside party). The mother company accesses large sums of financing at a cheaper cost than its subsidiaries can raise on a stand-alone basis; furthermore, it can afford to be staffed with the various finance, legal, tax, and accounting experts required to administer specialized services to the operating subsidiaries. Exhibit 9-19 presents a diagram showing a common organization structure.

EBIT valuation multiples enter into the sale process when the relevant subsidiary (or division as the case may be) does not have an independent capital structure. Its few long-term debts are owed to the mother company, which also owns its common equity. The concept of "subsidiary net income" does not exist on a stand-alone basis, since income tax obligations are consolidated at the parent company level. A

EXHIBIT 9-19   **Typical large corporation, financial and management structure of a holding company with four operating subsidiaries**

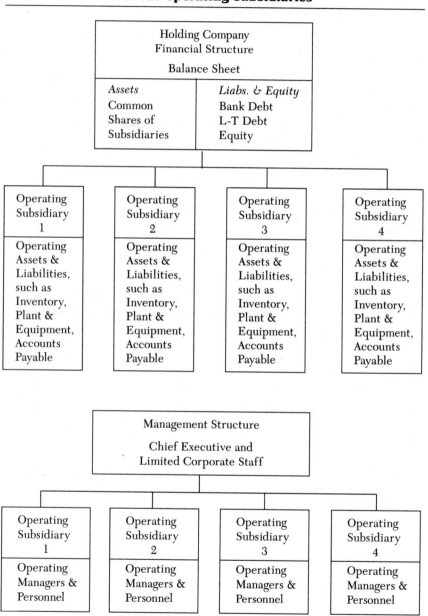

subsidiary's operating income, its EBIT, is frequently the best indicator against which to measure value in relation to independent firms engaged in the same business.

SUMMARY

Potential acquirers grapple with many valuation issues. The valuation of businesses is an inexact science. The valuation methods at hand provide, at best, a range of prices, rather than an exact number.

The primary valuation tools in the buyer's arsenal are derived from two frameworks: (1) the intrinsic value approach; and (2) the relative value method. Intrinsic value is the "academically pure" approach, which stipulates that a business is worth the discounted value of its future dividends. While theoretically correct, this dividend discounting carries little weight among practitioners, who decided long ago not to argue interminably among themselves about the merits of one projection against another. Nor do they care to debate the merits of one discount rate against another. Instead, most practitioner debates center on relative values. If the last steel manufacturing company was sold for 16× annual net earnings, then this 16× multiple is the starting point for valuing the next steel deal. If the new deal is a demonstrably better performer than the last acquisition, it deserves a higher multiple. If it has a worse record, it merits a lower multiple. Non-earnings-based valuation factors, such as "hidden" asset values or off-balance sheet liabilities, are then added or deducted from the benchmark value estimate.

10 VALUING MARGINAL PERFORMERS

In Chapter 9, we discussed the usefulness of applying earnings-based valuation ratios. P/Es and EBIT ratios are helpful indicators for solid, growing companies, but many firms lack a steady trend of improving sales and earnings. For these businesses, earnings-based multiples are less than an ideal means of discerning relative value. Alternative appraisal methods are used by professionals for these candidates, which generally fall into three broad categories:

Category 1. Corporate Value Based on Operating Track Record. A Category 1 company has a good historical trend, but it suffered a one year "earnings hiccup" over the past five years.

Category 2. Corporate Value Based More on Earnings Potential than on Past Performance. Sale candidates falling into Category 2 are erratic performers, cyclical businesses, or money-losers. The future earnings potential of these businesses is far more speculative than that of Category 1 companies.

Category 3. Corporate Value Based on Assets That Don't Provide Income Now, but That Have the Potential to Generate Income in the Future. Category 3 candidates frequently have substantial under-utilized real estate values or dormant natural resource assets, such as oil reserves, metallic ore reserves, or extensive timberlands. To generate income, the real estate must be sold or developed, while the natural resource assets must be extracted, harvested and then sold. A buyer calculates the likely future costs of real estate development, oil drilling, ore mining, or timber-cutting, and compares these costs with estimated revenues.

Underperforming government-mandated monopolies fall into Category 3. Examples include television stations, cellular bandwidths, and cable TV franchises. The key assets of these businesses are not "tangible assets" like timberlands, but they are nonetheless quite valuable if placed in the hands of an acquirer that can improve the franchise.

Harvesting underutilized assets can be both capital and management intensive. For example, the acquirer of a company with substantial iron ore reserves faces considerable expense to exploit the reserves. Mining equipment, rail spurs, utility connections, and start-up costs represent a huge investment. Constructing this infrastructure is for the buyer's account, as are the risks that the iron ore assets, after some development work, are not what they appeared to be at the time of purchase. The behavior of future iron ore prices is another uncertainty.

Set forth in the next section are some examples of businesses with erratic track records, along with the valuation methods applied to them.

CORPORATE VALUE BASED ON TRACK RECORD

Companies with Extraordinary Gains or Losses on the Income Statement

By definition, an extraordinary event is something that happens on rare occasions. Practitioners consider these items to be one-time occurrences that won't happen again. When using earnings multiples, they eliminate extraordinary gains or losses from the calculation of a target's net income and EBIT, providing the prospective buyer with pro forma data (i.e., as if the extraordinary event had never occurred). Needless to say, the valuation multiples of similar companies have to be adjusted in the same fashion to facilitate a comparison.

Companies with Discontinued Operations in the Income Statement

Large corporations regularly sell off divisions that do not fit in with their long-term goals. Following the divestitures, the sales and profits (or losses) of these discarded businesses are, for the most part, included in a separate part of the corporate income statement for accounting purposes, such as the "discontinued operations" section. For valuation purposes, practitioners eliminate a discontinued operation from the candidate's historical results, thereby producing pro forma data that can be used in a meaningful comparative analysis.

CORPORATE VALUE BASED MORE ON EARNINGS POTENTIAL THAN ON PAST PERFORMANCE

Companies with Uneven Earnings Records

Companies that do not exhibit smooth upward earnings trends are nevertheless valuable commodities, primarily because buyers think they can reform the inconsistent earnings pattern. Experts realize that a simplistic "estimated value," computed by multiplying (i) a one-year earnings statistic (such as net income or EBIT), by (ii) the recent transaction multiple, has much less meaning for an erratic performer than that same calculation performed for a consistent moneymaker. Several averaging methods exist to moderate the problematic effects of uneven track records. A common remedy is to "smooth" out the candidate's spotty performance by averaging three to five years of results. Instead of using the last year's earnings (or next year's estimated earnings), one calculates an average of the past three years' results. This average is multiplied by the one-year ratios applicable for similar acquisitions, thereby creating a meaningful estimate.

Besides averaging, other valuation methods are used to moderate the negative effect of an uneven earnings record, which corporate acquirers view unfavorably. A buyer's own constituencies may demand a steady stream of quarterly earnings increases, but this doesn't mean that Category 2 targets are unattractive. In fact, many such companies receive good offers. To rationalize the valuation process, practitioners rely on an additional set of approaches for erratic firms, cyclical companies, and money-losing enterprises.

Cyclical Firms

Many profitable firms have earnings streams that are highly sensitive to the business cycle of the economy. Typical cyclical enterprises are steel producers, car manufacturers, and home builders. "Boom times" for these firms are usually followed by "bust times" and their historical results show a repeated pattern of peaks and troughs. Other kinds of cyclical firms experience earnings patterns that do not correlate well to the general economy, but trend against other economic variables. Brokerage firms, for example, show cyclicality based on stock and bond prices, while agricultural firms exhibit earnings tied to the crop price cycle. M&A practitioners are hard pressed to place precise values on these enterprises. In practice, one-year and average earnings multiples are complemented by various other methods, including the following two earnings-based multiples:

- *Value as a Multiple of the Most Recent Peak Year Results.* Consider the multiple of Enterprise Value to peak year EBIT for recent acquisitions in the target's industry. Apply this multiple to the target's peak year EBIT to determine a reasonable valuation.
- *Value as a Multiple of the Most Recent Bottom Year Results.* Repeat the preceding exercise for bottom-of-the-cycle earnings.

Money Losing Companies

The first reaction of many corporate executives is to shy away from money-losing firms. The operating, managerial, and financial problems of the money-losers create headaches over and above those accompanying normal acquisitions. Furthermore, the risk of overpayment is magnified, since money-losers are hard to value, and their earnings, on a pro forma basis, are notoriously difficult to predict. These considerations increase the chances of the buyer not collecting the anticipated earnings on the investment.

While most large deals involve profitable firms, dozens of big money-losing companies change hands each year and, notwithstanding

the aforementioned complications, the acquirers of these underper-
formers represent a cross section of three buyer categories: the Bottom
Fisher, the Market Share/Product Line Extender, and the Strategic
Buyer. Each of these buyers expects a positive return on its investment, perhaps by liquidating the business for more money than the
purchase price, folding the target's product lines into its own (probably
without bringing over the related employees), obtaining access to
new technology, or reforming the loser into a winner through better
management.

While all these objectives are admirable, turnarounds are complicated. Buyers need to avoid being tempted into overpaying simply
because of promises of things to come. How does a rational buyer look
for valuation guideposts in these circumstances? Discounted cash
flow analysis is helpful only to facilitate the buyer's internal analysis.
Earnings-based multiples are of minimal use in appraising the worth
of a money-losing business since there are no earnings to multiply.
The primary attraction of the underperformer is its potential to make
money. How do buyers measure this potential in the real world, where
all earnings projections are suspect? They consider valuation benchmarks besides those derived from historical earnings. Many of these
tools are based on accounting statistics, while others rely on operating
data.

The following are popular accounting-based ratios for valuing a
money-losing company:

- *Cash Flow Multiple*. Even if the acquisition candidate loses
  money, it may have positive cash flow because of sizable depreciation and amortization expenses. The latest year's cash flow is
  then multiplied by a benchmark such as 5 or 6 to set a rough estimate of value.

- *Book Value Multiple*. A money-losing firm doesn't generate profits, but its shareholders' equity account is often positive, indicating that the accounting value of assets exceeds liabilities. The
  Price to Book Value Ratio of profitable manufacturing companies
  is usually 2–3×. Similar ratios for money-losers are 1× or less.

- *Sales Multiple*. A company with a high sales volume may have the
  potential to make money. Perhaps unneeded expenses can be cut,
  or prices raised. Recognizing this possibility, Wall Street bankers

representing an unprofitable firm often say something like, "Well, the proposed price is only 1× sales," as if this is a bargain for a money-losing business. To make sense out of this comment, buyers examine Price-to-Sales ratios of comparable publicly traded firms and acquisitions. A discount is then applied to establish a reasonable value. Thus, if the average Price/Sales ratio of the last three office supply deals was 0.6×, the asking price of a money-losing office supply firm might reasonably be 0.4×, a discount of 33%.

SHORTHAND RELATIVE VALUE RATIOS

For the most part, money-losing firms do not lend themselves to valuation tools based on accounting data, which work better for profitable firms with upward earnings trends. Nevertheless, comparable-company P/E, Value/EBIT, Value/Cash Flow, Price/Book, and Value/Sales ratios are factored into most distressed company appraisals, but the general lack of similar money-losing firms (or M&A transactions) limits the usefulness of these statistics. Practitioners consider a money-loser discount from profitable firm ratios in most cases, but practitioners do not always agree on the proper discount percentage. Projected cash flow analysis is also of questionable use in this marketplace because of the aforementioned uncertainty attached to the underperformer's prospects. Uncomfortable relying on either (1) value multiples based on historical results; or (2) future cash flows derived from doubtful projections, practitioners have developed numerous "shorthand" value ratios. These ratios depend on something other than historical and forecast financial data. Typically, they can be calculated quickly, using easily available asset or production statistics related to the sale candidate's business. Shorthand value indicators complement accounting-based ratios by providing alternative views on the price of "earnings potential."

Most shorthand value ratios are based on important operating criteria that relate specifically to one industry. For example, the value of a money-losing retailing company is often expressed in terms of its enterprise value divided by the number of stores. The money-loser's enterprise value per store statistic would then be compared with other retailing firms.

Shorthand calculations are in everyday use and unscientific as these calculations are, they are part of the valuation landscape. Most appropriate for erratic, cyclical, or money-losing firms, they also are calculated for businesses with long and successful track records, to ensure the completeness of an appraisal and to showcase possible discrepancies in the accounting-derived valuation techniques. Exhibit 10-1 shows common shorthand valuation ratios, segmented by industry.

The preceding list is not exhaustive. Almost every industry has its own set of shorthand ratios, which assist buyers and sellers in surmounting the problems of valuing a business without an ideal track record.

OTHER SPECIAL CASES

In addition to the preceding, a number of specialized valuation methods relate to particular acquisition strategies, including leveraged buyouts, asset liquidations, and "break-up" deals. These takeover techniques are the province of financial engineers, who aim to make money from each discrete transaction, as opposed to acquisitions, which are folded into a mother company in the pursuit of a unified corporate strategy. The deal-by-deal profit orientation of the financial engineer is diametrically opposed to the strategic goals behind the majority of corporate acquisitions. As such, it merits extensive coverage in this book and is discussed in detail in later chapters. In brief, a financial engineering firm determines its acquisition "bid" price in a two-step fashion. First, the likely amount of debt finance available from third parties is determined for the deal. Added to this amount is an equity down payment, perhaps 30% to 50% of the debt package. The resultant "affordability" calculation is then compared with the estimated market price for the sale candidate. If the affordability quotient exceeds the perceived market price, the financial engineer becomes an active bidder.

Small businesses represent a special valuation category. Any transaction with a value lower than $20 million qualifies as a small business in the eyes of most practitioners. For these smaller deals, buyers demand substantial discounts from the value which would otherwise be

EXHIBIT 10-1   Short-hand valuation ratios used in M&A analysis

Restaurants

$$\frac{\text{Enterprise value}}{\text{Number of restaurants in operation}} = \text{Value per restaurant}$$

Telephone Services

Hard line: $\dfrac{\text{Enterprise value}}{\text{Number of phone lines}} = \text{Value per phone line}$

Cellular: $\dfrac{\text{Enterprise value}}{\text{Number of persons in coverage area}} = \text{Value per PIP}$

Cable Television

$$\frac{\text{Enterprise value}}{\text{Number of subscribers}} = \text{Value per subscriber}$$

Cement, Steel, Petrochemical

$$\frac{\text{Enterprise value}}{\text{Ton of annual production capacity}} = \text{Value per ton of capacity}$$

Hotels

$$\frac{\text{Enterprise value}}{\text{Number of rooms}} = \text{Value per room}$$

Enterprise value = Average nightly room rate × Number of rooms × 1,000

Airlines

$$\frac{\text{Enterprise value}}{\text{Annual passenger miles}} = \text{Value per passenger mile}$$

$$\frac{\text{Enterprise value}}{\text{Number of annual seats filled}} = \text{Value per seat filled}$$

Movie Theater

$$\frac{\text{Enterprise value}}{\text{Number of movie screens}} = \text{Value per movie screen}$$

Oil, Gas, Timber and Mining

Equity value = The following sum:

+ Net working capital
+ Fixed assets
− Accounting liabilities
+ Value of natural resource reserves based on recent prices paid solely for such reserves (e.g., 1995 prices for oil-in-the-ground reserves were $6 per barrel, vs. above-the-ground price of $16 per barrel)

calculated using accounting-based multipliers or shorthand ratios. The pricing rationale is derived from the higher risks associated with the purchase of small businesses; many such firms exhibit earnings fluctuations or depend entirely on one or two executives. Small business discounts can be as high as 50% off large company multiples.

SUMMARY

The M&A market emphasizes the relative value approach, which compares transaction prices to earnings-based valuation ratios such as Price/Earnings and Enterprise Value/EBIT. These ratios are particularly appropriate for firms with upward earnings trends, but they are less helpful in evaluating companies with erratic performance records. Should the acquisition candidate have an uneven track record or an earnings problem, practitioners turn to averaging, peak-year, and shorthand value indicators. These items are based on the potential of the candidate to make money, as opposed to its actual profit history. Many indicators of potential are industry-specific, and include ratios based on sales, production capacity, or mineral reserves.

11 FINDING A DEAL

If a would-be acquirer has followed the process outlined so far in this book, then a substantial groundwork has been laid, and the potential buyer is ready to begin its search for suitable acquisition targets. A successful search program combines methodical hard work with occasional instances of pure luck, i.e., "being in the right place at the right time." But luck in the M&A business isn't just happenstance. Being in the right place at the right time is the result of months of considerable effort. Sifting through prospective acquisitions, evaluating actual deals, stroking M&A intermediaries, and initiating direct contacts with other companies are just four of the ongoing activities that require time and expense. The situation is analogous to the quote of one professional golfer, who said: "There's some luck in golf, and I found out that I'm luckier when I practice five hours a day."

LAYING THE GROUNDWORK

By way of review, an efficiently designed search program is preceded by these important buyer determinations:

- *Proposed Acquisition Strategy.* Having concluded that corporate growth needs can be fulfilled through buying other businesses, the buyer has made a self-assessment of its overall M&A objectives. Within this self-imposed framework for outside expansion, it has selected specific industry sectors and product lines. In doing so, the buyer has erected the "tent" under which acquisition ideas must fall.

- *Distilling the Strategy for the Practitioner Community.* Recognizing the insular, transaction-oriented focus of the M&A practitioner community, the buyer has accepted the fact that intermediaries will neither understand nor care about its acquisition strategy. The practitioner community will place the buyer's strategy into one of the five themes:

  1. Window Shopper.
  2. Market Share/Product Line Extender.
  3. Bottom Fisher.
  4. Strategic Buyer.
  5. Leveraged Buyout.

  To make life easier for the intermediaries who present potential transactions, the buyer has translated its acquisition strategy into one of these themes.

- *Buyer's Risk Parameters Defined.* In developing its acquisition objectives, the buyer has weighed its own skills in evaluating the three key acquisition risks—postclosing operating risk, overpayment risk, and added financial risk—and its ability to sustain the potential problems attendant to these risks. Only those acquisitions falling within the buyer's risk parameters will be selected for further study.

- *Affordability.* A proposed acquisition budget has been set by the buyer, limiting the buyer to examining those prospective deals with a value of between 10% and 40% of the buyer's own market value. This budget is flexible and can increase if larger opportunities become available.

- *Price.* The buyer has studied the prices paid for recent transactions in its target industries. Accordingly, the buyer's senior managers know what is, and what isn't, a reasonable asking price.

Valuation ratios such as P/E, Enterprise Value/EBIT, and Price/Book have been recorded by the buyer for recent deals. These accounting-based ratios are complemented in the buyer's analysis by numerous shorthand valuation ratios that are industry-specific. The numerous valuation criteria now at the buyer's fingertips form the basis for the quick elimination of acquisition proposals that have unrealistic price goals.

The buyer is now ready to enter the shark pit of investment bankers, business brokers, and dubious sellers.

STARTING THE SEARCH

For a larger company with annual sales of $100 million or more, the best way to begin a search is to alert the elite members of the M&A practitioner community to the buyer's interest in expanding through acquisition. Indeed, a firm of this size is already being showered with unsolicited acquisition ideas from New York investment bankers and commercial banks. For a small to medium-size firm with annual sales of less than $100 million, I recommend a similar "alert" tactic, but with an emphasis on the specialized and regional intermediaries, since the larger practitioners are not interested in working on the $5 to $20 million transactions consummated by such acquirers.

As mentioned earlier, the practitioner community encompasses a large army of businesspeople whose work focuses on the processing of merger and acquisition transactions. The principal members of this community include the following:

- Investment banks.
- Business brokers.
- Other intermediaries.
- Law firms.
- Accountants.
- Acquisition lenders.
- Leveraged buyout firms.
- Asset appraisal firms.

Each of these groups plays an important role in the M&A business, but not all generate a continuous stream of acquisition opportunities (i.e., "deal flow"). Deal flow is the lifeblood of an acquisition search. The primary originators of deal flow are the firms in the intermediary category, which primarily comprises investment banks and business brokers. Secondary sources of deal flow are the corporate financial advisory departments of certain large commercial banks, management consulting firms, and national accounting firms. Another common source is the finder, who is a well-connected member of the local business community with a sideline as a corporate matchmaker.

Investment Banks

Investment banks dominate the origination of large deals, considered to be those with a price tag of $50 million and up; they also play an important role in sourcing medium-sized transactions. The big New York-based investment banks have the largest concentration of advisory talent, while many regional investment banks have solid middle-market practices in the $10 to $50 million range. Business owners gravitate to investment banks because the banks offer them the experience and resources required to process transactions effectively. Typical services provided to sellers include (1) valuing the business to be sold; (2) preparing a descriptive memorandum that is sent to potential buyers; (3) conducting an orderly auction of the business; and (4) assisting in negotiations, legal work, financing, and other matters related to closing the deal. Because of their high overhead, most investment banks try to "weed out" clients that are not serious sellers. Their most effective device for screening clients is a $50,000 to $100,000 retainer fee, payable prior to the bank commencing substantial work on the client's behalf.

Business Brokers

Business brokers are small operations with either a regional focus or industry specialty. Many have only one or two principals, operating with little more than a phone, a desk, and a file cabinet. Small deals in the range of $1 million to $10 million are the province of business brokers, who usually represent businesses that are either family-owned companies or small corporate divisions. The fundamental strategy of most business brokers is the methodology of "throw enough . . . against the wall and some will stick." Dozens of clients are retained without up-front fees and little investigation is done by the business broker on his client's operations. Brief descriptions of the broker's clients are routinely sent to a laundry list of possible buyers with little forethought. Beyond a few earnings ratio clichés, brokers offer little valuation advice to their respective clients, and few brokers bother to understand their clients' businesses well enough to formalize a coherent marketing strategy or to draft a meaningful offering memorandum. This lack of service is a result of the inability of most brokers to charge up-front retainer fees that would cover a portion of their overhead. Their clients, who are typically hard-nosed small business owners, generally refuse to pay up-front fees by arguing that the broker cannot guarantee a successful transaction.

To maximize the chances of closing a deal, most business brokers carry a broad inventory of firms for sale. The majority of these are ill-suited for purchase because of the sellers' unrealistic price expectations, legal complications, income tax problems or stale inventories. This portrait of the business broker may be bleak, but the fact remains that this brand of practitioner carries a substantial amount of acquisition "inventory." A minuscule portion of this inventory is appropriate for serious consideration by a thoughtful buyer. A small minority of brokers have patterned their businesses after the services of the regional investment banks. This elite group of business brokers works only with the larger sellers having demonstrated commitment toward consummating a deal. Information memoranda are prepared and up-front fees are charged, just as with the larger intermediaries.

Other Intermediaries

Other professionals are found in the corporate finance advisory departments of large commercial banks, management consulting firms, and national accounting firms. These organizations seek to advise on deals $10 million and up. Like their investment banking brethren, these firms have the infrastructure to provide advisory services which are similar in many ways to the investment banking product, but the quality of their advice suffers from a limited deal flow relative to the investment banking competition. Knowledge, experience, and contacts count for a lot in the M&A business and these intermediaries are deficient in such areas.

The finder, the remaining type of intermediary, provides little more than an introduction between buyer and seller. While this may not sound like a major service to the average reader, an introduction that is made at the highest level in the buyer's organization, and in the right manner, can remove a lot of the bureaucratic underbrush present in many large companies. The finder thus facilitates the deal's orderly consideration.

Intermediaries are the source of many M&A deals because sellers hire them to provide advice on the sale process. Valuing, packaging, and auctioning a business are specialized tasks that are best handled by intermediaries which participate in the M&A market on a regular basis. A seller can accomplish the task itself, but it risks closing the deal under suboptimal terms. In the court of law, the saying goes that "a person who represents himself has a fool for a client." This admonition is appropriate for the M&A business.

Law Firms and Accountants

Law firms occasionally play a finder role by virtue of their extensive contacts in the business community. Accounting firms, exclusive of those with a formal M&A advisory practice, can perform the same function. Notwithstanding this sporadic finder service, law firms and accounting firms play their primary roles during the closing phase of a transaction. This phase of the deal process occurs after the seller's intermediary has negotiated the basic terms and conditions of the sale with the prospective buyer. At such time, both parties require comprehensive legal and accounting services.

Acquisition Lenders

Acquisition lenders do not source deals, but they are an important part of the acquisition scene. Many deals are financed with debt. Much of the debt financing for large acquisitions tends to be provided by a select group of New York money-center banks, large life insurance companies, and sizable finance firms. Other transactions are financed directly through the public bond markets (although the public markets are more effective in the refinancing of bank acquisition debt). For highly leveraged mergers, a significant lending community complements conventional debt financing with "junk bonds," i.e., lower-rated debt having a subordinated claim against the borrower's assets. Smaller financings do not attract the attention of large New York banks, so the small to medium-size buyer must look to regionally-based lenders for support.

Leveraged Buyout Firms

Leveraged buyout firms are a pillar of the M&A community because of the frequency with which they buy and sell companies. Barely active in the 1970s, the LBO industry boomed in the 1980s when over 300 investment firms specialized in arranging LBOs. The ranks of LBO investors thinned considerably in the 1990s, but the surviving firms are still a potent force, with billions of dollars to invest. As a result, LBO firms such as Kohlberg, Kravis & Roberts, Thomas H. Lee & Company, and Forstman Little & Company are constant sources of competition for the traditional operating corporation interested in expansion. With an acquisition turnover ratio that is higher than the average corporate buyer, LBO firms are also an indirect source of acquisitions. And LBO investors are not shy about listening to purchase offers for parts of their portfolios. The direct sources are the intermediaries, which are regularly retained by LBO firms to conduct orderly sales of their portfolio investments.

Asset Appraisal Firms

Asset appraisal firms such as American Appraisal Associates, Houlihan Lokey, and Arthur D. Little provide a needed service that facilitates the closing of a transaction. When one company purchases another, the acquirer and its accounting firm must assign values to the acquired assets for the purposes of constructing financial statements. In certain cases, the acquirer or its accounting firm requires a professional appraiser to assist in this value allocation progress. In other instances, such as a transaction involving substantial debt financing, the lender needs an independent asset appraisal to buttress its perception of the creditworthiness of its loan. At other times, appraisals provide independent corroboration of asset values assigned for income tax, capital gains tax, or estate tax purposes. Asset appraisers work in many deals, but they do not originate transactions. Accordingly, they should not be contacted during the search process.

FOUR STEPS IN BEGINNING A SEARCH

The beginning of a search covers four basic steps:

1. Initiating the search with intermediaries.
2. Starting your own search program.
3. Screening the candidates.
4. Implementing direct contact.

By following these steps, a would-be acquirer starts to generate leads.

Step 1. Initiating the Search with Intermediaries

If a company has annual sales of $100 million or more and its stock is publicly traded, top management is already responding to several acquisition proposals per week. Intermediaries introduce the majority of these proposals, but the prospective buyer is responsible for increasing the number of deals presented and boosting the quality of this "banker deal flow." It cannot rely on the practitioner community to serve its interests well. Improving deal flow can only be accomplished if the buyer is willing to dedicate one manager toward maintaining a constant line of communication between the buyer and the intermediary community. Too often, contact between potential acquirers and intermediaries is fragmented and incomplete, when it should be a vehicle for promoting the sharing of information.

The intermittent dialogue on acquisition suggestions between buyer and intermediaries is often less than satisfactory. Frustrations are evident through the following comments that I have heard repeatedly:

Potential Buyer Talking about an Intermediary

- "They (the intermediaries) always show me a lot of junk, never a good deal."
- "They don't understand my business or my acquisition strategy."
- "There's not enough analysis or information in their proposals."

Intermediary Talking about a Potential Buyer

- "They (the buyer) want to see every deal, so that they know they're not missing anything. I have no idea what they're really interested in."
- "They complain about every deal I show them. Either it's not the right 'fit,' or its too expensive."
- "That company doesn't know what it wants."

The best way for a buyer to avoid this miscommunication and to improve deal flow is to initiate and maintain continuous contact with a wide variety of intermediaries. For large conglomerates, this is not a major problem. They are besieged by investment banks proffering corporate finance services, including M&A advice and related acquisition ideas. For smaller companies, accessing investment banks for M&A product is more difficult, but it is achievable by implementing a direct approach. To begin, a small to medium-size company should make direct contact with a large number of intermediaries, perhaps 50 to 100. At a minimum, the top 30 investment banks, and the 20 largest commercial banks should be called, followed by the business brokers and the intermediaries specializing in the industry, product line, or region in which the buyer is interested. The names of these firms can be found in numerous directories, although the specific executive working in your target area may not be identified by name. Finding this individual is important. Once you identify the intermediary executive responsible for "M&A deals" in your target industry, begin contact with a short letter addressed to this person, describing the buyer's business, financial performance, affordability quotient, and target industry. One or two weeks later, the in-house staffer responsible for the acquisition search supplements this letter by a phone call. Where practicable, the in-house executive follows up the telephone call with a visit from the in-house executive to the intermediary's offices. Like any other business, the personal touch is important in the merger and acquisition industry.

Assuming the buyer has the wherewithal to finance a medium-size acquisition, perhaps in the $20 to $50 million range, the acquisition ideas and proposals should begin to roll in after 15 to 20 visits to intermediaries. The buyer, however, will soon discover that the vast majority of the proposals are unsuitable for its needs. Rather than dismissing the intermediaries as hopelessly poor listeners, the in-house executive makes a conscious effort to respond to each intermediary suggestion within 2 to 3 weeks. Rejections are phrased in the vocabulary used by the intermediary, such as the deal was turned down on the basis of:

- "The price is too high."
- "The size is wrong."
- "The proposal (or idea) does not fit with our Product Line Extension Strategy."

Rejections based on the proposed acquisition's asking price being too high, or its size being too large or too small, are understandable to the average intermediary. Problems with "fit" are usually less easy to convey. Many corporate executives fall into Harvard Business School-type explanations of the proper fit for their respective employers. Such responses are incomprehensible to the average intermediary. For example, corporate executives talk of acquisition criteria based on "supplementary skills and resources," "complementary skills and resources," or "financial fit-risk benefits." These are fine for the Boston Consulting Group crowd, but they mean little to merger practitioners. Such individuals need to have the buyer's acquisition strategy couched in Wall Street verbiage. This means the criteria have to be distilled into one of the five buyer categories discussed previously.

Step 2. Starting Your Own Search Program

Once the buyer has determined its target industries, communicated with the practitioner community, and started reviewing "deal flow," its next step is developing its own system for identifying promising acquisition candidates. Sometimes this is a simple process, particularly if the buyer knows the target industry well and has criteria so restrictive that only three or four companies, already reasonably well-known to the buyer, qualify. More often, the realistic acquirer looks beyond a handful of ideal candidates, and the stage is set for a systematic "search and screen" program designed to reach attractive businesses that are not openly for sale.

The principal benefit to the buyer of working with intermediaries is that many of their ideas involve true acquisition proposals where money has changed hands—the seller has retained the intermediary for an up-front fee, the intermediary has done a preliminary investigation into the seller's business, and the auction has commenced. A willing seller exists, as opposed to a reluctant owner that entered into merger discussions without formally retaining an intermediary. A seller who retains a large investment bank or commercial bank is strongly motivated to consummate a deal. By this time it has: (1) spent a small amount of intermediary "up-front money" to begin the sale process; and (2) risked the negative effects of the news getting out about a possible sale. Yet, while intermediaries remove a lot of the guesswork from the search process, a prospective buyer can't wait and react only to opportunities brought in by intermediaries; this is not a guarantee of a quality deal flow. The buyer doesn't provide the impetus for deal origination; and, as a result, the proposed transactions supplied by intermediaries are unlikely to fit well into the buyer's acquisition criteria. Why shouldn't the buyer contact directly those companies that fit its criteria?

The direct contact method is methodical, exhausting, and frustrating. Despite these serious drawbacks, many buyers use it successfully. About 20% of business owners are "silent sellers," willing to consider any reasonable offer, but they are reluctant to commit to an orchestrated auction. A diligent buyer takes advantage of this hesitancy by initiating discussions on its own. In this instance, the buyer makes the first contact with a possible seller, instead of the reverse situation when the seller's representative starts the process. Because the buyer is making the first move and has no knowledge of the owner's state-of-mind, it endures a lot of turndowns from the 80% of companies that are not selling. Besides these repeated rejections, the direct search method has another big negative. In early negotiations, the seller has the upper hand, since it is the "pursued" rather than the "pursuer."

The buyer's search program acknowledges first the broad landscape of American and international business. Many established industries are fragmented and include a melange of publicly traded companies, private firms, and corporate subsidiaries. Obtaining data on these candidates means consulting numerous sources besides the buyer's constituency and the practitioner community. Industry experts, product consultants and trade reporters have to be discreetly surveyed by the buyer, who collects the raw data on businesses participating in the target industry(ies). Data on publicly held companies is easy to find because U.S. public companies file detailed reports with the Securities & Exchange Commission. This information is available from either the SEC, the company itself, or private reporting firms, such as Disclosure, Inc., which keep libraries of all SEC filings. Overseas-based publicly held firms also file reports with their local securities regulators and this information is available to the general public. Private company data is harder to locate, but various business databases and reference publications are available for this purpose. In many of these reference sources, corporate and subsidiary information is arrayed in multiple formats that are helpful to the prospective acquirer, such as:

- Industry by SIC code (i.e., industry classification).
- Location of headquarters.
- Size of operations in terms of sales, assets, and employees.

Many of the private company business databases and directories are computerized, and buyers can screen companies for specific qualities, thus providing a quick glimpse of candidates qualified by one or two desired attributes, such as size or profitability. Candidate lists that are generated by the computerized databases are far from complete, however, since databases are not 100% accurate. As a result of misreporting, errors, or omissions, the lists exclude many important private firms, corporate divisions, and recent start-up businesses. An intelligent acquisition search therefore requires that a buyer executive painstakingly research each database and business directory with his or her own hands. Such detailed searches are akin to a detective's work, for even in the best directories SIC codes are inaccurate, statistical data regarding sales and employees is out of date, or important information is simply unavailable. The key for the in-house executive is to check one directory or database against another. Selected phone calls to the target may also unearth basic information that cannot be found elsewhere.

Common computerized databases are Datext, Dialog, and Dun & Bradstreet Credit Rating. Useful business directories are Standard & Poor's Corporate Register, Thomas Register, and Million Dollar Directories.

One alternative to the grinding work of playing acquisition detective is to hire a search/survey firm that can canvass entire industries, including private companies and corporate divisions. Companies that do this work charge from $50,000 to $200,000 per assignment.

The result of a buyer's foray into screening will be a long list of firms. These prospects will be classified into three broad categories of informational availability:

1. *Publicly Traded Companies.* SEC reports provide an excellent sense of financial strength and product line focus.

2. *Divisions of Publicly-Traded Companies.* SEC reports filed by the parent company often provide basic data on divisional product lines, including summary financial results. This information can be supplemented with database and directory data.

3. *Privately Held Firms.* Many privately held companies supply key financial and personnel data to Dun & Bradstreet and other credit firms, which, in turn, provide this information in written reports to trade creditors and other interested parties. Information on industry and principal products is generally available for large private firms (i.e., sales > $10 million) along with basic financial statistics. Obtaining data on smaller companies is problematic. Credit firms provide a credit history of the company without a financial summary. The buyer can continue the search in other areas. The small privately owned firms may participate in industry associations, have promotional brochures, or be the subject of magazine articles.

Step 3. Screening the Candidates

As the buyer develops a list of candidates from its in-house research efforts, the process reduces the potential acquisition universe from a large mass of eligible prospects to a smaller and smaller grouping. The principal screening factor is size, as most companies fitting the buyer's industry objectives will be either too small to merit the buyer's attention, or too large to be affordable. Nevertheless, in-house research can generate a substantial number of candidates, and an acquisitive management needs to generate hard-and-fast criteria to quickly eliminate those candidates that do not merit further study. Industry and size characteristics are usually the first hurdle for a candidate. Candidates making the "first cut" are carried through a sequence of further screens, based on the buyer's detailed acquisition criteria, exclusive of industry and size. Developing these subsequent screening mechanisms is discussed fully in the next chapter, but popular secondary screening criteria include price, industry subsector, product line within the subsector, profitability, leverage, unionized workforce, and market share position.

Step 4. Implementing Direct Contact

Depending on the scope of the would-be buyer's expansion strategy, the search and screen process may develop a substantial number of leads. Assuming a concerted effort has been made to study the various target businesses through public SEC filings (if applicable), industry contacts, computerized databases, business directories, and credit reporting firms, the buyer's management has assembled a "short list" of candidates. What's the next step? For small privately held companies (i.e., annual sales under $25 million) in which the buyer has no direct contacts, a vaguely worded introductory letter to the chairman or chief executive officer is a good start. The letter suggests the buyer's general interest in a joint venture or a marketing arrangement and advises the individual of a follow-up call, which the buyer's development executive places shortly thereafter. During this call the buyer discloses its true interest in pursuing a potential acquisition. If the buyer is targeting a medium-size business, privately owned company, or the small division of a publicly traded company (purchase price of $25 million to $100 million), the initial contact is better made through an intermediary such as the buyer's investment banker, its outside attorney, or a reputable finder. Outside board members of the buyer can fill a similar purpose if they know a top executive or a prominent shareholder of the candidate. In many cases, the buyer's intermediary conveys the buyer's intentions indirectly through another intermediary closely affiliated with the candidate, such as the candidate's investment bank or outside law firm.

Where the potential acquisition is a publicly traded company or a large division of a publicly traded company, the method of contact needs to be considered carefully. Any acquisition interest needs to be communicated with discretion. A publicly traded company management is understandably paranoid about any overt takeover interest—direct or indirect—because of the publicity that will surround such interest, no matter how preliminary. If the word gets out that "so and so is considering a bid for XYZ Company," intermediaries unaffiliated with either the prospective buyer or the potential seller look immediately toward putting the publicly traded acquisition candidate into "play."

"Putting a company into play" is an attempt by practitioners, particularly investment banks, to set up an auction of the candidate, without regard to the expressed wishes of its management. The investment banks have two motives: (1) to gain a fee by representing either a buyer or the candidate itself in closing or financing a transaction; or (2) to make a profit through trading the candidate's shares in the market, often in concert with the practitioner's risk arbitrage department.

A public company is vulnerable to being put into play. By law, it must consider serious offers and alert shareholders. If its managers lack a sincere desire to sell out, they are understandably reticent to respond favorably to any expression of interest, no matter how preliminary, from an unsolicited buyer of either the company's entire business or a key division. This natural reluctance places the burden of serious intentions on the buyer, which should conduct a serious study of the target's business before attempting a legitimate inquiry. The ensuing mating ritual with a public company must then follow a well-worn script prompted by the mutual desire of the parties to avoid damaging publicity and costly litigation. Dictated by highly paid practitioners who are mindful of the confidentiality requirement, who pay strict attention to legal precedent, and who have detailed knowledge of the regulatory environment, this script is now de rigueur for all public-market transactions.

No matter what kind of business a buyer approaches—a publicly traded company, a corporate division, or a privately owned firm—the unsolicited direct approach results in a high percentage of outright rejections. The lack of interest exhibited by many firms should not discourage the buyer. Many of these candidates can be contacted regularly, perhaps every year or so, to remind the owners that the buyer's door remains open if the candidate's situation changes. That minority of candidates that enter into a dialogue and allow the buyer into their respective businesses are funneled through the buyer's "sifting" process.

RETAINING AN INTERMEDIARY TO ASSIST IN THE SEARCH

Investment banks, business brokers, finders, and the other organizations that perform intermediary functions are not effective in the search process. The economics of these firms require that they generate a continual stream of advisory fees, which can only come about through deals that close (i.e., where money changes hands). While assisting with a search may eventually lead to a closed transaction in which the intermediary collects a fee, the search process is long and arduous, and the probability of success on any one unsolicited contact is small. Accordingly, intermediaries are poorly motivated to assist any buyer in an extensive "search and screen" process. A *large* retainer fee for an investment bank on a "search and screen" assignment might be in the $100,000 to $250,000 range, whereas the success fee, even on a *small* $10 million to $20 million deal, is typically $400,000 to $500,000. Larger transaction fees climb into the millions of dollars. As a result, intermediaries devote far more effort to advising clients on deals that appear to have a good chance of closing, rather than allocating resources to "long shot" search and screen activities. Besides this low motivation factor, a buyer is well advised to avoid using intermediaries in the search process for another reason: exclusivity. The intermediary retained to assist in the search function usually insists on the sole right to represent its client in all acquisitions over the retainer period, which usually ranges from 6 to 12 months. There is no need for a rational buyer to lock itself into this restrictive arrangement with what undoubtedly is a poorly-motivated adviser. The intelligent buyer's logical course of action is to bring a transaction to where the chances of a closing appear likely, and then to retain a skillful intermediary to assist in negotiating and closing the deal.

SUMMARY

To maximize its chances for success, an intelligent buyer takes a proactive approach toward increasing its acquisition opportunities. The buyer's first step in promoting "deal flow" is alerting the practitioner community about the buyer's acquisition interests. Regular communication with intermediaries is maintained, and personal visits from the buyer's executives to the intermediaries' offices are encouraged. These visits demonstrate the buyer's acknowledgment of the intermediaries as professionals in their own right and provide both sides with the personal touch that is so important in business life. Intermediaries are the source of many transactions, and they should be dealt with carefully. On receiving an inquiry from an intermediary, for example, a would-be buyer answers promptly. If the response is a form of "we're not interested," the buyer's rationale for turning down the idea is explained in terms which intermediaries can relate to easily.

Supplementing the deal flow provided by intermediaries is a stream of acquisition candidates generated by the buyer's own in-house search efforts. A variety of reference sources and outside contacts are used to develop lists of companies and corporate divisions that meet key acquisition criteria. The buyer contacts candidates making the first cut. Most of these contacts end with the candidate rejecting the buyer's acquisition overtures. In the case of a rejection, the buyer remembers to call the candidate again after a decent interval of time. For those firms that invite the buyer into an exchange of information, the sifting process begins.

12 SIFTING THROUGH POTENTIAL ACQUISITIONS

The buyer has now set up its proactive search program. Its management has provided dozens of intermediaries with the buyer's basic acquisition criteria and it has implemented a methodical in-house search to develop acquisition candidates aside from those presented by intermediaries. The resultant "deal flow" results in 10 or more candidates per week, derived from acquisition criteria based on the buyer's general industry, price, and size guidelines, but more specifics are needed. How does the buyer narrow the field of eligible candidates? How does it reduce this list to the few potential acquisitions that merit serious, and sometimes expensive, study? Thousands of companies and corporate divisions are open to purchase offers. As numerous acquisition prospects roll in through the front door every week, it is critical that the would-be buyer have a realistic system for separating the "wheat from the chaff." The vast majority of acquisition ideas are unsuitable for one reason or another, and the buyer's objective is to eliminate the castoffs from consideration as soon as possible, based on whatever information is on hand.

Assuming a selling company is represented by an investment bank or a similar professional intermediary, a fair amount of useful

EXHIBIT 12-1   The sifting process

Ideal corporate goals
↓
Written acquisition strategy
↓
Real-life screening criteria
↓
In-house screening decisions
(1) Eliminate candidates, or (2) Investigate further

information can be gleaned from the information memorandum prepared by the bank and then provided to the prospective acquirers. The information memorandum will have a fairly detailed description of the seller's business, along with a financial history. Other data can be quickly obtained from follow-up phone calls with the investment bank. For potential acquisitions developed through the direct approach, information gathered by the buyer's in-house executive is supplemented through conversations with the candidate's management. The data is sifted through the buyer's detailed acquisition criteria, which is based on a strategy designed to meet the buyer's corporate goals. While this strategy may be clearly outlined, the resultant sifting process is more complex than a mechanical activity such as matching candidate attribute "A" against acquisition criteria "B." Achieving ideal corporate objectives in the rough-and-tumble marketplace is a near impossible task and compromises are necessary. Corporate guidelines undergo a transformation at the screening level, where real-life businesses, with all their peculiarities and problems, are evaluated rapidly. The lofty corporate acquisition goals set forth on paper by top management are distilled in real time by the in-house sifter, who is faced with reviewing a hodgepodge of businesses with less than complete information. Exhibit 12-1 shows a schematic of this development executive's decision process.

Many times, a corporate strategy is overly ambitious and out-of-touch with the real world. As a hypothetical example, consider a Fortune 500 consumer food products manufacturer (the "Company") that requires the following 11 acquisition criteria in its search:

*Ideal Acquisition Criteria for Fortune 500
Consumer Food Company*

The Candidate Must:

1. Be involved in manufacturing and marketing consumer food products, including items such as prepared food, canned fruits and vegetables, dairy products, and bakery goods.
2. Have a brand-name orientation in its major product lines to restrict new competition.
3. Be able to benefit from the Company's marketing and distribution skills.
4. Participate in growing markets.
5. Have a leading position in its markets.
6. Earn a 35% or greater gross margin on sales, which is approximately the gross margin of the Company's product lines.
7. Generate a 15% pretax, unleveraged return on assets. No money-losing companies will be considered as acquisition candidates.
8. Register annual sales of $100 million or more as a stand-alone business, $50 million or more as an add-on to the Company's existing product lines.
9. Have a good management willing to stay after the closing.
10. Employ a nonunion labor force.
11. Be available at a reasonable price based on comparable transactions, which averaged 18 P/E, 3× Price/Book and 10× EBIT, respectively. Based on these price indications and anticipated synergies, the candidate will represent little or no prospective earnings per share dilution for the Company.

Taken separately, all the preceding criteria are reasonable. Depending on the Company's definition of its "product line" or its "market," the list boils down to a conventional "market share/product line extension" strategy. A conservative management might consider parts of the criteria to represent a "strategic diversification," although as diversification strategies go, this approach is pretty tame, since the Company is staying within related product lines, technologies, customer bases, and marketing/distribution channels. Anyway, this checklist has a fundamental flaw: It is unrealistic. Only one or two opportunities will meet each of these criteria in any given year, and competition for these properties will be stiff, leaving the Company's management totally frustrated in its search for profitable growth through acquisition. A better strategy is for the Company to be more flexible, leaving room for its acquisition criteria to fit the available businesses. This involves limiting key screening hurdles to a handful of attributes.

SCREENING CRITERIA

The first screen of an acquisition candidate should focus on three important criteria:

1. Industry.
2. Size.
3. Asking price.

This three-pronged screen can be accomplished by an executive at his desk with a minimum of research, particularly if the transaction is presented by an intermediary with a passing knowledge of his client's business and price thinking. Obtaining this fundamental information is more difficult when the buyer itself has approached a privately owned firm or corporate division though basic industry and size data, if unavailable from standard reference sources, can be gathered during a brief conversation with the candidate's managers. Or the buyer can estimate candidate sales and assets through applying known ratios to available operating statistics. The number of employees or the capacity of production facilities often bear a direct relation to annual sales. Without outside research, the vast majority of candidates can be eliminated through the use of the industry, size, and price criteria reasonably quickly. In the case of our hypothetical consumer food products manufacturer, we shrink the "initial hurdle list" considerably, from 11 items to these 3 items. Assume the Company's quick screen selects potential acquisitions with the following industry, size, and price attributes:

Key Screening Criteria for Fortune 500
Consumer Food Company

1. *Industry.* The candidate is involved in manufacturing and marketing of consumer food products, like the Company.

2. *Size*. The candidate has annual sales of $100 million or more, to merit senior management attention.

3. *Price*. The candidate's asking price is within the range of comparable public transactions, or within established benchmarks in the case of smaller, private concerns.

The Company will study candidates meeting these criteria.

MENTIONING PRICE FIRST

Of the three criteria, determining the seller's asking price is the most difficult exercise, even when the seller is represented by an investment bank. Although the investment bank has covered price expectations with its client, the bank is reluctant to talk price with the potential buyer for fear of quoting a number that is too low. Corporate valuation, as shown in Chapter 9, is an inexact science. Businesses, even those operating in the same industry, are different from one another, dimming value comparisons. Also, market circumstances change frequently. A Mexican brewery acquisition completed in 1997, for example, will have very different pricing parameters than one closed in 1993, the year before the 50% peso devaluation. The results of the sale process are thus difficult to predict for any individual business. Even experienced investment bankers prefer to predict sales prices within a large range that can have a spread of 20% to 30%.

The price-talk problem is compounded when dealing with unsophisticated sellers, many of which don't employ knowledgeable intermediaries, and thus lack access to any kind of intelligent financial advice. These sellers may have only a vague sense of their businesses' worth, likely obtained from reading business publications or talking to industry contacts. More often than not, they rely solely on an emotional view of what their respective business should bring in a sale. Without a real sense of value, they are hesitant to divulge their price expectations for fear of "leaving money on the table," although they in fact have little information on which to base a judgment. In an acquisition search involving candidates with annual sales exceeding $50 million, this latter scenario is unlikely. The candidate's owners are inevitably active in the acquisition business or are represented by knowledgeable advisers. In dealing with acquisitions of smaller companies in the $1 million to

$20 million sales range, the buyer confronts unsophisticated sellers with unrealistic price expectations.

Inevitably, the sale candidate or its agent will press the buyer to mention first a price range for the seller's business. The buyer wants to avoid this initial price talk, since it is operating on limited information in these early stages. Also, as its due diligence process unfolds, the buyer typically discovers more negatives than positives regarding the candidate's business, since the candidate will have exhausted its listing of positive attributes in the beginning rounds of discussions, while conveniently forgetting negative factors such as slow-moving inventories or IRS problems. After extending its initial price suggestion, the buyer may well find itself lowering its price thoughts as due diligence continues. This change of heart causes a problem in later negotiations. The candidate and its agent will ignore the results of the buyer's due diligence efforts and continue to use the initial price talk as an anchor for subsequent discussions. Thus, the disadvantages of the buyer mentioning price first are real, but there is little alternative if the candidate and its representative refuse to provide a valuation range. Confronted with this situation, the would-be buyer can reject the potential deal out of hand, provide a price range, or accept the only remaining alternative: the completion of a substantial amount of due diligence before the real price discussions begin. The risk in the latter course of action is obvious: the buyer expends significant effort only to discover later that its price thoughts are substantially lower than those of the seller. This disappointing result means one thing: the due diligence process has largely been a waste of the buyer's time and money. The prospect of this eventuality highlights the need for early discussions on mutual price expectations, and buyer tactics in this regard are set forth in Chapter 12.

QUICK PRICE ADJUSTMENTS

A prospective buyer reviews a candidate's asking price relative to market benchmarks such as the Price/Earnings, Enterprise Value/EBIT, and Price/Book ratios of recent transactions. During the preliminary evaluation an in-house executive considers pro forma adjustments to the seller's business that effectively lessen the asking price.

A common quick adjustment is to reduce, on a pro forma basis, the selling company's level of executive compensation. Many small to medium-size private companies are managed by their respective owner(s), who pay themselves far in excess of what they could earn as managers of a similar-size division of a larger company. (And these individuals typically run substantial personal expenses through their businesses' respective income statements.) Similarly, smaller public company executives generally earn more than their divisional counterparts in large public firms. If the buyer believes the prospective acquisition can prosper without its existing group of highly paid executives, it can assume they are replaced with managers earning lower salaries. In Exhibit 12-2, the in-house development executive suggests that a $2.0 million annual reduction in executive compensation is achieved by the buyer, postclosing. This presumed saving reduces the asking price expressed in terms of the P/E ratio. Note how the effective P/E ratio declines from 16.7× to 13.9× when the $2.0 million savings are included as a result of the quick adjustment.

Another quick adjustment is the assumed sale of underutilized assets. An acquisition candidate may own undeveloped real estate or carry excess inventory, neither of which are necessary for the continued

EXHIBIT 12-2   Screening for price, adjusting for executive compensation at Target Company, Inc.

(US$ million)	Historical Results	Adjustment[1]	Pro Forma Results
Sales	$100.0	—	$100.0
Operating expenses	88.0	(2.0)	86.0
Earnings before interest and taxes	12.0	2.0	14.0
Interest	2.0	—	2.0
Pretax income	10.0	2.0	12.0
Income taxes	4.0	0.8	4.8
Net income	$ 6.0	1.2	$ 7.2
Asking price	$100 million		$100 million
P/E ratio at asking price	16.7×		13.9×

[1] Adjusted to reflect pro forma decrease of $2.0 million in executive compensation.

viability of its core operations. In the screening analysis, the buyer can assume the liquidation of these assets, which may not be fully factored into the asking price. As noted in Exhibit 12-2, the Target Company's vital statistics are as follows, before any adjustments:

Target Company, Inc.

Asking price	$100 million
Historical net income	$6.0 million
P/E ratio at asking price	16.7×

Suppose the buyer's in-house executive believes the candidate has $10 million of unused real estate and $5 million of excess inventories. He therefore assumes the liquidation of $15 million of excess assets in his analysis:

Asking price	$100 million
Adjustment for excess assets	− 15
Adjusted asking price	$ 85 million
Net income	$6.0 million
P/E ratio at adjusted asking price	14.2×

Note how the prospective buyer reduces the asking price, expressed in terms of the P/E ratio, from 16.7× to 14.2×.

Combining the executive compensation and excess asset adjustments results in a significant change in the P/E ratio of the asking price. Inclusion of both changes reduces it by 29%, from 16.7× to 11.8×:

Asking price, after excess asset adjustment	$85 million
Net income, after executive compensation adjustment	$7.2 million
P/E ratio of asking price, after two quick adjustments	11.8×

Reductions in asking price P/E ratios (and other valuation benchmarks) can be accomplished through various quick adjustments. Executive compensation and excess assets are two of the more popular quick adjustments.

As one illustration, when Wells Fargo bid $11 billion for rival First Interstate Bancorp in 1995, Paul Hazen, Wells Fargo's Chief Executive, estimated that combined expenses of the two banks could be cut $800 million per year. First Interstate only made $670 million in annual net income, so the implicit savings reduced the proposed transaction's valuation ratios considerably.

In the preliminary evaluation stage, quick adjustments enable an otherwise high-priced deal to survive the buyer's price screen. The validity of these assumptions is verified later during the buyer's due diligence. In many deals, the intermediary or seller factors these adjustments into the asking price, thus diminishing their value from the buyer's perspective.

SCREENING ON REMAINING CRITERIA

Industry, size, and price are the key criteria used for the initial screening process. In most cases, these criteria are the easiest to cover without the benefit of the buyer doing anything more than reading an offering memorandum or reviewing in-house research reports. Screening an acquisition candidates for additional attributes may involve analytical work extending past the buyer's desk review. Such increased scrutiny may start to involve a meaningful commitment of the buyer's time and money, and it may present a difficult balancing act for the in-house M&A executive. On the one hand, he is probably working with a set of acquisition criteria developed by a top management committee that is unfamiliar with the day-to-day process of screening deals. The committee has developed a naive "wish list" that doesn't reflect the opportunities available in the marketplace at a reasonable price. On the other hand, the buyer's board of directors is sincerely interested in the buyer purchasing companies as a positive means of fostering growth. To resolve the contradiction, the in-house executive needs to decide which "wish list" guidelines can be compromised and which criteria must be maintained. At the same time, the level of subjectivity attached by top management to concepts such as a corporation's "market," "strategic direction," or "competitive strengths" makes this executive's job both difficult, and easy. (Microsoft's recent forays into the entertainment business illustrate this broad scope.) Ambiguity opens

EXHIBIT 12-3   Fortune 500 consumer food company acquisition criteria

DEAL KILLERS

Relevant Acquisition Criteria	Comments
The Candidate Must:	
Be involved in manufacturing and marketing consumer food products.	Industry—Candidate must meet this criteria.
Register annual sales of $100 million or more.	Size—Candidate must meet this criteria.
Asking price of seller should be realistic.	Price—Overly aggressive price expectations can sometimes be moderated through Quick Adjustments. Otherwise, the deal should be rejected.

PROBABLE DEAL KILLERS

Relevant Acquisition Criteria	Comments
The Candidate Must:	
Be profitable.	Many managements refuse to consider money-losing companies (i.e., turnarounds). Quick Adjustments may transform a historical loss into a pro forma gain.
Employ a nonunion labor force.	Many managements are reluctant to have any part of their labor force unionized.

HIGHLY DESIRABLE ATTRIBUTES BUT NOT ABSOLUTELY NECESSARY

Relevant Acquisition Criteria	Comments
The Candidate Must:	
Have a brand-name orientation that restricts competition.	The buyer may be able to pump life into tired regional or national brand names of the candidate.
Be able to benefit from the buyer's marketing and distribution skills.	The likely buyer may compromise on this point, if other criteria are in place.

EXHIBIT 12-3 *(Continued)*

Relevant Acquisition Criteria	Comments
Participate in growing markets.	Desirable, but not critical, particularly if the deal is an add-on to the buyer's existing lines or markets.
Have a leadership position in its markets.	Desirable. If the candidate does not have a leadership position, perhaps the buyer can assist in future market share increases.
Earn a 35% or greater gross margin on sales.	Arbitrary hurdle that may not be relevant to the candidate's business.
Have a good management team, that is willing to stay postclosing.	Retaining management is important if (1) the buyer doesn't have its own managers available to take over the helm of the acquired business, or (2) the acquisition isn't going to be "folded into" an existing buyer business that already has management.

the door for innovative acquisition concepts, but it also gives others latitude in which to criticize the development executive's screening ideas, should they fall into disfavor at the board level.

As a practical matter, development executives are well advised to segment acquisition criteria into three categories: (1) Deal-Killers; (2) Probable Deal-Killers; and (3) Highly Desirable Attributes but Not Absolutely Necessary. A Deal Killer defines an attribute the candidate must have to advance to the next step in the screening process. If not, the candidate is eliminated. Typical Deal Killers are industry, size, and price criteria. A Probable Deal Killer is an attribute about which the buyer management feels strongly, although they may consider buying a business that lacks this particular quality. Profitability and labor unions often fall into the Probable Deal Killer category. Criteria belonging to the Highly Desirable but Not Absolutely Necessary category are harder to pinpoint because they vary widely by industry and company. This three-tier segmentation of acquisition criteria accelerates the process of separating the wheat from the chaff. An hypothetical example of these three categories for the Fortune 500 Consumer Food Company appears in Exhibit 12-3, alongside related commentary.

How might the development executive implement these screens in real life? The following 10 acquisition ideas crossed the executive's desk during a one-month period:

Fortune 500 Consumer Food Company
One Month of Sample Acquisition Candidates

1. *Ottomanelli Macaroni Company*
   Description: Family-owned pasta manufacturer with a solid brand name in the Philadelphia area. Profitable. $30 million in sales.

   Source: Reputable business broker.

   Deal Killers

   Industry: *Pass.*

   Size: *Fail.* Doesn't meet the $100 million annual sales hurdle.

   Asking Price: *No grade.* Price is undetermined

   Screening Decision: The Ottomanelli Macaroni Company is rejected on size criterion, which is a Deal Killer. No further study is required by the Company.

2. *CTC Corporation*
   Description: Second largest distributor of prepared Mexican foods in the United States. Profitable, with solid growth potential. Annual sales of $110 million.

   Source: Regional investment bank.

   Deal Killers

   Industry: *Fail.* CTC is a food products *distributor.* It is not a *manufacturer* as required by the industry criteria.

   Size: *Pass.*

   Asking Price: *Pass.* The investment banker's price talk is in line with recent food distributor deals.

   Screening Decision: CTC Corp. is rejected because it failed the industry criterion.

3. *Queen Anne Premium Chocolate Company*
   Description: National manufacturer of premium chocolates sold to the carriage trade. Established, quality brand

name. Profitable. Family owned. $10 million in annual sales.

Source: Board member of the Fortune 500 Consumer Food Company, who works part-time as a finder.

Deal Killers

Industry: *Pass.*

Size: *Fail.* Queen Anne doesn't meet the $100 million annual sales hurdle.

Asking Price: *No grade.* Undetermined.

Screening Decision: Queen Anne Premium Chocolate Co. is rejected on size criterion.

4. *Indian Maid Dairy Company*
   Description: Strong regional producer of brand-name dairy products, including milk, butter, and cheese. $400 million in annual sales. Two straight years of losses. Division of major conglomerate. Asking price is book value, which is reasonable compared with recent transactions.

Source: Major commercial bank.

Deal Killers

Industry: *Pass.*

Size: *Pass.*

Asking Price: *Pass.*

Screening Decision: Indian Maid Dairy Co. passes all Deal Killer criteria. The next step is an examination of its suitability given the Probable Deal Killers.

Probable Deal Killers

Brand Name: Fail. Brand name appears to be ineffective against competing private-label dairy products.

Benefits from Buyer's Skills: Pass. The Company's marketing skills are complementary.

Growing Market: Pass. Candidate's industry growth is roughly equal to population growth, since dairy demand is highly correlated to food consumption.

Leadership Position: Pass. Strongest regional producer.

Profitable: Fail. Indian Maid is a turnaround candidate. Quick adjustments used by the in-house executive are not significant.

Nonunion: No grade. Undetermined from material at hand.

Screening Decision: Indian Maid is rejected for failing to meet two key attributes (i.e., an effective brand name and a profitable track record).

5. *Tasteful Frozen Fruit Ices, Inc.*
   Description: Manufacturer of frozen food novelties. Leading brand name in growing, niche market. Profitable. $55 million in sales. Division of leveraged buyout firm, which is suggesting a 30× P/E multiple as its asking price.

   Source: Major investment bank.

   Deal Killers

   Industry: *Pass.* Tasteful Frozen Fruit represents an "add on" to the Company's successful frozen desserts line.

   Size: *Pass.* $55 million in annual sales passes Buyer's $50 million sales guideline for an add-on deal.

   Asking Price: *Fail.* Growth potential of Tasteful does not merit a 30× P/E, particularly in light of the Company's price guideline which is based on recent transactions' P/E range of 18×—22×.

   Screening Decision: The Tasteful Frozen Fruit proposal is rejected due to unreasonable price indications.

6. *Delson Food Services, Inc.*
   Description: Manufactures "Delson Quality" brand-name ice cream to national institutional market (i.e., schools, restaurants, and hospitals). Marginally profitable because of a high debt load originating from earlier leveraged buyout. $350 million in annual sales. Owned by management and several large institutional investors. Price talk of 8× EBIT is in line with recent deals.

   Source: Major investment bank.

Deal Killers

Industry: *Fail.* Delson's products are sold and marketed to the institutional market, as opposed to the consumer market favored by the Company.

Size: *Pass.*

Asking Price: *Pass.*

Screening Decision: Delson Food is rejected on industry grounds.

7. *Wisconsin Food Processors Corporation.*
   Description: Manufactures private-label canned vegetable products for supermarket chains. $60 million in annual sales. Losing $1 million per year, but the owner's family is receiving $2 million annually in excess compensation.

Source: Business broker.

Deal Killers

Industry: *Pass.*

Size: *Pass.* Possible add-on to buyer's vegetable line.

Asking Price: *No grade.* Undetermined price.

Wisconsin Food Processors proceeds to the next screening step.

Probable Deal Killers

Brand Name: Fail. Wisconsin Food has no brand name. In fact, the private label goods it manufactures compete with the Company's own sales. The private label market, however, could be an outlet for the Company's excess production capacity. The brand-name hurdle is thus rendered less important.

Benefit from Buyer's Skills: Pass. The Company's canned vegetable business is larger and more sophisticated, so it can provide technological expertise to Wisconsin Food.

Growing Market: Pass. The private label business is expanding rapidly in supermarkets.

Leadership Position: Fail, but the private label vegetable production market is fragmented. There are few participants with market shares over 2%–3%.

Profitable: Pass, if a quick adjustment of $2 million is made for excess compensation.

Nonunion: Pass.

Screening Decision: The Wisconsin Foods transaction is reserved for further study. Key decision factors include (1) the owner's price expectations; and (2) the Company's willingness to consider a private-label operation.

8. *Movie Time Popcorn, Inc.*
    Description: Late-stage start-up venture with a patented formula for non-salt, non-fat popcorn that tastes like the real thing. $4 million in annual sales. No profits over 3-year history. $10 million in assets, negative net worth. The owners are seeking outside capital through a joint venture or a merger with a larger operation.

    Source: Venture capital firm that holds a 30% ownership position.

    ### Deal Killers

    Industry: *Pass.* Movie Time's popcorn has the potential to be a branded consumer food product.

    Size: *Fail.* Too small for the Company.

    Asking Price: *No grade.* Price hasn't been suggested.

    Screening Decision: Movie Time has the makings of a true growth company if its product quality can be assured. As an acquisition candidate, it fails the size guidelines. For the Company, now might be the time to break the rules and investigate Movie Time further.

9. *Prince Charcoal Company*
    Description: Established division of a conglomerate that is restructuring its operations. Prince Charcoal is the market leader in charcoal for outdoor barbecuing. $150 million in annual sales. Highly profitable even after the parent company's allocation of $7 million in corporate overhead. The management is willing to stay after the closing.

    Source: Major investment bank.

Deal Killers

Industry: *Fail.*

Size: *Pass.*

Asking Price: *No grade.* Investment bank has said it "will let the market decide."

Screening Decision: Prince Charcoal Company sells to the same consumers who purchase the Fortune 500 Consumer Food Company's products. Furthermore, charcoal is sold through the same supermarkets that sell the buyer's product lines. Marketing and distribution systems are therefore similar to those of the Company. Although Prince Charcoal fails the Deal Killing test on industry grounds, it is an interesting diversification candidate that falls outside the Company's standard industry criteria. Opportunism should thus overtake preset guidelines.

10. *Collins Soups, Inc.*

   Description: Established leader in the fast-growing powdered soup market. Well-recognized brand name. 30% market share. Profitable with annual sales of $175 million. Owned by a foreign-based conglomerate.

   Source: In-house search. The Company's initial contact with the owner uncovered an interest in selling. Preliminary price talk is in line with recent transactions.

Deal Killers

Industry: *Pass.*

Size: *Pass.*

Asking Price: *Pass.*

Probable Deal Killers

Brand Name: Pass.

Benefit from Buyer's Skill: Pass.

Growing Market: Pass.

Leadership Position: Pass.

Nonunion: Pass.

Screening Decision: Collins Soup, Inc. is an ideal acquisition candidate for the Company. It meets all the Fortune 500 Food

Company's key criteria. Unfortunately, it will also meet the acquisition criteria of numerous large food concerns, industrial conglomerates and leveraged buyout firms. If Collins' foreign parent decides to contact other prospective acquirers, the deal could deteriorate into a high-priced auction, leaving the "winner" to pay top dollar for Collins Soups. Nevertheless, Collins Soups merits serious study and the Company's due diligence process should commence immediately.

While reasonably complete, the 11 criteria set forth in the Fortune 500 Food Company's hypothetical screening list are not all-encompassing. Certain opportunities require bending—if not breaking—the rules. In certain cases, where the candidate passes the initial screen, the subsequent due diligence effort may reveal serious incompatibilities between the operations of the Company and the candidate that cannot be papered over with good intentions. Poor technology fits, customer conflicts, and cultural differences are only three examples of potential problems on the operational side. Antitrust issues, tax liabilities, environmental uncertainties, and a host of other problems may also hinder an acquisition that successfully passes the initial screening criteria.

STRATEGIC SEARCHES

The Fortune 500 Consumer Food Company's search criteria focused on candidates that were related to the would-be acquirer's core business. The Company's acquisition strategy was a clear-cut Market Share/Product Line Extension approach. Suppose this Company believed that the consumer foods business was too slow-growth to warrant further investment. How might the acquisition criteria change if its management decided to purchase businesses that either: (1) diversified the Company out of the consumer packaged foods business; or (2) enabled it to obtain a new set of skills and resources that complement its core business? Where would the company start in implementing such a strategic search, and how would it define "The Vision Thing"?

In today's acquisition environment, a strategic deal that resembles pure diversification is hard for corporate managers to rationalize to their constituencies—their shareholders, bondholders, bank lenders, employees, customers, and suppliers. Many pure diversification acquisitions have been dismal failures, costing untold millions of dollars for the constituencies of the unfortunate purchasers. Given this backdrop of dysfunctional deals, the justification for today's strategic acquisition must rest on a foundation that stresses a logical connection between the buyer's operation and the candidate's business. Thus, a marriage between a steel manufacturer and our Fortune 500 Consumer Food Company has little strategic purpose. The Company's acquisition of a brand-name luggage manufacturer, on the other hand, makes more sense since the consumer goods orientation of a luggage producer is similar in certain respects to the Company's brand-name packaged foods business.

Certain strategic deals do not involve an extensive search and screen exercise. For reasons related to changing aspects of its core business, the Strategic Buyer may require special functional skills or resources that can only be found in a handful of known candidates. A good example of this targeted approach is IBM's $3.5 billion acquisition of Lotus Development Corporation. Only a handful of software companies filled the unique needs of IBM in its goal to accelerate its entry into the software business. Vertical integration—a company overseeing every step a product takes from its source to the customer—prompts many strategic mergers. Entertainment companies have been active in this respect. Walt Disney, Time Warner, and TCI Communications have built up vertical media empires. They found acquisition candidates among suppliers and customers.

Most strategic buyers have a daunting exercise. Which acquisition candidates, out of the many available, have a rational connection to the buyer's base business? So much depends on what the buyer defines as desired strategic attributes and what importance it attaches to them in its planning process. Consider the notion of a strategic acquisition: Should it bring a new set of functional skills and resources to the buyer, or should it merely complement the buyer's existing skills and asset base? The Fortune 500 Consumer Food Company may want a diversification outside the food business, yet the deal should have some logical connection with its existing customer base, marketing strength, and manufacturing technology. This objective appears rational, but it is fraught with ambiguity. The Company's definition of these three elements of its business could occupy a broad berth, leaving the Company's search process with little direction. A narrow interpretation of

EXHIBIT 12-4   Fortune 500 consumer food company establishing the framework for linking the buyer and a strategic acquisition

CUSTOMER BASE CONNECTION

Narrow Definition of Customer Base Connection	**Broad Definition of Customer Base Connection**
Acquisition candidate should sell its products to the same U.S. supermarkets and convenience stores that feature the Company's packaged food products.	There is a global marketplace for the Company's products. It includes all consumers. Retailers and wholesalers are also "customers" because of their ability to "push down" products to the ultimate consumer. A prospective acquisition candidate can thus service any portion of this customer base.
Examples of Eligible Candidates:	
• Detergent manufacturer	*Examples of Eligible Candidates:*
• Greeting card firm	• Foreign consumer business
• Cigarette producer	• Manufacturer of consumer products that are sold in any retailing business
	• Consumer furniture maker
	• Companies providing services to retailers

MARKETING STRENGTHS CONNECTION

Narrow Definition of Marketing Strengths Connection	**Broad Definition of Marketing Strengths Connection**
The Company is adept at mass marketing low-ticket, repeat purchase brand-name items sold to individual consumers through the chain store channel. The candidate's products should fit into this same marketing and distribution thrust.	The candidate should provide the Company with an entry into alternative consumer marketing channels, such as direct mail, telemarketing, and the Internet.
Examples of Eligible Candidates:	*Examples of Eligible Candidates:*
• Manufacture of low-cost, brand-name apparel (e.g., Fruit of the Loom)	• Direct mail catalog firm
• Manufacturer of school supplies (i.e., pens, pencils, notebooks)	• TV marketer such as Home Shopping Network
• Manufacturer of children's toys	• Door-to-door sales company such as Avon or Encyclopedia Britannica

EXHIBIT 12-4   *(Continued)*

MANUFACTURING TECHNOLOGY CONNECTION

Narrow Definition of Manufacturing Technology Connection	Broad Definition of Manufacturing Technology Connection
The candidate's manufacturing technology should be compatible with the Company's, or should have the potential to be enhanced through an affiliation with Company.	The candidate's technology should be adequate to provide its products or services to its customer base at a reasonable cost.
Examples of Eligible Candidates:	*Examples of Eligible Candidates:*
• Restricts the Company to candidates engaged in low-tech manufacturing businesses	• Opens the search process to many firms with technologies that may be new to the Company

these factors, on the other hand, ties the hands of the executive who is on the lookout for a good transaction. Exhibit 12-4 sets forth examples of how the Food Company might define the appropriate connection between its core business and a strategic acquisition.

The broader definitions of "candidate connections" provide the Food Company with a wide range of discretion in pursuing strategic acquisitions. In practice, it would have to narrow this range to a manageable level. Ranking the strategic attributes in terms of priority is a good start. Since management's objective is a "strategic connection" that enhances its core business, the search and screen guidelines must address this concern, but not at the expense of making the search resemble a market share/product line extension. The following criteria focus the Company's efforts:

Fortune 500 Consumer Food Company
Strategic Diversification Criteria

Deal Killers

The strategic candidate must:

1. Be involved in *manufacturing* and *marketing* a nondurable consumer *product* that involves repeated purchases, or in providing a consumer *service* that involves repeated purchases.

Author's Comments: The prospective acquisition must serve the consumer sector, which is the current market for the Company's products. The connection is obvious.

2. Register annual sales of $100 million or more.

   Author's Comments: The proposed diversification should be a sizable commitment to merit the attention of the Company's top management.

3. Have an asking price that is realistic in the context of recent transactions. The deal should result in minimal EPS dilution, taking into account all pro forma adjustments.

   Author's Comments: The Company has no interest in either overpaying for a deal or incurring substantial EPS dilution.

4. Be profitable.

   Author's Comments: The Company can't gamble on a money-losing business as a diversification. Numerous operating risks come with acquiring a firm outside the Company's core food businesses. Why compound these risks with the purchase of a turnaround business?

5. Have good management willing to stay after the closing.

   Author's Comments: Since the Company has no direct experience in the strategic candidate's industry, the chances of the acquisition's success are enhanced if management remains after the closing. If the candidate's management becomes wealthy as a result of the deal, the Company has to be wary of their motivation for hard work subsequent to the closing.

Probable Deal Killers

6. Participate in growing markets.

   Author's Comments: A strategic acquisition is justifiable if the buyer's base business is stagnating, or if the buyer's long-term survival requires new functional skills or resources that can only be obtained on the outside. Diversifying into a shrinking market runs counter to these goals unless the seller's functional skills and resources are truly unique.

7. Employ a nonunion labor force.

   Author's Comments: Many companies are reluctant to have any part of their labor force unionized.

Highly Desirable, But Not Absolutely Necessary

8. Have as a key success factor the need for a brand name, a heavy advertising budget, and an extensive distribution system.

   Author's Comments: The acquisition should be able to take advantage of the Company's strengths in these areas.

9. Low technology and low degree of technical know-how.

   Author's Comments: The company is uncomfortable with high-tech businesses, even if they hold the promise of growth.

10. Have a leadership position in its markets.

    Author's Comments: The Company likes businesses with market leadership positions.

11. Have a "culture fit" with the Company.

    Author's Comments: Culture is an intangible attribute that is difficult to pinpoint. Most acquirers, however, know culture fit when they see it.

The preceding criteria provide the Company with a great deal of flexibility in selecting a diversification while at the same time preserving a sense of rationality. The Company can select from industries as diverse as restaurants, home hardware, and income tax preparation. Almost any low-ticket consumer business applies. The number of candidates to be screened is much larger than the number that would have been generated under the previous Market Share/Product Line Extender approach. As a result, the strategic program dramatizes the need for the Company to develop a review system that eliminates candidates quickly. Otherwise, the development effort will be swamped with acquisition proposals that inevitably turn out to be inappropriate with further scrutiny.

It is unlikely that the intermediary community could grasp the finer points of the Food Company's strategic acquisition guidelines. Every manner of private company, corporate division, or public company would be shown to the Company by investment banks and business brokers, particularly since this acquirer can easily afford a large transaction. Many of these intermediary-generated candidates would not be officially for sale, adding another layer of complexity. The Company would not be sure whether the business in question is a real candidate or exists only in the mind of the investment banker placing the phone call. Notwithstanding the unfocused nature of most intermediary suggestions, the development executives should respond to them within a reasonable period of time with a well-thought-out response.

Concurrently with the intermediary responses, the Company's in-house search process should be generating dozens of possibilities, which are followed up in an appropriate manner. It is imperative, therefore, that the executive's desk review is a quick arbiter of "good" versus "bad" ideas. Casting too wide a net over the candidate universe will dilute the development efforts, which must hone in on *finding* an attractive deal and then *closing* the transaction. The Company cannot allow its search process to deteriorate into a window-shopping exercise.

To minimize the time spent on wasteful proposals, strict attention must be paid to Deal Killing criteria, which, in this example, covered five critical attributes:

Strategic Acquisition—Key Attributes

1. Industry.
2. Size.
3. Price, EPS dilution.
4. Profitability.
5. Carryover management.

The remaining criteria were secondary during the desk review. Confirming the candidate's suitability on secondary criteria requires more research, which is unwarranted at the initial screening level.

THE LEVERAGED BUYOUT AND BOTTOM FISHER SEARCH PROCESS

Leveraged buyout firms function on a different plane than an operating company. Buyout investors are on the lookout for companies that can finance the bulk of their respective purchase prices through borrowings. Industry fit is unimportant. For the most part, LBO candidates meeting this self-financing prescription are (1) classified as medium-size to large businesses (i.e., purchase price of $25 million plus); (2) engaged in a low-tech manufacturing or service sector; and

(3) established with a profitable operating history. These three attributes attract the sophisticated lending institutions that finance buyouts, and enable LBO firms to put up a small amount of the deal's purchase price in the form of equity. LBO firms provide few opportunities for operating synergies with their acquisitions, so they find it difficult to compete with corporations seeking Market Share/Product Line Extensions. The corporate acquirers can afford to propose purchase prices that incorporate the benefits of such synergies, which means their price thinking can be higher than that of the LBO firms, all other things being equal. As a result, LBOs tend to occur in out-of-favor industries, where the leading participants are deemphasizing their investment commitments. Corporate strategic buyers, meanwhile, tend to look at industries that are more fashionable and more growth-oriented than those sectors where the market leaders are curtailing investment.

Bottom Fishers are eclectic financial investors. Their prime screening criterion is a low Ratio of Asking Price to Perceived Asset Value. This kind of sale candidate is considered a bargain relative to other available acquisition opportunities. Not surprisingly, many of the deals meeting this objective turn up in out-of-favor industries, turnaround businesses, or financial restructurings. Bottom Fishers like the complex analytical exercises found in such situations, whereas the standard corporate buyers and large LBO players find this work to be an ineffective use of their resources. As a result, one can find Bottom Fishers circling around almost every distressed corporation.

SUMMARY

Thousands of companies are open to purchase offers. Unless a buyer's acquisition needs are extremely focused, finding the right deal involves working with the intermediary community as well as developing the proper in-house capability to search for quality acquisitions. A well-designed and executed search program results in a steady stream of acquisition ideas, the vast majority of which are ill-suited for the buyer's needs. Separating attractive opportunities from the many available requires strict attention to a few key acquisition criteria that can colloquially be called Deal Killers. With few exceptions, any acquisition candidate that doesn't meet the Deal Killer criteria should be discarded quickly to narrow the focus on likely targets.

The search and screen effort only justifies so much time and effort. At some point, the would-be buyer has to take the plunge by bidding for, performing due diligence on, and purchasing a business. If, after a period of 24 to 36 months, few candidates have survived the buyer's screening process, and no meaningful deals have been closed, top management should consider changes in its acquisition guidelines, since the criteria apparently do not reflect real-world opportunities.

13 FINANCIAL PROJECTIONS: EVALUATING THEIRS

Once the would-be buyer has narrowed its choices to a few prospects, it defines the relative contribution of each potential acquisition to the buyer's future earnings and cash flows. The first step in this process is to gain an understanding of the historical performance of each individual target company. From this analysis, a base of knowledge is created to project a prospective acquisition's operating results on a stand-alone basis, *without* the synergistic benefits of a combination with the buyer's business. This stand-alone projection is then adjusted to reflect the synergies of the acquisition affiliating itself with the buyer. Common synergies of mergers are cost savings from reducing duplicate overhead, sales gains from improved market access and lower capital costs due to the parent's favorable financing sources. After the stand-alone projections have been modified to reflect likely synergies, the buyer "folds in" the proposed acquisition's operating results with its own forecast results. Occasionally, the buyer's own business may realize synergies from the deal. The Burlington Northern's claim in 1995 that the Santa Fe Pacific takeover would provide $300 million in added revenues for Burlington's railroad business was a recent example of this theme. Following the inclusion of synergies, the buyer includes the proposed financing for the transaction (stock, cash, debt or a combination

147

of the three) along with the requisite accounting adjustments, such as increases in depreciation and goodwill expenses. The buyer's final step is constructing the combined firm's financial statements. In sum, the process of making M&A projections unfolds in five stages:

1. Complete historical financial analysis of acquisition candidate.
2. Prepare stand-alone projections of acquisition candidate and buyer.
3. Include synergies and cost cuts in combined financial statements.
4. Structure finances and allow for purchase accounting adjustments.
5. Complete pro forma combined projections.

After the pro forma combined projections are finished, the buyer analyzes how the proposed deal impacts the buyer's future financial picture and resultant equity value. Does EPS growth increase? Is added financial risk a potential problem? Will the market value the buyer's stock more if the transaction is consummated? Or less? The analysis begins to answer these questions.

In those cases where the seller is represented by a knowledgeable intermediary, the buyer receives an information memorandum that provides the seller's written version of what is going to take place in the future. The target business' prospects are inevitably presented in an optimistic light: Sales and margins are forecast to increase steadily, and profits rise accordingly. In 20 years of doing deals, I have not seen a single projection indicating a decline in sales and profits. Since no one really knows what is going to happen in the future, the seller's projections are really the product of educated guesswork. Despite this failing, the seller's numbers often set the "anchor" from which the buyer's projections are derived and they have a tendency to influence unduly the seller's own thoughts about what its business is worth.

It is important that a prospective buyer defer making definitive projections until it has taken the time to meet with the seller's management and review its business. Face-to-face due diligence meetings answer many questions about the key factors influencing sales and earnings in the target's business. The substance of these conversations should focus heavily on the seller's recent *historical* results, since 95% of all projections are based on assumptions tied directly to past experience. This is why historical financial analysis is a critical part of the buyer's up-front effort. As the would-be buyer understands the seller's explanation of the main drivers behind its past financial performance, the groundwork is laid for an appreciation of the target's future prospects. Personal meetings go a long way toward providing the buyer with the seller's justification for its rosy projections.

Historical financial analysis and financial forecasting are topics on which many books have been written. This chapter does not duplicate these efforts. It is intended to be a brief guide in completing a historical financial analysis of a company as well as a short lesson in noticing the warning signs of an overly aggressive forecast.

TARGET "STAND ALONE" HISTORICAL FINANCIAL ANALYSIS

Before forecasting the financial statements of a prospective acquisition, an analyst has to understand the target's past performance. Why did sales go up? or down? Why did profit margins change? Is there a specific reason for the increase in the inventory-to-sales ratio? The historical analysis section of an acquisition study is the beginning of an investigation, and a search for knowledge. Eventually, this information is put to practical use in the development of a series of financial projections. The buyer relies on this data to make a rational business decision about whether or not to buy the target business.

A financial statement analysis of a company must begin with the assumption that the statements provided to the buyer are not fraudulent. The risk of material misstatements is small if the statements are audited by a certified public accounting firm. Audited data is always the case for publicly traded firms and is generally the case for larger private companies. While there is no requirement, many small to medium-size private firms also use outside accounting firms to audit the books, either for their own purposes or to satisfy outside parties such as bank lenders or governmental clients that need this information to enter into contractual relationships. Even under the supervision of CPAs, most firms have significant flexibility in their use of accounting methods, which may, at times, promote earnings inflation. By permitting liberal accounting techniques at times when the more conservative approach is justified, CPAs risk economic misstatements in audited data; and while they try to police outright fraudulent reporting, they are sometimes fooled by crafty clients. Indeed, the history of deals is replete with buyers suffering from the effects of inaccurate financial statements certified by accountants who were unable to detect faulty ledger entries. For most smaller companies, in the $1–$10 million sales range, the books are not audited. With these smaller businesses, the incidence of sellers inflating their performance is high, and the buyer typically awaits its own audit of such reported results before relying too much on the by-the-books historical analysis. While important, the buyer's self-audit of the seller's accounts is expensive, and for reasons of seller confidentiality, it is usually one of the last steps in the purchase process. As a result of the preceding factors, the initial development of acquirer projections and historical analysis uses the data more or less as presented in the seller's written statements and oral representations.

Having accepted the possibility of inaccurate financial data, the buyer executive studying the acquisition candidate's statements aims at preparing a *reasonable* estimate of current earnings power. In this context "reasonable" means he doesn't look for perfection in the early rounds of study. This "current earnings" estimate is subsequently used as the platform from which to base future earnings projections. For example, suppose the executive concludes that Braveheart Corporation earned approximately $20 million per year in each of the past three years, after stripping out the effects of all extraordinary items and asset sales during the period. All factors being equal, he has a logical basis for assuming that $20 million is a reasonable earnings objective in 1996, as indicated in Exhibit 13-1.

EXHIBIT 13-1   Possible acquisition Braveheart Corporation (US$ millions)

	Year Ended December 31			
	Actual			Projected
	1993	**1994**	**1995**	**1996**
Sales	362.0	374.5	381.0	390.0
Net income[1]	19.8	20.4	20.2	20.0

[1] Adjusted to eliminate unusual items.

Basing earnings forecasts solely on past performance is akin to driving your car by looking in the rearview mirror. Many acquirers fall into this trap and pay dearly for their mistakes, but a total separation of the future from the past is illogical. Most businesses have a number of fairly stable elements which are readily predictable, so the present and immediate past are good first steps in departing for the future.

STARTING THE HISTORICAL FINANCIAL ANALYSIS

What are the raw materials from which a historical financial analysis is created? Start with the three key financial statements and the attached footnotes:

1. The income statement.
2. The balance sheet.
3. Sources and uses of funds statement.
4. Notes to financial statement.

This accounting data provides a wealth of information from which certain trends and patterns can be discerned. Financial analysis gives us four primary tools to evaluate historical corporate performance:

1. Absolute amount changes.
2. Percentage changes in growth.
3. Common size percentage statements.
4. Financial ratios.

Typically, these tools are applied over a 3- to 5-year period, since interyear comparisons are the best means of facilitating the discovery of trends, patterns, or anomalies. But, be forewarned. This sort of analysis is a lot of work. For example, by applying the preceding four analytical tools to each of the three financial statements in Exhibit 13-2 for just a one-year period, you will have made *twelve* snapshots of the candidate's finances for that year. This means plenty of number crunching.

Luckily, the advent of technology has reduced the effort involved in preparing the raw data. Various off-the-shelf analysis software

EXHIBIT 13-2 **Financial statement analysis matrix of accounting data and analytical tools**

	Absolute Amounts	Percentage Changes	Common Size	Ratios
Income statement	1	2	3	· 4
Balance sheet	5	6	7	8
Source and uses of funds	9	10	11	12

packages are available to assist in the process, or the buyer can customize its analytical program in house with the involvement of MBAs who are familiar with Lotus and similar software products.

BEGINNING THE FINANCIAL ANALYSIS

As an illustration of the recommended approach to financial analysis, consider Payless Cashways, Inc.'s results for the three years ended November 30, 1987. Payless was a full-line buildings materials retailer serving the home improvement, maintenance, and repair market. As of November 1987, the Kansas City-based company operated 193 stores in 26 states. Sales for fiscal year 1987 totaled just under $1.8 billion. In early 1988 Payless became a takeover target of Asher Edelman, a New York corporate raider, who headed an investor group that bought 8% of the company's outstanding shares. After a spirited search for a white knight, the retail chain was taken over in August 1988 in a $909 million leveraged buyout sponsored by Goldman, Sachs & Company, a leading investment banking firm, Masco Corporation, a Michigan-based manufacturer of hardware products, and the top management of Payless. Pre-buyout income statement and summary balance sheet data are shown in Exhibit 13-3.

A cursory glance at this information enables the reader to reach the following conclusions: (1) Payless was profitable and growing; (2) its principal expense was cost of goods sold, which is to be expected for a retailer that resells products made by others; (3) the company was conservatively leveraged; and (4) 1987's EBIT was reduced sharply by special charges totaling $24 million.

EXHIBIT 13-3   Payless Cashways, Inc., summary financial data (in millions)

	Fiscal Year Ended November 30		
	1985	1986	1987
Income Statement Data			
Net sales	$1,390	$1,528	$1,770
Cost of goods sold	971	1,058	1,250
SG&A expense	307	343	390
Depreciation	25	29	36
Special charges[1]	—	—	24
Earnings before interest and taxes (EBIT)	86	97	69
Interest on debt	18	15	17
Earnings before taxes	68	82	52
Provision for income taxes	30	40	24
Net income	$ 38	$ 42	$ 28
Earnings per share	$ 1.12	$ 1.22	$ 0.81
Balance Sheet Data			
Working capital	$ 128	$ 132	$ 123
Total assets	606	708	813
Long-term debt, less current maturities	120	132	180
Shareholders' equity	333	370	379

[1] To reflect expenses associated with store closings, interest rate swap termination and transfer of private-label credit card operation.

"NORMALIZING" RESULTS

This latter item needs to be considered before the reader proceeds. Management was clearly trying to characterize the multiple store closings, the interest rate swap termination, and the transfer of private credit card operation as "one-time" items, which would not be repeated. That was why the related costs were designated as special charges and footnoted in Exhibit 13-3. A review of Payless Cashway's results over the preceding five years indicates that these events were true aberrations. Thus, from an analyst's viewpoint in 1988, these developments obscured the "normal" earnings power of Payless and so should not have an adverse effect on earnings in future years. In keeping with this interpretation of the facts, our historical analysis of the

EXHIBIT 13-4   Payless Cashways, Inc., normalized income statement data (in millions)

	Fiscal Year Ended November 30		
	1985	**1986**	**1987**
Original EBIT	$86	$97	$69
Add back: special charges	—	—	24
Normalized EBIT	86	97	93
Interest on debt	18	15	17
Normalized earnings before taxes	68	82	76
Provision for income taxes	30	40	35[1]
Normalized net income	$38	$42	$41
Normalized earnings per share	$1.12	$1.22	$1.19

[1] Income taxes are assumed to increase proportionally to the higher normalized earnings before taxes.

EXHIBIT 13-5   Payless Cashways, Inc., normalized financial data, absolute amount changes (in millions)

	Fiscal Year Ended November 30		
	1985	**1986**	**1987**
Income Statement Data			
Net sales	+214	+138	+242
Cost of goods sold	+145	+87	+192
SG&A expense	+55	+36	+47
Depreciation	+8	+4	+7
Earnings before interest and taxes (EBIT)	+7	+11	−4
Interest on debt	+6	−3	+2
Earnings before taxes	+1	+14	−6
Provision for income taxes	—	+10	−5
Net income	+1	+4	−1
Earnings per share	+.03	+.11	−.03
Balance Sheet Data			
Working capital	−9	+4	−9
Total assets	+52	+102	+105
Long-term debt, less current maturities	−41	+12	+48
Shareholders' equity	+76	+37	+9

Company's "earnings power" eliminates 1987's $24 million of special charges so as to normalize 1987's data. As a result, normalized EBIT for Payless exhibited a consistent trend over the three-year period (see Exhibit 13-4).

Having modified the historical data to reflect an improved perception of future potential, the analyst proceeds to the next step, which is a review of the changes in each financial statement item expressed in terms of absolute dollar amounts. Many practitioners tend to "eyeball" such changes, rather than make the calculations that appear in the Exhibit 13-5.

ABSOLUTE AMOUNT ANALYSIS

The big jump in 1987 sales was primarily the result of the acquisition of a 10-store chain, whose results were fully included in the year. Operating income (EBIT) declined slightly in 1987 as expenses were slightly higher than the gain in sales. The large additions to total assets in each year illustrated the incremental asset base that was needed to support sales growth.

PERCENTAGE CHANGES

Financial analysts make extensive use of year-to-year percentage changes in a company's financial results. As discussed earlier, percentage growth statistics in net income and dividends are key drivers in establishing stock prices. The analyst's ability to predict with confidence future earnings is heavily influenced by his ability to determine constant relationships between sales, expenses, and the additional investment required to sustain growth. Financial statements expressed in terms of percentage changes are quite helpful in making these determinations. The related information for Payless Cashways appears in Exhibit 13-6.

Considering that inflation was only 5% annually over the 1985–1987 period, Payless appears to be a growth company since it recorded annual sales changes of 18%, 10%, and 16%. EBIT and net income increases were less consistent; however, and EPS advances

EXHIBIT 13-6 Payless Cashways, Inc., normalized financial data, percentage changes

	Fiscal Year Ended November 30		
	1985	1986	1987
Income Statement Data			
Net sales	+18%	+10%	+16%
Cost of goods sold	+18	+9	+18
SG&A expense	+22	+12	+14
Depreciation	+47	+16	+24
Earnings before interest and taxes (EBIT)	+8	+13	−4
Interest on debt	+46	−17	+13
Earnings before taxes	+1	+21	−7
Provision for income taxes	−1	+33	−12
Net income	+3%	+11%	−2%
Earnings per share	+3%	9%	−2%
Balance Sheet Data			
Working capital	−8%	+3%	−7%
Total assets	+9	+17	+15
Long-term debt, less current maturities	−26	+10	+36
Shareholders' equity	+30	+11	+2

failed to keep pace with the sales gains. The data show that the growth in several expense categories exceeded the growth in sales, indicating that obtaining new sales dollars was an expensive proposition, and perhaps raising a red flag regarding the company's expansion strategy.

COMMON SIZE ANALYSIS

Another popular tool in financial analysis is the common size statement. In this presentation, income statement and balance sheet items are expressed as a percentage of sales and total assets, respectively. Since all accounting results are reduced to percentages of the same line item, the data arranged in this way is referred to as "common size." Information for Payless Cashways appears in Exhibit 13-7.

The common size data facilitates comparisons of operating results between years. Exhibit 13-7 shows that profitability declined as a

EXHIBIT 13-7   Payless Cashways, Inc., normalized financial data, common size data

	Fiscal Year Ended November 30		
	1985	1986	1987
Income Statement Data			
Net sales	100.0%	100.0%	100.0%
Cost of goods sold	69.9	69.2	71.6
SG&A expense	22.1	22.4	22.0
Depreciation	1.8	1.9	2.0
Earnings before interest and taxes (EBIT)	6.2	6.3	5.3
Interest on debt	1.3	1.0	1.0
Earnings before taxes	4.9	5.4	4.3
Provision for income taxes	2.2	2.6	2.0
Net income	2.7%	2.8%	2.3%
Earnings per share	—	—	—
Balance Sheet Data			
Working capital	21.1%	18.6%	15.1%
Total assets	100.0	100.0	100.0
Long-term debt, less current maturities	19.8	18.6	22.1
Shareholders' equity	55.0	52.3	46.6

percentage of sales. EBIT decreased from 6.2% to 5.3% while net income dropped from 2.7% to 2.3%. A primary contributor to the decrease was cost of goods sold, which rose from 69.9% to 71.6%. Other income statement items were stable. The balance sheet data indicates a decline in liquidity and an increase in leverage. Working capital, as a percentage of assets, shrunk from 21.1% to 15.1%, and equity decreased from 55.0% to 46.6%.

RATIO ANALYSIS

Ratio analysis relates income statement, balance sheet, and cash flow statement items to one another. Like the other forms of analysis reviewed herein, ratio analysis provides clues in evaluating a firm's current position and in spotting trends toward future performance. Ratios fall into four broad categories:

1. *Profitability Ratios.* Measure return on assets and equity investments. Profits margins, expressed as a percentage of sales in the common size income statement, are also defined as profitability ratios.
2. *Activity Ratios.* Measure the efficiency with which the firm is managing its assets.
3. *Credit Ratios.* Measure the firm's ability to repay its obligations, its existing leverage situation, and its resultant financial risk.
4. *Growth Ratios.* Measure the firm's performance in expanding its business, a key criterion in valuation.

Each category utilizes many different ratios. Commonly used ratios are calculated for Payless Cashways in Exhibit 13-8.

EXHIBIT 13-8 Payless Cashways, Inc., selected financial ratios

	Year Ended November 30		
	1985	**1986**	**1987**
Profitability Ratios			
$\dfrac{\text{EBIT}}{\text{Total assets}} =$	14%	14%	11%
$\dfrac{\text{Net profit}}{\text{Stockholders' equity}} =$	11%	11%	11%
Activity Ratios			
Asset Turnover $= \dfrac{\text{Sales}}{\text{Assets}} =$	2.3×	2.2×	2.2×
Inventory Turnover $= \dfrac{\text{Average inventory}}{\text{Sales}} =$	3.7×	4.0×	4.2×
Credit Ratios			
Current Ratio $= \dfrac{\text{Current assets}}{\text{Current liabilities}} =$	2.0	1.7	1.5
$\dfrac{\text{Long-term debt}}{\text{Stockholders' equity}} =$	0.4	0.4	0.5
$\dfrac{\text{EBIT}}{\text{Interest}} =$	4.8×	6.5×	5.5×

GROWTH RATIOS

Five-year compound annual growth ratios, using normalized data, are as follows:

Payless Cashways, Inc.	1982–1987
Sales	12.0%
EBIT	2.3
Earnings before taxes	(0.1)
Net income	(0.2)
Earnings per share	(1.1)

A review of the Payless Cashways financial ratios paints a picture of a company that was, at best, a mediocre performer. The profitability ratios show the EBIT/assets ratio declined from 14% in 1985 to 11% in 1987. The net profit/stockholders' equity ratio was mired at 11%, far lower than the 15% to 20% expected by most investors in publicly traded stocks. Indeed, "AA" corporate bonds were yielding 9% at the time, indicating that these blue-chip investments were providing a handsome return compared with Payless Cashway's business, which carried substantially more investor risk. The activity ratios indicate some progress in boosting inventory turnover, an important element of the retailing business, but at the same time, the credit ratios show a deterioration of the Company's financial strength. The current ratio declined from 2.0 to 1.5 over the three-year period and the long-term/equity ratio increased from 0.4 to 0.5. Perhaps the growth ratios demonstrate the real failure of the Company. While sales grew at a 12% compound annual rate, Payless was unable to bring any of this growth to the bottom line. EBIT, net income, and earnings per share were virtually flat over the 1982–1987 period. The ratio analysis does not provide a flattering portrait of Payless Cashways.

In part, management ascribed these negative developments to a weak economy in several key geographic areas where the Company had a concentration of stores. Consider the following quote from David Stanley, Chairman, in the 1987 Annual Report, "The farm economy, which has affected our performance for several years, showed modest signs of improvement. Of even greater importance to us, the oil patch economy appears to have bottomed out and may indeed be recovering."

This final bit of optimism may have spurred the Edelman takeover inquiries; but prior to his interest, the general investing public was noncommittal, as the common stock price declined from 1982 to 1987.

INDUSTRY-SPECIFIC INDICATORS

In the preceding financial analysis, we reached a few tentative conclusions through the use of several standard ratios and the evaluation of financial data arranged in various ways, but it cannot be overemphasized that each financial analysis situation is unique. Part of the art of analyzing corporate financial performance is selecting which data must be the focus of an investigation. Which ratios are meaningful? What trends are important? What are the best comparative indicators? How reliable is the analysis of past results in predicting future performance? A sober consideration of these questions prior to the start of any detailed financial analysis is going to represent a huge time-saver for the buyer executives involved in doing the actual work product.

Notwithstanding the importance of financial statement analysis, the interpretation of a company's results usually extend past the information contained in audited data. Most companies record certain industry-specific statistics that over time have proven to be useful performance indicators. The home-improvement retailing industry is no exception. Exhibit 13-9 presents selected industry-specific data calculated by Payless Cashways over the 1985–1987 time period.

EXHIBIT 13-9   Industry-specific statistics

	Year Ended November 30		
	1985	**1986**	**1987**
Growth in "same store" sales	5.0%	4.4%	2.9%
Growth from acquisitions and new stores	13.2%	5.5%	13.0%
Sales per store (MM)	$8.1	$8.8	$9.1
Sales per sq. ft. of selling area	$301	$312	$324
Sales per employee (000)	$105	$117	$117

Because retailers can increase sales volume easily by opening new stores, analysts developed a statistic that isolated the sales growth accruing from established properties from the sales growth resulting from new stores. This statistic is termed the growth in "same store" sales. An examination of this statistic shows the strength of a retailer's underlying growth, without the added capital expense of new stores. In the case of Payless Cashways over the 1985–1987 period, same store sales growth was less than the inflation rate, auguring poor growth prospects in the firm's base business. Recognizing shareholder concerns, management responded to the low 2.9% same store sales growth number in 1987 with the following commentary: "Sales for comparable stores (those open a year or more) increased 2.9 percent. Approximately one-third of our stores operate in the oil-affected states of Texas, Oklahoma, and Colorado. Comparable sales in stores outside of those states increased 7.8 percent."

Same stores sales data enable an analyst to separate the sales growth from acquisitions. In the case of Payless, this separation was important because acquisitions provided the bulk of sales improvements. Sales efficiency—measured by sales per store, sales per square foot of selling area, and sales per employee—is also a monitor of performance. If inflationary effects are excluded from the data, Payless showed few positive advances.

COMPARABLE COMPANY PERFORMANCE

Historical financial analysis of a company cannot be conducted in a vacuum. Statistics ratios and profit margins are not meaningful numbers in and of themselves; they must be compared with something before they become useful. Much depends on the type of industry involved. For example, a brokerage firm, with a preponderance of liquid assets, can operate with a much higher degree of leverage than a home improvement retailer such as Payless Cashways, whose primary assets are real estate and merchandise inventories. Evaluated within the same industry grouping, however, single-company financial data takes on new meaning, as it provides the basis for comparisons and facilitates analytical conclusions. For this reason, most of the tools used to evaluate corporate performance are compared with identical data prepared for companies operating in the same industry. The business that is the object of study is then measured against its peer group. Has it done better, or worse, than the competition? Do its financial yardsticks meet the averages for its industry? Are its results trending with those of the industry? The answers to these and other comparable company questions are useful in appraising the relative merits of a business.

In 1987, Payless Cashways had two major competitors whose financial results were publicly available: The Home Deport, Inc., and Lowe's Companies, Inc. A short description of each company follows:

The Home Depot, Inc.

Home Depot operated 75 retail warehouse stores that sold a wide variety of building supplies and home improvement products. Sales and net income for the fiscal year ending January 31, 1988, were $1.5 billion and $54 million, respectively.

Lowe's Companies, Inc.

Lowe's operated 295 retail stores selling building supplies and home improvement products. Sales and net income for the fiscal year ended January 31, 1988, were $2.4 billion and $61 million, respectively.

Payless' sales and net income (normalized) for its fiscal year ended November 30, 1987 were $1.8 billion, and $41 million, respectively.

Because Payless and the other two companies were similar in size, but not identical, comparable analyses are more helpful in the context of common size percentages and ratios.

Common size data is a typical starting point in a comparative financial analysis and Exhibit 13-10 sets forth relevant information from the income statement and balance sheet. Referring to the income statement data, Payless ranked in the middle of its two publicly traded competitors in terms of the EBIT/sales ratio, which was 6.7% for Home Depot. Cost of goods sold for Payless is the lowest at 71.6%, but the benefits of this number are overshadowed by the Company's relatively high SG&A expense. Bottom-line performance for Payless, as summarized in the net income/sales ratio was the smallest of the group, owing to its relatively higher interest costs, a direct result of its increasing debt as shown in the earlier ratio analysis. Payless was slightly more

**EXHIBIT 13-10   Comparable common size normalized
             financial results**

	Payless Cashways[1]	Home Depot[2]	Lowe's Companies
Income Statement Data			
Net sales	100.0%	100.0%	100.0%
Cost of goods sold	71.6	72.2	76.1
SG&A expense	22.0	20.3	17.4
Depreciation	2.0	0.7	1.6
Earnings before interest and taxes (EBIT)	5.3	6.7	4.9
Interest on debt	1.0	0.2	0.8
Earnings before taxes	4.3	6.5	4.1
Provision for income taxes	2.0	2.8	1.5
Net income	2.3%	3.7%	2.6%
Balance Sheet Data			
Working capital	15.1%	20.8%	31.2%
Total assets	100.0	100.0	100.0
Long-term debt, less current maturities	22.1	9.8	18.1
Shareholders' equity	46.6	60.6	56.7

[1] Fiscal year ended November 30, 1987.
[2] Fiscal year ended January 31, 1988.

leveraged than its companion companies, both of which had lower
working capital/assets and debt/assets ratios and commensurately
higher equity/assets ratios.

Comparable ratio analysis, as shown in Exhibit 13-11, indicates
that Payless ranked third among its competition in financial performance. In virtually every ratio category (Exhibit 13-12), Payless was at
the bottom of its peer group. Profitability and activity ratios were
below the competition, while the credit ratios indicated a higher use of
leverage. The five-year growth statistics were probably the most worri-
some from the standpoint of an equity investor. EBIT growth for Payless stood at an anemic 2.3%, compared with the impressive statistics
turned in by Home Depot, 50.1%, and Lowe's, 14.4%. Net income and
EPS growth for Payless, correspondingly, were much lower than the
other two retailers.

EXHIBIT 13-11   Comparable financial ratios, normalized data

	Payless Cashways	Home Depot	Lowe's Companies
Profitability Ratios			
$\dfrac{\text{EBIT}}{\text{Total assets}} =$	11%	19%	12%
$\dfrac{\text{Net profit}}{\text{Stockholders' equity}} =$	11%	10%	11%
Activity Ratios			
$\text{Asset Turnover} = \dfrac{\text{Sales}}{\text{Assets}} =$	2.2×	2.8×	2.4×
$\text{Inventory Turnover} = \dfrac{\text{Average inventory}}{\text{Cost of good sold}} = 4.2×$		5.6×	5.0×
Credit Ratios			
$\text{Current Ratio} = \dfrac{\text{Current assets}}{\text{Current liabilities}} =$	1.5	1.7	2.4
$\dfrac{\text{Long-term debt}}{\text{Stockholders' equity}} =$	0.5	0.2	0.3
$\dfrac{\text{EBIT}}{\text{Interest}} =$	4.8×	6.5×	5.5×

EXHIBIT 13-12   Selected growth statistics—latest five years

	Payless Cashways	Home Depot	Lowe's Companies
Sales	12.0%	54.3%	18.8%
EBIT	2.3	50.1	14.4
Earnings before taxes	(0.1)	49.9	16.2
Net income	(0.2)	51.7	19.8
Earnings per share	(1.1)	41.7	15.8

EXHIBIT 13-13   Industry-specific statistics

	Latest Fiscal Year—1987		
	Payless Cashways	**Home Depot**	**Lowe's Companies**
Growth in same store sales	2.9%	18.0%	4.0%
Growth from acquisitions and new stores	13.0	36.3	3.0
Sales per store (MM)	8.1	19.9	8.0
Sales per sq. ft. of selling area	301	265	289

The industry-specific data was less conclusive in pinpointing Payless as the underperformer. Summary data for the 1987 fiscal year appears in Exhibit 13-13.

Interpreting this data in a meaningful way required a knowledge of the workings of the do-it-yourself (DIY) retailing industry in 1987. Home Depot's stellar performance in same store sales growth was the result of a large proportion of its stores being relatively new compared with the competition. New stores typically have an accelerated ramp-up in sales during the first 3 or 4 years after start-up. By the fourth or fifth year of operation, the stores become "mature" and experience less frenetic growth. Home Depot was also in the middle of an extensive rollout of its warehouse store program, a concept that both Payless and Lowe's were attempting to copy. A Wall Street darling, Home Depot was able to raise enormous sums to finance this rapid buildup, shown by the 36.3% growth in sales from new stores. The lower sales per store recorded by Payless and Lowe's at the time indicated that they were operating smaller-sized units relative to Home Depot.

REVIEW OF PAYLESS FINANCIAL ANALYSIS

Any comparable analysis is flawed because few companies are totally homogeneous in their activities and characteristics. Another drawback lies in the differences found among the accounting practices used by companies in the same industry. Finally, the analysis of past performance is only a guide to future success. Thus, historical financial analysis can only be the base from which financial projections and corporate valuations are determined, not the *end-all* for the M&A practitioner.

The financial analysis for Payless Cashways reached the following conclusions:

- *Sales growth* was overly dependent on acquisitions, as many existing stores were located in economically depressed areas.
- *Earnings growth* was nonexistent.
- *Liquidity and credit ratios* were strong, but were showing signs of deterioration.
- *Comparable analysis* placed Payless behind two important competitors.

The evidence indicated that Payless was not an outstanding performer. Reflecting this fact, its stock price languished in early 1988 at $11 per share. At this price, the shares traded at only 9.2× normalized earnings and 1.0× book value. (Compare these multiples with Home Depot's 16.8× and 2.6×, and Lowe's 10.9× and 1.3×.) The relatively low stock price and mediocre operating performance set up Payless for an approach by a corporate raider. As noted in Chapter 19, there is money to be made in buying mediocre businesses when the purchase price is low enough to minimize the risks of adverse operating results. Payless fit this situation in 1988.

Given its low stock price relative to earnings power and assets, Payless represented an attractive takeover target for Asher Edelman. As his interest became known, the stock price quickly climbed from $11 into mid-teens and then into the 20s. The eventual leveraged buyout was consummated at $27 per share. At this price, the Company's equity had a value of 22.1× normalized earnings and 2.3× book value.

MANAGEMENT'S PROJECTIONS

Postbuyout, the "new" Payless Cashways had a debt-to-equity ratio of 10:1. A key element of the debt financing was a $335 million junk bond financing, which was subordinated to $600 million of secured bank debt. In a prospectus furnished to prospective investors in the bonds, the management of Payless provided financial forecasts prepared "to the best of management's knowledge and belief." The forecasts exemplify the optimism found in the vast majority of deal-inspired projections: sales continually go up, operating profit margins increase, and working capital needs shrink relative to sales volume. Neither a recession nor a new competitor is contemplated. Exhibit 13-14 provides the relevant data.

Several key assumptions used in preparing the projections seemed at odds with the past history of Payless. Consider the following information.

Forecast Assumption: Sales

The following quote appeared in the prospectus:

> The overall annual sales growth rates forecast by Payless are 8% in 1988, 11% in 1989, 11% in 1990, 10% in 1991, 8% in 1992 and 7% in 1993. At the beginning of the forecast period Do-It-Yourself customers sales are estimated to comprise approximately 70% of total sales and Professional Contractor (Pro) sales are estimated to comprise approximately 30%. Payless forecasts that by the end of the forecast period Pro sales will represent approximately 40–50% of total sales. Payless believes that the Pro market offers greater growth opportunities than the DIY market where Payless was principally focused in the past.

This sales assumption does not withstand close scrutiny. Payless was planning to achieve this 8% to 11% annual sales growth with minimal new store openings—only 4 in 1988 and one each in 1989 through 1993—so the revenue increases were totally reliant on "same stores" sales growth, which averaged less than 5% historically. By way of explanation, management pointed to a new sales strategy focusing on the Pro market, although the effectiveness of the proposed strategy was untested.

Forecast Assumption: Gross Margins

> *Prospectus:* Payless forecasts gross margins as a percentage of sales to remain relatively constant during the forecast period: 29.3% in 1988 (four months), 30.5% in 1989 and 1990, 30.2% in 1991, 30.3% in 1992 and 30.4% in 1993.

EXHIBIT 13-14 Payless Cashways, Inc., condensed forecast financial data[1] (in millions)

	Actual 1987	Estimated 1988[2]	Forecast 1989	Forecast 1990	Forecast 1991	Forecast 1992	Forecast 1993
			For the Fiscal Year Ended November 30				
Income Statement							
Sales	1,770	1,911	2,102	2,543	3,077	3,384	3,723
Gross margin	520	566	644	716	782	851	911
Selling, general, administrative	(390)	(425)	(455)	(495)	(531)	(560)	(584)
Depreciation and amortization	(36)	na	(62)	(59)	(56)	(53)	(51)
EBIT	93	na	127	161	196	237	276
Interest	(17)	na	(158)	(158)	(159)	(157)	(153)
Earnings (loss) before taxes	76	na	(31)	3	37	81	122
Income taxes (benefit)	(35)	na	(7)	(6)	(19)	(36)	(52)
Net income (loss)	41	na	(24)	(3)	18	45	70
Balance Sheet							
Working capital	123	120	90	92	61	76	94
Total assets	813	1,522	1,480	1,461	1,466	1,471	1,502
Long-term debt, less current mats.	180	1,086	1,052	1,023	961	917	856
Shareholder's equity	379	98	73	70	69	79	115

[1] Prepared on October 14, 1988.
[2] Not applicable items for 1988 cannot be estimated because of accounting adjustments due to July 1988 leveraged buyout of Payless.

The Company's optimism flowed through to profit margins. The gross margin was projected to climb 1.1% over the period, from 29.3% to 30.4%. No justification was offered for the increase, although the historical record showed gross margin dropping from 30.2%, in 1983 to 29.4% in 1987.

Forecast Assumption: Selling, General, and Administrative Expense

Prospectus: The forecast includes annual increases in selling, general and administrative expense of 4.0% in 1989, 8.9% in 1990, 7.2% in 1991, 5.6% in 1992 and 4.2% in 1993. (Author's note: These increases are less than sales gains.) Selling, general and administrative expense as a percentage of sales are forecast to be approximately 21.0% in 1988 (four months) 21.6% in 1989, 21.1% in 1990, 20.5% in 1991, 20.0% in 1992 and 19.5% in 1993.

Here, the historical results again fail to support the Company's assumptions about the future. The management team increased SG&A expense from 20.6% of sales in 1983 to 22.0% of sales in 1987. In 1988, when they needed money to buy the Company, the forecast showed a dramatic reversal in the SG&A expense trend. SG&A expense was estimated to drop to 19.5% of sales in 1993. One hopes the junk bond investors understood the ancient admonition "caveat emptor."

Working capital improvements are a common source of operating improvements in projections. This fact is demonstrated by another assumption listed in the Payless prospectus.

Forecast Assumption: Inventories and Accounts Payable

Prospectus: Payless forecasts that it will lower the level of inventories and improve inventory turnover as a result of the opening of the Sedalia distribution center and the implementation of its new inventory management system. Inventory and accounts payable leverage (trade accounts payable as a percentage of inventories) are forecast as follows:

	1989	1990	1991	1992	1993
Inventory turnover	4.2	4.5	4.6	4.7	4.8
Accounts payable leverage	35%	35%	35%	35%	35%

In this instance, the historical record was more supportive of management's numbers. Inventory turnover rose from 3.7× in 1985 to 4.2× in 1987, so a further increase in turnover didn't appear to be out of line. In general, however, the overall forecast assumptions in the prospectus anticipated a turnaround in Payless's performance, despite a mediocre track record.

ACTUAL RESULTS 1989–1993

It is interesting to compare management's projections with what really happened. After all, who can predict a company's future better than its management? Exhibit 13-15 compares the projected data with the Company's actual results for the five years ended November 30, 1993.

Actual sales consistently failed to meet management's targets because same store sales projections couldn't be achieved in the real world marketplace. An increase in Pro sales was obtained by Payless, but the gain wasn't large enough to cover overall growth objectives. Actual net income exhibited shortfalls throughout the period as management's optimistic assumptions regarding gross margins, SG&A expense and inventory turnover proved to be unreliable. The comparison of projected and actual data shown in Exhibit 13-16 illustrates the differences.

The inability of the Company to achieve its projections resulted in many nervous moments for holders of the senior subordinated debentures issued pursuant to the prospectus. For many months, the debentures traded below their original offering price, amid rumors of Payless having debt service problems. In 1993, the debenture holders' anxieties

EXHIBIT 13-15   Payless Cashways, Inc., condensed financial data (in millions)

	Fiscal Year Ended November 30				
	1989	1990	1991	1992	1993
Projected sales	$2,110	$2,346	$2,592	$2,808	$2,999
Actual sales	2,007	2,229	2,392	2,500	2,606
Projected net income	(24)	(3)	18	45	70
Actual net income	(32)	(21)	(13)	(16)	44

**EXHIBIT 13-16   Payless Cashways, Inc., 1993
operating results**

	Projected	Actual
Gross margin	30.4%	30.0%
SG&A expense	19.5%	21.9%
Inventory turnover	4.8×	4.4×

subsided when, after four years of losses, Payless completed a major debt and equity refinancing in a favorable stock market. A short time later, the debentures were repaid in full. Shareholders in the leveraged buyout, in contrast, were considerably more frustrated. According to management's projections, earnings per share for the new LBO were supposed to be $3.02 in 1993. In fact, EPS were only $0.16 in 1993, a negative difference of 95%. Earnings recovered in 1994 and 1995, but by August 1995 the LBO investors' shares were worth only the same $11 that the group had paid at the original time of the buyout seven years earlier.

SUMMARY

Any evaluation of an acquisition target's future prospects is based on prior events. Thus, a historical financial analysis must precede any projection of future results. Historical financial analysis is conducted systematically using the seller's financial statements as the raw materials and the four primary analytical tools—absolute amounts, percentage changes, common size statements, and financial ratios—as the tools. The would-be buyer also prepares industry-specific statistics to measure the candidate's financial health. All this information is typically used in comparison with data from similar businesses.

Seller-derived projections are typically prepared through rose-colored glasses. While a buyer can obtain a sense of management's thinking and a business's direction by reviewing these forecasts, the buyer is better off preparing its own detailed projections.

14 FINANCIAL PROJECTIONS: DOING YOURS

The Payless Cashways forecast relied heavily on what had happened in the past. Key statistics such as same store sales, gross margins, and SG&A expenses were anticipated to improve modestly over historical results, and neither a recession, a new competitor, nor a major market change was predicted. The vast majority of M&A financial projections follow this pattern of the future reflecting the past. Indeed, it is difficult in many industries for investors to argue against the rearview-mirror approach. Financial analysts, economists and other investment experts are notoriously poor at gauging when a reasonably stable company, such as Payless, is going to face either a serious downturn or a rejuvenating upturn. As a result, most financial projections involving established businesses involve an extension of historical performance into the future, usually via a loosely derived mathematical model such as a regression, moving average, trend line or exponential smoothing.

ALTERNATE MEANS OF FORECASTING

To prevent a total reliance on historical data for established concerns or to construct projections from the ground up for new companies, analysts use other forecasting methods. These alternates means are most appropriate for businesses that have no historical track record or that participate in a rapidly changing market. Examples of the former are start-up ventures. Examples of the latter are innovative high-growth businesses relying on rapidly changing technology. Fashion-oriented businesses also require specialized projection techniques. Clothing, toy, and entertainment businesses fall into the fashion category.

The most important component of any corporate financial forecast is the revenue projection. Many expense and balance sheet items flow directly from sales. Thus, the first assignment for the financial analyst is determining which technique is best for estimating sales. The initial reaction of most analysts in this regard is to look at past sales as the anchor for predicting future revenues. While this technique is valid for many businesses, it must be tempered with a considered review of prospective changes in the candidate's product offerings, product prices, competitive environments, and required technologies. Even when firms operate in the same industry, they tend to contain many unique elements, and these make each company-specific projection a situational exercise. Many of the elements have a strong historical bias; others require an independent analytical interpretation.

A common approach to sales forecasting is to place the target company in the "corporate life cycle" chart. Alternatively, the candidate is designated as falling into a certain industry type. As shown in Exhibit 14-1, both the corporate life cycle positions and industry categories carry sales growth patterns that are well-known to investors.

When the fit between the candidate, its industry, and its corporate life cycle position has been established, the analyst is in a good position to consider which projection technique is most applicable to the target. The primary sales projection techniques can be segmented into three categories: (1) time series, (2) causal, and (3) qualitative. Each category tends to favor a particular industry or life cycle position.

TIME SERIES ANALYSIS FORECAST TECHNIQUES

The basic assumption underlying time series analysis is that the future will be like the past. Sales forecasts, therefore, are prepared by examining historical results, which are then brought forward through the

EXHIBIT 14-1   Defining the candidate for sales forecasting

Corporate Life Cycle	Expected Sales Performance
Pioneer	Unpredictable and volatile sales movements.
Growth	Steady growth in sales as product acceptance widens.
Stable	Moderate sales increases as market for the company's product matures.
Decline	Sales decrease as customers are attracted to newer, innovative products.

Industry Characterization	Expected Sales Performance
Growth	Steady growth in sales as product acceptance widens.
Cyclical	Established business in sector where sales are dependent on the economic cycle (e.g., autos, home construction).
Defensive	Sales movements are resistant to changes in the economic cycle (e.g., bread, beer, and cigarette companies).

use of moving averages, exponential smoothings, or trend lines. Using this technique, a company with a 5-year growth rate of 10% likely has an estimated future growth rate around 10%. This rearview-mirror approach is difficult to counter effectively unless the opposing analyst has a fresh reason for promoting a dramatic change.

The time series analysis technique has proven itself well in many basic industries such as food, electricity, and publishing. As a result, it is popular in projections of stable and defensive concerns. Accurate projections in these industries are still difficult at the company-specific level unless the business controls a significant market share. Budweiser's 40% in the beer market would be a useful proxy for the entire industry.

The key weakness of the time series technique is its inability to predict turning points in a company's sales performance. For many firms, such turning points are the result of hard-to-predict new competition or product innovation. How could a time-series analysis forecast the total demise of record player sales in the 1980s after 30 years of

LP's dominating the recorded music sector? Or, the almost complete collapse of U.S. television manufacturing in favor of Japanese, Korean, and Taiwanese TVs? The explosive growth in four-wheel drive vehicles, after these products had been consigned to the outdoor recreation and contractor markets?

CAUSAL METHODS

The causal methods forecast a company's sales by establishing relationships between sales and certain variables that are independent of the business in question. At times, these relationships relate to broad economic variables such as gross national product or housing starts. To illustrate, cement demand is tied closely to GNP growth, so a cement industry sales projection may rely heavily on GNP estimates. In other instances, demographic factors may influence strongly a firm's future sales. For example, the "greying" of the U.S. population inevitably has led to predictions that the nursing home business is a "growth industry." With many companies, industry-related factors may play a large role in driving sales. In the 1980s, for example, videotape sales and rentals were related directly to consumer purchases of VCRs.

Company-specific factors may be causal. In lodging, a hotel chain's future sales can be influenced strongly by its new hotel construction program. A computer chip company's future revenues can be impacted directly by a new production plant.

Quantifying these various causal relationships to produce usable forecasts involves regression formulas or econometric calculations. Complementing these results can be customer surveys and feasibility studies that connect future sales to variables which are less observable than those derived from the past. For example, hotel room rentals went up sharply in Florida after the construction of Walt Disney World there. A tourist survey would have made that connection.

Causal forecasting is used frequently for companies in the "stable" and "decline" phases of the corporate life cycle. It is also commonly applied to established firms operating in so-called "cyclical" or "defensive" industries. Companies in the later stages of their growth phase are causal forecasting candidates since their operating record is usually long enough to evaluate in relation to external economic variables.

QUALITATIVE METHODS

Qualitative projection techniques are applied often to "pioneer" or "growth" companies offering relatively new products and services. With little history to act as a guide, the sales forecaster is left with expert opinions, market research studies, and historical analogies as his analytical tools. Sometimes, the result is nothing more than educated guesswork. The market reaction of truly new products is very hard to gauge. Questions such as "What will be the level of acceptance? What price can the customer bear?" are difficult to answer, even for experienced professionals. The current debate over future revenues for Internet companies has compared the Internet to the introduction of telephones and cable television, and sales estimates have wide ranges.

Any would-be acquirer is well advised to consider the use of several qualitative techniques in evaluating the projections of a takeover candidate, even if the business has a consistent sales record. The added research is another part of an effective due diligence. Important qualitative methods for predicting sales of a business are set forth in Exhibit 14-2.

Confronted with a historically derived projection from an established company such as Payless Cashways, a careful buyer would have considered alternate means of forecasting future results. In 1988, the

EXHIBIT 14-2   Qualitative forecasting methods

Experts	The buyer consults with an industry expert(s) to develop assumptions on sales projections.
Market Research	Consumer studies are made to estimate future demand and pricing for a potential or existing product line.
Historical Analogy	The buyer makes a connection between the seller's potential sales and those of firms that offered a related product concept in the past. For example, CD player manufacturers examined the prior introduction of the TV set and VCR into the American household.
Futurists	A long view, say 5–10 years into the future, may require an unconventional interpretation. The force, intensity, and speed of contemporary business brings unpredictable change. Every industry has its visionaries who try to look beyond obvious near-term developments.

do-it yourself (DIY) retailing industry was in the process of consolidation, as the larger, national chains were gathering market share from smaller participants. The handful of national players, which included Payless, resembled a growth industry in this regard. Payless's own sales performance certainly exceeded the growth in total DIY sales, despite the company's mediocre earnings results, which indicated a business in the "stable" phase of the corporate life cycle. Causal forces affecting DIY sales such as home starts and home sales would have been interesting items for projecting into the future alongside Payless' forecasted sales. And, while the company's home improvement product line appeared invulnerable to dramatic changes in technology, qualitative factors could have had a large impact on the forecast. Home Depot was in the midst of introducing a warehouse "superstore" concept that had achieved wide consumer acceptance—and industry experts agreed Payless needed to fight back over the long term. The emergence of this superstore concept would have had to affect the Company's results negatively over the long term. An equally important qualitative aspect—with a more positive result—would have been the anticipated rebound of the "oil patch" Payless stores, since the region wouldn't remain depressed forever.

PREPARING STAND-ALONE PROJECTIONS

Accompanying the analysis of "top line" sales projections are the conclusions garnered from the historical financial review. How will the gross margin change in the future? Will SG&A expense stay constant as sales rise? Will inventory turnover jump in the upcoming years? Applying the answers to these questions provides the buyer with the framework for developing its own projections for the seller on a stand-alone basis. In the case of Payless, a rational investor would likely have prepared a forecast that was somewhat less sanguine than the data provided in the prospectus. Exhibit 14-3 shows the projected numbers given in the prospectus alongside hypothetical data developed by a possible financial buyer.

Note how the hypothetical financial buyer assumes a mild recession in 1990 and 1991, reducing DIY sales activity because of lower home sales. Profit margins increase but fail to reach the levels presumed

EXHIBIT 14-3 Payless Cashways condensed forecast financial data (in millions)

	Forecast				
	1989	**1990**	**1991**	**1992**	**1993**
Prospectus					
Sales	2,110	2,346	2,592	2,808	2,999
EBIT	127	161	196	237	276
Sales growth	10%	11%	11%	8%	7%
EBIT margin	6%	7%	8%	8%	9%
Hypothetical Buyer					
Sales	2,030	2,120	2,210	2,340	2,530
EBIT	100	120	130	160	180
Sales growth	6%	5%	4%	6%	8%
EBIT margin	5%	6%	6%	7%	7%

in the prospectus. Both sets of forecasts assume a highly leveraged corporate structure. Without a heavy debt load, Payless could be expected to grow faster than indicated. Cash flow targeted to LBO debt service payments could instead be invested in expanding the business.

CORPORATE BUYER PROJECTIONS

When Payless was being evaluated by Asher Edleman in early 1988, the Company was shown to numerous large retailing firms as a potential acquisition candidate. Many rejected the deal outright because of "price" or "strategic fit" reasons, while others took a hard look at the potential of the business. As noted in Chapter 13, many of these buyers followed these five steps:

1. Complete historical financial analysis of acquisition candidate.
2. Prepare stand-alone projections of acquisition candidate and buyer.
3. Include synergies and cost cuts in combined financial statements.
4. Structure finances and allow for purchase accounting adjustments.
5. Complete pro forma combined projections.

STEPS 1 AND 2

The historical analysis presented in Chapter 13 would be a good start for any corporate buyer. The follow up step would be a forecast of Payless on a stand-alone basis, before the inclusion of the effects of a takeover. In the case of another retail acquirer, rather than an LBO, Payless' future balance sheets would not be so encumbered with debt, leaving open the possibility of new store openings and acquisitions. A related-industry buyer, therefore, might use a projection showing 10% compounded annual sales gains and constant EBIT margins—neither assumption being out of line with general industry expectations (see Exhibit 14-4).

STEP 3. INCLUDE SYNERGIES AND COST CUTS

The degree of synergies and the amount of cost cuts depend in large part on what kind of buyer is making the projection. A Payless competitor, for example is going to realize more synergies and savings than a firm that intends to use Payless as a strategic diversification. For the sake of illustration, assume Lowe's Companies was interested in buying Payless in 1988. What kind of synergies and cost cuts might it have assumed?

Although operating in the same business and having a combined $4 billion in sales, the two companies had different geographic coverage in 1988. Payless focused on the Midwest and Northeast, while Lowe's emphasized the South and Southeast. In only three states did

EXHIBIT 14-4   Retail buyer stand-alone forecasts for Payless Cashways[1] (in millions)

	1989	1990	1991	1992	1993	5 Year CAGR
Sales	2,100	2,250	2,430	2,700	3,080	10%
EBIT	115	125	135	150	170	10
Net income	50	55	61	67	74	10
Debt/equity ratio	50%	50%	50%	50%	50%	

[1] Assumes no leveraged buyout.

EXHIBIT 14-5   Retail buyer stand-alone forecasts for Payless Cashways, with synergies (in millions)

	1989	1990	1991	1992	1993
Sales	2,100	2,250	2,450	2,700	3,080
EBIT	115	125	135	150	170
Add: Synergies	42	45	49	54	62
Revised EBIT	157	169	184	204	232
Revised net income	75	82	91	99	110
Debt/equity ratio	50%	50%	50%	50%	50%

the two firms compete head on. This lack of market overlap limited the potential benefits from market concentration, but there were numerous other potential synergies in the areas of corporate overhead, advertising, buying, and distribution. Assume Lowe's believed these synergies totaled 2% of the annual sales of Payless over the projected period. The EBIT forecast of Payless would increase accordingly (see Exhibit 14-5).

By including these estimated synergies, Lowe's would have increased the earnings power of Payless by 36%. The next step is gauging how much to pay for the deal and how to finance the acquisition. Purchase accounting adjustments, such as asset write-ups and goodwill expenses, also need to be included.

STEP 4. STRUCTURE FINANCES AND ALLOW FOR PURCHASE ACCOUNTING ADJUSTMENTS

In Step 4, the buyer's own historical performance, stock market value, and creditworthiness play an important role. These factors, along with the proposed integration of the acquisition, are the critical determinants behind the financing assumptions incorporated in the projections. A buyer with a strong track record and conservative balance sheet will have an easier time raising debt financing than a high-flying technology business with an aggressively priced stock and a volatile operating history. The latter company is more likely to use its common shares as currency for an acquisition.

In early 1988, Lowe's Companies was a very creditworthy business. Sales and cash flow had increased steadily over the previous five years, and the balance sheet showed only $186 million of long-term debt against $582 million of stockholders' equity. EBIT covered interest charges by factor of six times in 1987. Being the largest independent DIY chain, Lowe's was in a good position to attract financing for the takeover of the third largest independent chain. As its investment banker, I would have projected Lowe's future results in a optimistic light given its solid record. These projections would have been combined with the Payless operating forecasts, adjusted for synergies. From the combined EBIT one would subtract purchase accounting adjustments of increased depreciation and goodwill. Summary forecast data for an assumed $900 million Payless acquisition appears in Exhibit 14-6.

Since Lowe's had only $40 to $50 million cash on hand in early 1988, the money for a Payless acquisition would have been obtained from external sources. Banks and institutional lenders would have been the sources for the bulk of the financing, bearing in mind that they would have required certain pro forma interest coverage and debt ratio requirements in order to offer attractive interest rates. As noted in

EXHIBIT 14-6 **Hypothetical Lowe's/Payless merger, condensed forecast financial data (in millions)**

	1989	1990	1991	1992	1993
Sales					
Lowe's Companies	2,950	3,250	3,550	3,900	4,300
Payless Cashways	2,100	2,250	2,430	2,700	3,080
Combined sales	5,050	5,500	5,980	6,600	7,380
EBIT					
Lowe's Companies	132	145	160	175	195
Payless Cashways	115	125	135	150	170
Add: Synergies	42	45	49	54	62
Less: Depreciation[1]	(8)	(8)	(8)	(8)	(8)
Goodwill[1]	(10)	(10)	(10)	(10)	(10)
Combined EBIT	271	297	326	361	409

[1] Assumes $528 million allocation of purchase price over book value: $128 million to fixed assets and $400 million to goodwill.

Chapter 8, these credit standards vary by industry. In the case of a hypothetical Lowe's/Payless transaction, the lenders likely would have required a pro forma EBIT/interest expense coverage factor of 2× or higher and a debt/equity ratio of no more than 2:1. Under this scenario, Lowe's had the ability to borrow practically the entire $900 million purchase price. In this example, management selects a more conservative tact, borrowing $600 million from the banks and selling $300 million of new common shares (at a price of $20 per share). As shown in Exhibit 14-7, the end result is a combined company that is operating within credit limits and realizing EPS improvements.

The $0.18 pro forma increase in Lowe's EPS does not come without a cost. Pro forma leverage increases significantly, as the debt/equity ratio rises from 0.3 to 1.0, implying more financial risk for shareholders. Pro forma balance sheet data appears in Exhibit 14-8.

The financial risk of the deal could be lessened by Lowe's selling more equity, but the consequence of more shares outstanding would

EXHIBIT 14-7   Lowe's acquisition of Payless 1989 income statement data (in millions)

| | Before Acquisition | | | |
	Lowe's Companies	Payless Cashways	Acquisition Adjustments	Pro Forma Combined
Sales	2,950	2,100	—	5,050
Operating income	132	115	42[1]	271
			(18)[2]	
Interest expense	(20)	(15)	(60)[3]	(95)[6]
Pretax income	112	100	(36)	176
Income taxes	42	44	—	70
Net income	70	56	—	106
Earnings per share	1.75	1.60	—	1.93
Shares outs. (MM)	40	35	(35)[4]	55
			15[5]	

Adjustments
[1] Assumed cost synergies totaling 2% of Payless sales.
[2] Added depreciation and goodwill expense of $18 million annually.
[3] 10% interest on $600 million debt financing.
[4] Cancellation of Payless shares.
[5] Addition of 15 million new Lowe's shares.
[6] EBIT/Interest expense coverage is 2.9×.

EXHIBIT 14-8   Lowe's acquisition of Payless 1989 balance sheet data (in millions)

| | Before Acquisition | | | |
	Lowe's Companies	Payless Cashways	Acquisition Adjustments	Pro Forma Combined
Current assets	580	352	—	932
Fixed assets	490	420	128[1]	1,038
Goodwill and other assets	30	—	400[2]	430
Total assets	1,100	772	528	2,400
Current liabilities	250	230	—	480
Other liabilities	30	20	—	50
Long-term debt	200	150	600[3]	950
			(372)[4]	
Stockholders' equity	620	372	300[5]	920
Total liabilities & stockholders' equity	1,100	772	528	2,400
Debt/equity ratio	0.3:1	—	—	1:1

Adjustments

[1] $128 million fixed asset write-up.
[2] $400 million goodwill allocation.
[3] Addition of $600 million acquisition debt.
[4] Cancellation of Payless equity.
[5] Lowe's sale of $300 million in new equity.

lower pro forma EPS and, in all likelihood, reduce the stock price. Most acquirers carefully weigh the benefits of reduced leverage against the costs of lower EPS. Matrix analysis is helpful in this respect. A matrix for the Lowe's/Payless combination appears in Exhibit 14-9.

During the refinement of such analysis, buyers evaluate numerous combinations of debt and equity finance. The financing scenarios begin with the "all debt" case, which means no ownership dilution for existing shareholders. In many deals, this case is unrealistic from the lenders' standpoint or too laden with financial risk for the buyer's shareholders. The "all debt" case is then followed by alternative scenarios, including larger and larger amounts of equity finance. In certain instances, selling a portion of the target's assets is projected as a source of financing. This was the case in the 1995 Westinghouse/CBS

EXHIBIT 14-9   The trade-off between leverage and earnings per share

Credit Objectives		Lowe's/Payless Combination		
Debt/Equity Ratio	Interest Coverage	Required Equity Financing	Estimated Market Price of Lowe's Share	Pro Forma EPS
1:1	2.9×	$300MM	$20	1.93
0.8:1	3.3×	420MM	19	1.79
0.6:1	3.9×	550MM	18	1.76

deal, in which Westinghouse obtained a short-term bridge loan in return for promising to sell its Defense Electronics division for an estimated $2.5 billion price tag.

Most large corporate buyers take the various financing scenarios and sensitize them to different offering prices. In the Lowe's/Payless data shown earlier, a price of $900 million was assumed for Payless. What would the pro forma EPS look like if the proposed offer price was $850 million, or $950 million? Exhibit 14-10 shows the results for these prices, assuming management retained debt/equity and interest coverage ratios of 1:1 and 2.9×, respectively.

Changing the proposed purchase price in concert with multiple financing scenarios produces many forecasts to consider. The process is further complicated by buyers when they adjust the projections of operating performance for both the buyer and seller. In the end, most

EXHIBIT 14-10   Pro forma earnings per share under different price scenarios, Lowe's/Payless combination

Payless Purchase Price (in millions)	Required Equity Financing (in millions)	Pro Forma EPS
$850	$275	$1.98
900	300	1.93
950	325	1.87

buyers consider three sets of operating forecasts: upside case (optimistic), base case (best guess), and downside case (pessimistic). Such operating forecasts for the Lowe's/Payless merger appear as in Exhibit 14-11.

The downside case is of the greatest interest to lenders, who have everything to lose if the deal doesn't work out and a moderate amount to gain if it does succeed. Included in the downside case can be the effects of potential recessions, price wars, and turning points, along with the possibility that the synergies will be less beneficial than expected. Many buyers "pooh pooh" downside case analysis as too pessimistic, but thoughtful lenders need to examine the financial cushion of a transaction if things go bad. In any case, the final result of a merger financial analysis is a bewildering array of deal permutations that use differing price, leverage, and operating scenarios.

Adding asset sales or other restructuring alternatives to this mix can easily result in 20 to 30 acquisition scenarios for what might appear to be a relatively straightforward transaction. As an extreme example of complexity, when Shearson Lehman Brothers was considering an equity investment in the RJR Nabisco leveraged buyout, the Merchant Banking Group prepared over 150 scenarios, each of which was 120 pages in length and required approximately 20 minutes of computer calculation time before printing.

EXHIBIT 14-11   **Lowe's/Payless combination, three operating forecast scenarios (in millions)**

	1989	1990	1991	1992	1993
Base Case					
Sales	5,050	5,500	5,980	6,600	7,380
EBIT	271	297	326	361	409
Upside Case					
Sales	5,150	5,750	6,400	7,200	8,000
EBIT	310	345	390	430	500
Downside Case					
Sales	4,950	5,000	5,300	5,800	6,300
EBIT	220	230	250	290	350

At some point, the buyer settles on a few scenarios from which to make a business judgment. With these selected projections, the buyer's executives view the acquisition's likely impact on the buyer's EPS growth, financial risk, and share price. If EPS growth is higher with the acquisition, the industry fit is reasonable and the new leverage does not get out of hand, the buyer is likely to assume that its P/E ratio will stay the same or increase. Applying this ratio to a higher EPS in the near future (after any dilution has been eliminated) results in a higher stock price. For many buyers, the financial decision process centers around this summary analysis. For others, this information is complemented by a discounted cash flow (DCF) analysis that measures the acquisition's ultimate contribution to the buyer's net present value (NPV) per share. If the buyer's NPV/share is greater after the deal than before it, the acquisition is attractive from the shareholders' point of view.

Suppose Lowe's projections for itself indicated that Lowe's stock had a fundamental value, based on DCF analysis, of $25 per share. Including any new shares or debt issued to purchase Payless, the "combined company" DCF analysis would have to indicate a per share value in excess of $25 per share. Otherwise, there is no point in proceeding with the deal. Merger-oriented DCF analysis is dependent on a few critical variables including the operating forecasts of buyer and seller, the prospects for synergies, the purchase price expectations of the buyer, and the discount rates used in the NPV calculations. All these variables are subject to manipulation by a motivated buyer. Perhaps the most difficult number for an outside portfolio investor to pin down is the synergy estimate, since it is highly dependent on the opinions of experienced operating personnel. The appropriate discount rate for the combined enterprise is another question mark. This number (i.e., the k statistic in the Capital Asset Pricing Model) is difficult to approximate for a publicly traded, stand-alone business. Attempting to determine reliable discount rates for numerous acquisition scenarios is problematic. Moreover, a motivated buyer may be tempted to lowball these discount rates to justify an overpriced deal. The many valuation issues brought on by DCF analysis means that it plays a secondary role in most merger financial evaluations, although its use is still trumpeted by many academics and management consulting firms.

SUMMARY

In preparing a financial forecast for an acquisition, the analyst's first objective is to estimate sales, the key variable from which many financial statement items flow. Most corporate sales projections rely heavily on past results as a guide, and this modus operandi is widely accepted in corporate America. Nevertheless, most would-be buyers are well advised to apply causal and qualitative forecasting techniques to test historically based assumptions.

Most financial projection exercises follow a tried-and-true formula incorporating five basic steps. The end result is a "base case" forecast, which is then adjusted to reflect different operating, pricing, and financing scenarios. After reviewing this information, the buyer is in a position to determine its level of interest in the proposed deal.

15 THE OPERATIONS SCREEN

By now, the buyer has concluded that a prospective acquisition is attractive. The business fits in with the buyer's strategy and looks worthwhile from a financial point of view. Making a bid for the company is a serious option.

In most large U.S. firms, the acquisition review process up to this point has been localized in the corporate development department, finance department, or chairman's office. Many of the executives in these offices are staff personnel with little operating experience. Their review of the operational side of the candidate has been limited to a few broad areas such as industry, product line, and market share. Failure of the acquisition to meet relevant criteria in these categories resulted in a rejection. For those deals that have passed the initial Deal Killer stage, a new host of concerns will arise, and now is the time for the buyer to look beyond the seller's broad financial and development attributes and into its specific operational characteristics. With minimal line experience, the staff executives need to consult with operating personnel to learn if there are obvious operational issues that can "kill the deal." This secondary review stage can be called the "preliminary operations screen."

In the case of a Market Share/Product Line Extension acquisition, where the buyer is already familiar with the seller's industry, this evaluation may only involve consultations with executives from the buyer's key divisional and functional departments. In contrast, the Strategic, Leveraged Buyout, or Bottom Fisher acquirers may not have the luxury of the Extender's in-house expertise. For those acquirers venturing into new industries, an in-depth knowledge of the seller's business must be obtained through outside consultants. Although neither outside consultants nor "inside" operating executives have veto power over proposed transactions, these individuals provide important insights regarding the seller's product line, manufacturing facilities, marketing efforts, distribution networks, labor relations, customer loyalties, market regulations, and other notable matters. This information influences the buyer's decision about whether to proceed with the time-consuming and expensive process of making a bid, conducting due diligence, and closing the deal.

The preliminary operations screen is a good system for most transactions, but it may be inappropriate for some deals. In certain situations, the buyer's chief executive officer believes he has screening knowledge in his head, so consultation with the principal divisional personnel is therefore unnecessary. In transactions involving public companies, broadening the preliminary efforts to the divisional level is too risky. A rumor of either the buyer's potential involvement or the seller's interest in "selling out" could be counterproductive. "Loose lips sink ships" was a popular government slogan in World War II, and it is an appropriate warning in the delicate world of mergers and acquisitions. Nevertheless, the opinions of selected operating personnel—independent of the in-house development staff—can provide valuable assistance in the secondary stage of the evaluation process.

Like the sifting process utilized to eliminate inappropriate candidates quickly, the operations screen seeks to uncover characteristics of the seller's operations that are so out of line with the buyer's requirements as to make the transaction untenable, even though the numbers work. If such a characteristic is found and the problem appears insoluble, the buyer should withdraw from its evaluation of the deal without looking back. The in-house M&A executive then can continue to search and screen for additional acquisition candidates.

SELLER RESISTANCE TO OPERATIONAL SCREEN

Most sellers resist providing detailed operating data to a buyer that has not made a bona fide offer (and remember a preliminary offer is not written in concrete; it has many "outs" for the buyer). This resistance is grounded in several rationale. First, many sellers and intermediaries have experience with the Window Shopper, a denizen of the M&A world that is constantly visiting companies and interrogating managements, without ever buying a business. Sellers thus waste time and resources with Window Shoppers that could be far better spent elsewhere, such as negotiating with a Market Share/Product Line Extender, Strategic Buyer, or Leveraged Buyout firm. Second, the most logical buyer for a seller is a direct competitor. The seller's reluctance to provide detailed operating data to competitors is completely natural, particularly if there is no written bid on the table. Finally, although the prospective buyer may have signed a confidentiality letter at the beginning stage of the courting process, there is no guarantee that sensitive information provided to the would-be buyer won't leak out to third parties.

Thus, the prospective buyer will feel pressure from the seller to make an offer on the basis of a minimal due diligence effort, such as merely reviewing the financial statements, reading the offering memorandum (if one has been prepared), visiting one or two of the candidate's facilities, and talking to a small group of the sellers's management team. While this level of study gives the buyer a good sense of the seller's business and its general fit with the buyer's objectives, such an effort is hardly the foundation from which an intelligent buyer makes a firm bid. And furthermore, at this stage, experience tells us that the buyer's analysis is littered with inadequate information and seller half-truths. This lack of information leaves the buyer exposed to the necessity of renegotiating any hasty offer, or withdrawing from the deal altogether, once it has the facts in hand. This sort of result is an embarrassment to both parties.

Nevertheless, buyers must be prepared to accede to the seller's repeated requests for a written offer, even after undertaking the minimal due diligence effort I have just described. This written offer, which is called a "letter of intent," describes the buyer's proposed purchase price, the form of the purchase price (e.g., cash, stock, contingent earn-out), the contemplated structure of the deal (e.g., asset purchase, stock purchase) and the proposed schedule for completing due diligence, firming up legal documentation, and financing and closing the transaction. A smart buyer attempts to extract as much information as possible in its preliminary investigation before responding favorably to the seller's pleas for a letter of intent. While most letters of intent carry numerous escape clauses for the buyer's benefit, and are not fully binding in a court of law, they present potential legal problems for the buyer if they aren't handled properly. Further, these letters represent an immediate up-front cost for the buyer if an outside law firm is retained to draft the letter. Sometimes the lack of a letter becomes a bone of contention and the seller closes the "due diligence door" to further buyer analysis. Before ending the stand off by negotiating a letter, the intelligent buyer should have at least sufficient data to conduct its operations screen. (Letters of intent and negotiating strategy are covered in Chapters 16 and 17.)

The scope of the buyer's preliminary investigation is occasionally restricted due to factors that are unrelated to the motives of the seller. If the seller is the subject of a hostile takeover, and time is of the essence, a broad, in-depth due diligence is a practical impossibility. The time constraints imposed on a public company that is the target of a hostile bid can be measured in two or three weeks. The seller's stockholders are solicited by the hostile bidder, and the takeover price, which usually incorporates a large premium to the preannouncement market price, has a finite life, usually about 30 days. Within this short period, the target's management has to find a well-capitalized "white knight," willing to respond quickly with a topping bid that is fully financed. The search for a white knight is a tall order in a hostile deal and one that permits prospective rescuers little time to investigate the target thoroughly.

OPERATIONAL SCREENING

The operations screen should cover a variety of subjects. Many of them can fall out of the range of expertise of the buyer's in-house corporate development team. Despite this weakness, the team should be sufficiently "heads up" to know which raw data should be gathered to facilitate a meaningful discussion with a broader set of operating and staff personnel. Perhaps a summary memo is written beforehand by the team, describing its preliminary findings on important operations subjects. On receiving the information, the operating and staff personnel included in the larger grouping can then "weigh in" with a reality check on the team's acquisition review.

Important operations screening items are as follows:

- Long-term trends in seller's industry.
- Seller's business plan versus reality.
- Major products and potential obsolescence.
- Degree of real and potential competition:
    - Barriers to entry.
    - Degree of current competition.
- Major customers:
    - Ability to retain them postacquisition.
    - Loyalty of major customers to specific salesperson.
- Synergies:
    - Can buyer really cut costs of the target without reducing sales volume?
    - Can buyer truly enhance sales volumes, postacquisition?
- Technology.
- Distribution and marketing.
- Employee compensation and benefits.
- Antitrust implications.
- Reputation of the seller and its management.
- Government regulations, environmental issues, and legal problems.

LONG-TERM TRENDS IN THE SELLER'S INDUSTRY

The buyer has selected the seller's industry for expansion, so the buyer's management has taken a positive outlook. Many industries, however, comprise a myriad of products or services. For example, computer software is considered to be a growth industry, yet sellers of DOS-based computer software are rapidly becoming dinosaurs. This shrinking subset of the software industry would therefore be a poor candidate for a growth-oriented acquirer. Such questions might be answered easily enough by the buyer's development executives, but the input of line personnel is important, particularly in Market Share/Product Line Extender deals, since the operating executives should have strong views on competitors and complementary businesses.

SELLER'S BUSINESS PLAN VERSUS REALITY

By now, the buyer's senior development executive has analyzed carefully the target's business plan. In forming his views, he has consulted with other executives in preparing an analysis of the seller's over-optimistic designs. New product introductions and new market penetrations proposed by the seller, for example, have been questioned by the buyer's marketing and production personnel, who realize how difficult new product introductions are in the real world. The viability of the seller's base business is also considered by these personnel, who know how tough it is to maintain even the momentum of existing products.

MAJOR PRODUCTS AND POTENTIAL OBSOLESCENCE

In many industries, the product life cycle has shortened. Women's clothing, first-run movies, and children's toys are good examples of products with a short shelf life. Manufacturers of these products rely on a continual stream of new ideas and innovative merchandise. Past history, therefore, can be a poor indicator of future results. Operating personnel with their fingers on the pulse of such markets have a good gut sense of the future sales of a target's product line. Mattel Corporation's $1.2 billion acquisition in 1993 of fellow toymaker Fisher-Price is an example of a successful merger in a volatile business.

DEGREE OF REAL AND POTENTIAL COMPETITION

Real competition can be judged in the marketplace. How well are competitors' products selling versus those of the acquisition candidate? Is the relevant industry subsector profitable? Are competitors implementing expansion plans or strategies that can affect the growth of the target? These questions can be answered more accurately by line executives than by staff personnel.

Many of the sellers with whom I worked as an investment banker liked to maintain that they sold a proprietary product or service. The sellers told prospective suitors that their businesses were immune from new competition. Although this sales pitch occasionally was effective, few companies sell anything that is truly proprietary. In almost every industry, products and services come and go, and successful items are quickly copied by the competition. Patented products provide some degree of protection, but patents are only useful in a few industries. Brand names and corporate reputation are valuable assets also, yet their durability is open to question. Economies of scale are formidable barriers to entry, as evidenced by the $3 billion price tag for entering the North American TV network business, if Fox's UPN start-up costs are used as a guide. Closely guarded production technology presents a considerable obstacle for new competition, particularly if the technology provides a measurable product cost and quality advantage. Truly, many of the preceding factors can keep a company in business. Evaluating which attributes effectively restrict competition and promote enhanced profitability is one of the buyer's most difficult jobs. The operations screen facilitates reaching the right conclusion.

MAJOR CUSTOMERS

Many businesses are reliant on the patronage of a few key customers. During the initial screen, it is incumbent on the prospective acquirer to identify which customers are important to the future success of the acquisition candidate. At the same time, the buyer must determine the strength of the relationships between the candidate and these major customers. For Market Share/Product Line Extension deals, the buyer's in-house marketing personnel may be able to ascertain whether those customers will continue the relationship with the candidate after the deal closes. For Strategic Buyers or Leveraged Buyouts, an outside industry consultant may be able to provide guidance along these lines. After a letter of intent has been signed and initial due diligence has been completed, the buyer should seek the candidate's permission to contact its principal customers, to ensure their intentions of continuing with the merged operation in the future. Any doubts regarding customer retention that are generated by this investigation should be factored into a reduction of the purchase price.

In several of my transactions, a major customer of the seller had a strong loyalty to a particular executive. In an office supply acquisition, one salesperson represented over 25% of the seller's sales. The ties of this individual to his clients were of long standing and had withstood various and sundry corporate upheavals. In this instance, it was important that my client, the buyer, recognized these allegiances early on. By doing so, it was able to tailor a transition strategy that retained this salesperson customers. In that particular case, a concerted effort was made to retain the key executive. He accepted an attractive employment contract, effective immediately after the deal's closing.

SYNERGIES

In enabling the candidate to pass through the initial price screen, the in-house development executive may have assumed certain operating synergies, such as pro forma cost reductions, asset sales, or revenue gains. Without these pro forma adjustments, the seller's asking price may have been too high to sustain an attractive return on investment or to limit dilution of EPS. The operations screen is the appropriate stage for the executive to double-check important synergy assumptions with real-life operating personnel. For reasons of confidentiality, this "reality" check may be limited to two or three senior operating personnel.

Questions on the size and likelihood of cost reductions and asset liquidations are best directed to general management or manufacturing personnel. Such reductive actions are frequently assumed to be totally positive by buyers, but decreasing the seller's head count or inventories, for example, can involve negative implications. Sales may decline if the marketing department is cut back, or if regional distribution centers are shut down. In-house line personnel need to consider the impact of such changes on future growth, and the fact that immediate benefits in cost reductions may jeopardize future gains in earnings.

Many deals are justified in part by the buyer assuming that its skills and resources, once applied to the seller's business, will ratchet up the seller's sales performance. One recent example of this synergy was Pillsbury's acquisition of Häagen Dazs, a regional producer of ice cream. After Häagen Dazs gained access to Pillsbury's national distribution system, sales skyrocketed. During the operations screen, similar synergies included in the buyer's projections should be reviewed by one or two marketing executives. Do the sales enhancement predictions have a footing in the real world marketplace?

Sales synergies are found most often in Market Share/Product Line Extender deals, although increasingly they are being used to justify transactions involving vertical combinations (i.e., Strategic Acquisitions). For example, in the Disney $19 billion takeover of Capital Cities, analysts predicted that Disney might increase sales by selling a *Pocahontas* TV series to the ABC network.

In general, Strategic Buyers, LBO Firms, and Bottom Fishers have less foundation than Market Share/Product Line Extenders on which to base pro forma sales increases. In the expense department, however, these three buyer categories typically include numerous cost reductions into forward results. LBO Firms and Bottom Fishers are notorious for implementing draconian cost-cutting programs that result in numerous layoffs. While these expense reductions increase the acquisition's income in the near term, their effect on medium- to long-term results appears mixed. Oftentimes, the cost cutters "throw out the baby with the bathwater." Research and development funding is dropped and customer development investment is diminished. The eventual results are less innovations and fewer new customers, in time leading to sales stagnation and profit decline.

TECHNOLOGY

On the subject of technology, the buyer is unlikely to gain much specific data from the seller prior to signing a letter of intent. Conversations with the seller's management, one or two plant tours and a few industry studies will provide some factual information. This material can be handed over to the relevant operations executive, but a deeper understanding of proprietary technology must await the intensive due diligence phase, which follows the signing of the letter of intent.

For many businesses, cutting-edge technology is not important to overall results. For others, the latest technology is a critical competitive factor, and it may represent a barrier to entry that is comparable in importance to the economies of scale or the well-known brand names that provide formidable barriers in many other industries. Accordingly, the prospective buyer has to recognize early in the process the value of technology to the seller's business. The focus of the buyer's investigation efforts may shift if technology appears to be a key to success.

In Market Share/Product Line Extender deals, the buyer's first objective in technology research is to ensure applicability and proprietary. When Sandoz A.G., a major drug company, acquired Genetic Therapy, a gene researcher for $295 million in 1995, you can be sure Sandoz thought gene research was going to produce the next wave of new drugs. In such transactions, the seller's product, service, and systems technology have to be understood well enough so the buyer knows the postclosing melding of buyer and seller won't result in substantial integration problems. Most LBO Investors and Bottom Fishers have a different perspective in the technology arena. For the most part, they seek low-tech businesses that are not susceptible to rapid obsolescence through technological changes—low-tech firms are preferred by lenders, who view such businesses as better credit risks for the highly leveraged deals preferred by these two buyer categories. Not surprisingly, in their respective operations screens, the LBO Investor and Bottom Fisher have a tendency to confirm as soon as possible whether an acquisition candidate is truly "low-tech." If their lenders believe otherwise, there can be no deal.

In selected strategic acquisitions, the access to new technology is a principal buyer objective. Before wasting a lot of time examining every facet of the proposed transaction, the Strategic Buyer in these circumstances focuses its operations screen closely on the candidate's technology. How new and innovative is this technology? IBM bought Lotus Development Corporation for $3.5 billion in 1995 largely to gain access to software's then hottest product, Lotus Notes, which enabled many PC users to work on the same document. In such transactions, one question is: Does the technology provide a meaningful barrier to entry in the candidate's industry? For the Lotus situation, a comparable program would have cost IBM's competitors hundreds of millions of dollars to develop. Another question: Can the technology assist the buyers' base business? Lotus Notes enhances IBM's already large role as an integrator of corporate computer networks.

DISTRIBUTION AND MARKETING

The distribution and marketing functions are prime candidates for expense reduction in Market Share/Product Line Extender deals. Combining these functions with those of the buyer often provides cost cuts through less duplication and more centralization. Developing an accurate estimate of the pro forma savings from the consolidation is a key objective of the Buyer's operations screen.

Another important point is confirming whether any aspect of the seller's distribution or marketing efforts is the subject of a long-term contract with a third party. This point is relevant to all buyer categories. Continuing such a fixed arrangement may be detrimental to the buyer's future plans for the candidate, so any restrictions have to be discovered early in the game.

EMPLOYEE COMPENSATION AND BENEFITS

The buyer's preliminary study of employee compensation usually consists of a cursory review of personnel policy manuals and, if applicable, union contracts. This gives a sense of how similar the buyer's compensation and benefit packages are to the seller's. Severe differences cost money if the buyer, like many companies, follows a policy of conforming the new subsidiary's personnel benefits to the parent company's policies. For example, if the seller's commission structure for marketing representatives is far higher than the buyer's, reducing these commissions may lead to loss of the seller's salespeople and, eventually, to a decrease in revenues. Likewise, if the seller doesn't offer its employees medical insurance, and the buyer's policy is to do so, pro forma insurance costs go up.

In many acquisitions, the buyer increases efficiencies by removing layers of management and by cutting overhead that is already duplicated in the buyer's existing organization. When the acquirer is contemplating layoffs right after the closing, it is imperative to check the employees' rights to severance payments. For middle managers and lower-ranking workers, this information may appear in the seller's personnel manuals, but top executives may have individual employment contracts that spell out specific severance amounts. Obtaining this kind of information for top management prior to the signing of a letter of intent is a delicate matter. In the early stages, therefore, the buyer has to rely on industry practice as a guide in developing estimates for severance costs.

Other important employee benefit concerns in the operations screen are the seller's future obligations with respect to employee pension and postretirement benefits. Audited companies disclose in the footnotes of their financial statements whether their pension plans have sufficient assets from which to pay the related pension obligations. A significant underfunding, or a dubious actuarial report on the plan's future liabilities, can be a Deal Killer. Bethlehem Steel, for example, has a $1.4 billion underfunding of its pension plans, representing a serious obstacle to a takeover. Another item deserving attention is an obligation for postretirement medical benefits. This employee prerequisite can be an unpredictable wild card in terms of future costs for the buyer. If possible, significant liabilities in this regard should be flushed out by the buyer in the preliminary due diligence effort.

ANTITRUST IMPLICATIONS

One of corporate America's favorite deals is "buying the competition." This sort of transaction offers the buyer the immediate opportunity to increase its market share and broaden its product line. Besides offering the buyer lower operating risks and more synergies than other deals, buying the competition also provides the buyer with the real chance of increasing prices after the deal has closed.

With certain exceptions, such as electric utilities, federal laws discourage the formation of oligopolies (or monopolies) through acquisitions. Unregulated oligopolies, in the view of the government, limit price competition and stifle product innovation. In doing so, if left unfettered, they damage the U.S. economy and hurt the U.S. consumer. Pursuant to legislation, the federal government has the right to prohibit mergers that substantially decrease competition. The laws governing when a merger is uncompetitive are complicated and apply in general only to large-size deals (i.e., when the seller has annual sales or assets of at least $10 million and the buyer has annual sales or assets of at least $100 million or vice versa). However complicated their interpretation, the policy goals of the antitrust regulations are clear—to promote competition.

For the sake of illustration, assume a buyer is seeking to acquire a direct competitor. During the operations screen, the buyer obtains basic market share data of the seller. A pro forma calculation of the combined entities' market share is calculated and compared with the existing level of industry concentration. At this point, common sense takes over. If the acquisition provides the buyer with a 25% to 30% share of a market that already is limited to a handful of participants, there is a good chance of an antitrust problem. On the other hand, a 35% combined share in a market with 20 strong players is probably not a concern. Close calls require more work. In these cases, an analysis of the competitive situation has to be prepared in line with antitrust guidelines issued by the Department of Justice and Federal Trade Commission. Outside counsel specializing in antitrust matters can be retained to do this specialized sort of work. For any sizable merger, the signing of the acquisition agreement requires a formal filing to be made before the federal government. Such filing outlines the deal in question, provides related information and requests permission from the government for the merger to proceed. Transactions involving potential antitrust problems receive intense government review.

Key antitrust issues revolve around legal definitions of business terms such as "market," "product," and "present and prospective competition." The meanings of these words are fuzzy. When Federated Department Stores acquired Macy's, the department store business was characterized as "general merchandising," a market that could theoretically include numerous other retailers such as Sears, Kmart, and Wal-Mart, even though the product offerings of department stores are typically more upscale. When I advised Youngs Drug Products Corporation, the manufacturer of Trojan condoms, one bidder was a direct competitor in the condom business. This firm believed it could avoid antitrust problems by defining condoms as part of the larger birth-control-device market, which in its view included birth control pills, diaphragms, and protective gels. In a $55 million drug distribution merger, the combined company had a 55% share of a regional market for wholesaling prescription drugs to pharmacies. The federal government registered no objections to the transaction, most likely because of the ease of entry of potential competitors into the wholesale business. In another transaction, The Great Atlantic & Pacific Tea Company (A&P), a national supermarket chain, bought Waldbaum's Inc., a regional supermarket operator that covered the New York metropolitan area. The combination did not create undue concentration in the large metropolitan "market," so the FTC did not object on this basis. However, when certain neighborhoods were defined as "individual" markets, many New Yorkers were faced with their local supermarkets being owned by either A&P or Waldbaum's—soon to be combined into one company. The FTC subsequently ordered A&P to divest 12 stores having these uncompetitive elements.

The operation screen needs to eliminate candidates that pose obvious antitrust problems as soon as practicable.

REPUTATION OF SELLER AND ITS MANAGEMENT

If the buyer's in-house M&A team has no personal knowledge of the seller's reputation, a few discreet checks with internal operating executives or outside consultants are in order prior to signing the letter of intent. This informal checking should be enough effort if the seller is a large, well-known firm. If the seller is a small, privately held business, or maintains a low public profile, information can be hard to obtain using standard reference sources. A private investigation firm can be retained to assist in the process.

GOVERNMENT REGULATIONS, ENVIRONMENTAL PROBLEMS, AND LEGAL ISSUES

Evaluating the impact of arcane government regulations, environmental problems and legal issues on the seller's assets, values, and future earnings is usually left for the intense due diligence effort that follows the signing of a letter of intent. Any significant negatives in these areas can be Deal Killers, so the buyer should look for warning signs during the preliminary evaluation. For related-industry deals, in-house operating personnel may be helpful in pointing out areas for special concern. Outside consultants do the same for diversification-type acquisitions.

Environmental regulation can play a critical role in defining purchase arrangements. In a chemical company merger, my client, the seller, placed 80% of its sales price, $22 million, into an escrow account for the payment of environmental cleanup costs that couldn't be calculated precisely at closing. The actual cleanup came in at less than $3 million, far below the escrow amount, but the degree of protection required by the buyer reflected the uncertainties in the environmental area.

Legal issues can sometimes be spotlighted early. For example, the risk of product liability lawsuits or insurance coverage shortages are endemic to certain industries such as pharmaceuticals, medical services, and construction materials. Buyers have to be wary as a result.

MODIFYING PROJECTIONS

Assuming the operations screen hasn't produced a Deal Killer objection by either internal personnel or outside consultants, the in-house team needs to plug whatever intelligence it has gathered from these sources into the deal's earlier financial projections. Was the candidate's business plan too optimistic in the opinion of the buyer's marketing chief? If so, revenue forecasts need to be trimmed. Did the candidate fail to note the probable entry of a major foreign competitor? Then, projected margins should be decreased. Are the team's assumptions regarding expense synergies too conservative? Greater cost reductions should be forecast. Does the buyer need to make up a shortfall in the seller's pension plan assets? The projections have to be adjusted for this obligation.

The resultant modifications to the financial forecasts provide the buyer with a clearer picture of what to expect if it "wins" the deal. At the same time, the buyer's opinion of the candidate's value changes. If this value assessment increases after the modifications, so much the better. If the opposite occurs, the buyer needs to take a fresh look at the deal's pricing.

FINANCING "REALITY CHECK"

Suppose the proposed transaction has survived both the search and screen and the operations screen; the in-house team has made a big step in winning the battle for top management's hearts and minds. The next step is to find out whether the newly modified projections conform to the real world of acquisition financing. Because acquisitions that are large in size relative to the buyer affect its financial status, the team needs to consult informally with several financing sources on large transactions. The discussions will center on determining if the deal, as conceived in the projections, can be funded by the appropriate issuances of debt or equity.

In "running the numbers" for the proposed deal, the in-house M&A group has made reasonable assumptions about the availability of debt and equity finance. Standard lender credit ratio tests were applied to the pro forma combined company's results. The debt-to-equity ratio and interest coverage ratio were in line with industry standards. At the same time, the projections on combined earnings per share and EPS growth indicated the deal's long-range ability to increase shareholder value. Having completed its homework, the buyer now has to step back and provide this information—perhaps without revealing the name of the seller—to a trusted commercial bank or to its traditional investment banker. These financial advisers can evaluate the likelihood of the buyer receiving financing on the terms assumed in the projections. They can also suggest important items to consider prior to making a bid. Taking this advice into account, the buyer's financing and valuation assumptions can be adjusted accordingly.

At times, these advisers can play a valuable strategic role—cautioning the buyer when the proposed purchase price is too high, the suggested leverage is dangerous, or the "business fit" too complicated for the investor community to understand. More often than not, the strategic advice from these advisers has to be approached somewhat skeptically. Despite intentions to provide objective advice, they have a built-in conflict. Overwhelmingly, their major objectives are short-term in nature (i.e., to generate transaction fees), while the buyer's goals are long-term in nature (i.e., to maximize shareholder value). Wall Street advice is better utilized in developing tactics—structuring and negotiating the final deal, followed by developing and marketing the acquisition financing package. The "buy" decision rests solely with the buyer's managers, and their instincts.

GO/NO GO DECISION

Within the limits of its preliminary due diligence effort, the buyer has examined the would-be acquisition from both a financial and operations point of view. While not all the buyer's questions have been answered, management has enough information on which to make a decision about whether to proceed. Furthermore, it knows what *it doesn't know*. Thus, a letter of intent can be crafted to provide the buyer with a lot of "outs" if subsequent due diligence shows that the seller has misrepresented its financial or operational health. Thus, it's time to "fish or cut bait." On finishing the operations screen, the buyer needs to make an offer or walk away.

SUMMARY

For the most part, a buyer's in-house evaluation team will not have all the answers. Acquisition analysis, once past the Deal Killer hurdles, should be refined in consultation with the buyer's operating executives or outside industry consultants. A final step in the operations screen should be a run-through of the proposed deal with a trusted financial advisor, who can provide a reality check on the buyer's assumptions regarding the availability of acquisition financing.

16 THE FIRST OFFER PRICE

That we have reached Chapter 16 before taking up the subject of making an offer exemplifies the complexity of mergers and acquisitions transactions. An enormous amount of preparation is involved before establishing a rational acquisition program. Having reached this point, our buyer's next job is to select an initial offer price for the seller's consideration.

Choosing the first price is a tricky proposition. On the one hand, the buyer wants to pay as little as possible. Too low an offer, however, will cast the buyer in an unfavorable light, and the seller could easily conclude that working with this particular buyer represents a poor use of the seller's time. Thus, a lowball number can be self-defeating. On the other hand, the buyer needs to avoid making an offer that is significantly more than the seller can reasonably expect from a competing bidder. Why pay more? While a high-priced offer may win the "prize," it reduces the buyer's financial return on the deal. A premium first offer is thus also self-defeating, and its negative impact be a drag for years on the buyer's earnings results. Knowing these two sides of the coin, the buyer wants a first offer to draw the seller into meaningful negotiations that provide a fair price, not a premium price. With this opening bid, the buyer wants to reach first base, rather than hit a home run by foolishly proposing a take-out offer that immediately eliminates other bidders.

VALUATION METHODOLOGIES

As Chapter 9 demonstrated, the valuation of companies is far from a science. There is room for a significant difference of opinion in almost every corporate valuation, and most transactions provide a variety of elements over which reasonable people can disagree. Moreover, each of the primary valuation methodologies used by corporate appraisers and investment bankers is highly judgmental and unscientific. This inexactitude provides a clever buyer with a lot of ammunition for negotiation.

In a specific deal-pricing situation, a buyer must know how to evaluate the seller's market value using methodologies that reflect four basic points of view:

1. *Comparable Public Companies Analysis.* The target price is compared with the value of publicly traded stocks of similar businesses. The companies relate market value to various financial statement results such as net earnings, EBIT, and book value. In many industries, the market value is considered in relation to operating data such as production capacity, mineral reserves, or subscribers.

2. *Comparable Merger Transactions Analysis.* The target's price is compared with the purchase prices of acquisitions involving similar businesses.

3. *Discounted Cash Flow Analysis.* The target's net cash flows are projected into the future and then discounted to the present. The resulting net present value is compared with the purchase price.

4. *Leveraged Buyout Analysis.* A LBO purchase price is estimated from the target, using the operating assumptions that are similar to those relied on in the DCF analysis. A LBO capital structure is then superimposed on the target and the resulting affordability price is compared with the acquisition price.

Each method relies heavily on the qualitative judgments of the appraiser. With *Comparable Public Companies Analysis,* few targets have exact comparisons, and differences between the businesses, operations and prospects of a target company and those of companies in a comparable grouping make a strict side-by-side numbers review impracticable. Thus, one can't properly say "Marriott has a 23 P/E ratio, so Hilton should have a 23 P/E ratio," because the two hotel firms have many unique qualities. *Comparable Public Companies Analysis* involves a substantial amount of qualitative judgment concerning the differences between the financial and operating characteristics of the target and the comparable grouping. *Comparable Merger Transactions Analysis* suffers from the same lack of exactness among comparable companies. *Discounted Cash Flow Analysis* is highly dependent on the appraiser's selection of the target's future growth rate, cost of capital, and ultimate terminal value. As shown in Chapter 9, even small changes in these three variables produce large differences in a target's net present value (NPV). *Leveraged Buyout Analysis* faces similar problems in its reliance on unreliable projections. As a result of the many judgmental decisions involved in this process, corporate appraisers typically provide a range of fair values. Rather than saying a business is worth $100 million, they provide a range, indicating that the value of the business is between $85 million and $115 million. Acquisition proposals falling into this range should be considered reasonable from the seller's point-of-view.

Done properly, these pricing analyses involve a significant amount of number crunching, M&A experience and, in certain cases, proprietary information. For this reason, many would-be buyers without extensive experience enlist investment bankers to assist in crafting an offer price and assisting in the related due diligence needed to refine the price. The comparable analyses, for example, encompass a bewildering array of calculations that tend to be confined in the practitioner community. For publicly traded comparables, much of the raw data used in these statistics is available from the SEC and other reference sources, but calculations on private deals, which are an important component of the M&A scene, reside mainly in the files of the advisory community. Even publicly disclosed merger transactions have important valuation issues that stay hidden from public view, such as underutilized real estate assets, undisclosed environmental liabilities, or large postclosing executive severance contracts. With the practitioner community having little respect for DCF analysis, it is incumbent on the buyer to have access to the universe of comparable deals relevant to the prospective transaction. Otherwise, the unprepared buyer is at a disadvantage with any seller represented by an experienced advisor.

In the balance of the chapter, I provide a case study that illustrates how a rational buyer approaches setting an initial price. The first step is determining what the fair price of an acquisition is likely to be. The second step is examining the effects of a fair price purchase on the buyer's financial results and its own valuation. If the deal contributes to the buyer's shareholder value, an offer is made to the target, within a tactical framework designed to limit the risk of overpayment.

CASE STUDY: BUYERCO

Determining a Fair Price

Buyerco (or the "Company") was a diversified industrial manufacturing company with three principal product groups: the Fasteners Division made automotive and industrialized fasteners; the Industrial Division components made pumps and instrumentation devices; and the Industrial Materials Division made plastic compounds and powdered metals. With 1994 sales and net earnings of $1.5 billion and $75 million, respectively, the Company had an active program of seeking complementary acquisitions to build its product base.

In November 1995, Buyerco's Chairman, Jack Wilson, was contacted by Tim Smith, an investment banker with Gordon Hull & Company, which represented Stewart Jones, owner of Quality Products, Inc., an old line manufacturer of industrial fasteners. Approaching retirement, Mr. Jones intended to sell his business to a corporation that could continue Quality's profitable operations after a short transition period. Supporting Mr. Jones at Quality Products was a capable management team, which included only one family member, a nephew who functioned as in-house counsel. Jack Wilson was acquainted with Stewart Jones, and in the course of Buyerco's acquisition search activities, they had engaged in several conversations over the years. After a brief discussion with Tim Smith, Mr. Wilson concluded that Quality Services passed Buyerco's primary acquisition criteria and he requested Gordon Hull's information memorandum describing Quality Products.

The memorandum arrived the next morning, accompanied by a confidentiality agreement.

After reading the memorandum, Mr. Wilson convened a small team to complete an acquisition review: Buyerco's Vice President-Corporate Development, Ann Insalaco; Vice President-Finance, Jerry White; and President-Fastener Division, Phil Petrowski. All knew the seller's company by reputation and they quickly decided that Quality Products represented an attractive product line extension; it served many of the same customers as Buyerco's Fastener Division, but with a slightly different product array. A quick read of the offering brochure suggested no Deal Killers, so the group's focus turned to price. In response to Mr. Wilson's earlier question on this subject, Tim Smith had replied, "Gordon Hull will let the market decide," but he pointed out that "recent comparable industrial deals were consummated in the 10×–12× EBIT range." Interpreting these remarks as a bottom asking price of 10× EBIT for Quality Products, Ann Insalaco suggested to the group that their merger analysis begin with this price. She believed the 10×–12× range was realistic, but she promised to check comparable transactions to confirm that this was in fact the case. In the meantime, Jerry White and Phil Petrowski agreed to prepare a due diligence list.

Gordon Hull & Company's 10×–12× EBIT range placed an enterprise value on Quality Products of $350 million to $420 million, based on the company's estimated results for the year ending December 31, 1995. Summary income statement and balance sheet data appeared as set forth in Exhibit 16-1. The investment banker's projection was optimistic, but not wholly unrealistic noted Ms. Insalaco, as she considered Quality's historical results. Observing the target's good operating record and strong balance sheet, she searched her records for comparable public companies and transactions. Because her database on private deals was quite limited she didn't use them in an analysis. Based on the results of her research, she thought a 10×–12× EBIT range was within reason. Comparable public companies were trading in a range of 6×–12× EBIT, but she realized this lower range excluded the requisite acquisition premium. Assuming a 50% premium, the public company EBIT multiples climbed into the 9×–18× area. Comparable merger multiples provided similar ranges. During the previous two

EXHIBIT 16-1 **Quality Products, Inc., summary financial data (in millions)**

| | Year Ending December 31 | | | | | |
| | Actual | | | Projected | | |
Income Statement	1993	1994	1995	1996	1997	1998
Sales	$335	$340	$360	$390	$420	$455
EBITDA	42	42	45	49	52	57
EBIT	32	33	35	38	41	44
Net income	15	16	18	20	22	25

Balance Sheet	At October 31, 1995
Cash	$ 20
Net working capital, incl. cash	70
Fixed assets	90
Total debt	30
Stockholders' equity	120

Where

1995 results were actual through October 31.
EBITDA = Earnings before the deduction of interest, taxes, depreciation and amortization.
EBIT = Earnings before the deduction of interest and taxes.

years, similar deals were struck for the most part in the 10×–12× range, although she couldn't account for higher multiples in two acquisitions, Moorco and Mark Controls. The statistics were as shown in Exhibits 16-2 and 16-3.

Gordon Hull suggested a 10×–12× EBIT multiple. As a double check, Ann Insalaco compared the $350 million to $420 million price range against other accounting variables such as Quality Products' net earnings, book value and EBITD. The resultant valuation multiples were in line with similar statistics for the comparable groupings, as shown in Exhibit 16-4.

Knowing that Gordon Hull & Company was adept at shopping companies, Ann didn't expect Quality Products to be sold for a bargain price. Accordingly, she decided to use a $400 million price tag in her Buyerco/Quality Products merger analysis. The calculation appears in Exhibit 16-5.

With this $400 million number in mind, she turned to Buyerco's most recent business plan, which included projections for the next

EXHIBIT 16-2   Comparable public companies, November 1995

	$MM Equity Values	Equity Value as of Multiple Of		Enterprise Value as a Multiple Of	
		Net Earnings	Book Value	EBIT	EBITDA
Companies with Normal Leverage					
Barnes Group	$ 244.0	9.4×	2.2×	6.2×	4.0×
Danaher	1,781.2	17.6	3.2	12.2	9.4
Park Ohio	139.8	17.0	1.9	11.1	8.4
Standex	460.0	13.3	3.7	10.0	8.2
Companies with High Leverage					
Ametek	$ 584.3	14.3×	6.5×	8.7×	6.0×
IMO Industries	102.0	10.0	Neg.	11.5	7.8

EXHIBIT 16-3   Comparable transactions, November 1995

		$MM Purchase Price	Purchase Price as a Multiple Of			
Target/Acquirer	Date		Net Earnings	Book Value	EBIT	EBITDA
Elco/Textron	10/95	$179.3	17.4×	2.4×	11.2×	8.3×
Joslyn/Danaher	9/95	244.6	15.4	2.8	10.8	8.8
Auto. Inds/ Lear Seating	8/95	619.4	17.4	2.7	1.6	8.9
Moorco/FMC	6/95	213.0	22.3	2.2	15.2	10.5
Welbilt/Berisford	12/94	301.1	14.4	7.3	9.5	8.2
Mark Controls/ Crane Co.	5/94	104.2	33.6	3.8	17.6	13.0
Rexnord/BTR	1/94	414.4	17.5	4.0	9.9	7.2

Where
Multiples are calculated on normalized earnings data.
EBIT and EBITDA multiples are calculated using enterprise value, which equals equity value plus net debt.
EBIT = Earnings before deduction of interest and taxes.
EBITDA = Earnings before deduction of interest, taxes, depreciation, and amortization.

EXHIBIT 16-4   Valuation multiples

	$350 to $420 MM Estimate for Quality Products	Same Multiples for Comparable Groupings
Enterprise value/EBITDA	7–9×	7–11×
Equity value/net earnings	16–20×	15–22×
Equity value/book value	2.8–3.4×	2.2–4.0×

three years. She needed the business plan because she wanted to start the process of combining Buyerco and Quality Products' respective earnings forecasts. This combination was the start of the pro forma merger analysis.

PRO FORMA MERGER ANALYSIS

Buyerco's reputation as a well-run business was reflected in its operating results and high valuation multiples. Sales and profits had increased steadily. Management constantly expanded existing product lines, and it regularly sought acquisitions that granted the company immediate access to markets that otherwise would have taken years of product development to enter. Summary financial and market data in November 1995 are shown in Exhibit 16-6.

The Buyerco business plan had aggressive growth targets, and these contributed to the Company's 18 P/E multiple, when most diversified industrial manufacturers were trading in the 12-14 P/E

EXHIBIT 16-5   Quality Product's acquisition cost estimate

	Millions
Buy 100% of Quality's equity	$380
Repay debt	30
Cash	(20)
Enterprise value	390
Expenses	10
	$400

EXHIBIT 16-6   Buyerco summary of financial and market data (in millions, except per share and ratios)

Income Statement	Year Ended December 31					
	1993	1994	1995	1996	1997	1998
Sales	$1,100	$1,300	$1,500	$1,800	$2,050	$2,350
EBITDA	130	200	230	265	305	340
EBIT	95	145	170	200	240	270
Net income	60	85	100	120	140	160
Earnings per share	1.30	1.75	2.00	2.40	2.80	3.20

Balance Sheet	At October 31, 1995
Cash	$ 20
Net working capital, incl. cash	190
Fixed assets	350
Total debt	100
Stockholders' equity	510

Market Data	At October 31, 1995
Buyerco share price	$36.00
P/E multiple	18.0×
Price/book	1.8×
Enterprise value/EBIT	11.1×
Dividend yield	0.3%

Where

Actual through October 31, 1995.
1996–1998 are company projections.

range. Could a $400 million acquisition contribute to Buyerco's EPS growth and increase the hefty P/E multiple already being enjoyed by shareholders?

Before her assistant ran a few "what if" scenarios combining the two companies, Ann called Jerry White for his read on financing sources. Because of the need to repay Quality Products' debt on a change of control, Jerry said that Buyerco would require the full acquisition cost—$400 million—in cash at closing. He suggested that $250 million of the purchase price could be raised from the banks without endangering Buyerco's "A" investment-grade debt rating. The remaining $150 million could be obtained through a common stock issue. Her next call went to Phil Petrowski, who had telephoned her earlier about a visit to Quality Products' head office. After confirming the arrangements, she asked

Phil about prospective synergies. He pointed out that the sales overlay
was about 50%, and then explained his "best guess" estimates on overhead reductions, marketing, and distribution expense savings, and
manufacturing efficiencies. The total synergies added up to approximately $8 million annually; with the preliminary synergies and finan-
cial plan in hand, she stopped by her assistant's office to discuss setting
up the initial "what if" financial projections.

To begin, her assistant, Mike Paul, decided to establish pro
forma results for 1996 and then follow through with the outer years.
He left the Buyerco business plan intact, but made changes in the
Quality Products projection furnished by Gordon Hull. On seeing
the 5% inconsistency between Quality's historical annual growth rate
(3%) and its projected growth rate (8%), he shaved three percentage
points off the projected growth and ran his first series of forecasts

EXHIBIT 16-7 **Buyerco acquisition of Quality Products, 1996
income statement data (in millions)**

	Buyerco	Quality Products	Adjustments	Pro Forma Combined
Sales	$1,800	$378	—	$2,178
EBITDA	265	47	+8[1]	320
Depreciation and			+6[2]	
amortization	65	9	+5[2]	85
EBIT	200	37	−3	234
			+20[3]	
Interest expense	10	6	−4[3]	32
Pretax income	190	31	−19	202
Income taxes	70	13	−7	76
Net income	$ 120	$ 18	$−12	$ 126
Earnings per share	$2.40	—	—	$2.32
Shares outs. (000)	50,000	—	+4,200[4]	54,200

[1] $8 million of cost-saving synergies
[2] $60 million fixed asset write-up amortized over 10 years; $200 million goodwill amortized
over 40 years.
[3] 8% interest on $250 million debt financing and cancellation of $4 million of interest on
quality debt to be repaid after the acquisition.
[4] Addition of 4.2 million new Buyerco shares from proposed public offering.

EXHIBIT 16-8   Buyerco acquisition of Quality Products, 1996 balance sheet data (in millions)

	Buyerco	Quality Products	Adjustments	Pro Forma Combined
Assets				
Current assets	$470	$140	$-10[1]	$ 600
Fixed assets	350	90	60[2]	500
Goodwill	100	—	200[2]	300
Total assets	920	230	250	1,400
Liabilities and Equity				
Current liabilities	280	70	—	350
Long-term debt	100	30	-30[3]	350
			+250[3]	
Postretirement liabilities	30	10	—	40
			-120[4]	
Stockholders' equity	510	120	+150[4]	660
	$920	$230	$250	$1,400

Adjustments

[1] Reduction of Quality's cash balance to pay costs of acquisition.

[2] Allocation of excess of purchase price over book value: $60 million to fixed assets and $200 million to goodwill.

[3] Repayment of Quality debts and incurrence of $250 million of new acquisition debt.

[4] Elimination of Quality equity and issuance of $150 million new Buyerco equity.

with a 5% annual growth rate. The results of these calculations appear in Exhibits 16-7 and 16-8.

On reviewing his data, Mike noticed immediately that the Quality acquisition would reduce Buyerco's prospective earnings per share in 1996. From a $2.40 EPS target in 1996, the deal would decrease 1996 EPS to $2.32, a 3% dilution. While the difference (8 cents) was small in absolute terms, he realized that it could cause a $1.44 drop in Buyerco's stock price (18 P/E multiple × $.08 EPS = $1.44 price change) unless Wall Street analysts were convinced that the deal would contribute eventually to Buyerco's long-term growth. Accordingly, he extended his forecast to 2000 (Exhibit 16-9).

After the first year, the Quality deal increased Buyerco's EPS. By 2000, the gain was $0.34 per share, a 9% jump over Buyerco's business

EXHIBIT 16-9 Buyerco acquisition of Quality Products, pro forma earnings per share forecast ($)

	1996	1997	1998	1999	2000
Acquisition	$2.32	$2.90	$3.31	$3.77	$4.24
No acquisition	2.40	2.80	3.20	3.50	3.90
Difference	−0.08	+0.10	+0.11	+0.27	+0.34

plan. Overall, annual EPS growth went from 13% under the business plan to 16% with the Quality purchase. This would impress Wall Street analysts, and, furthermore, the new debt needed to finance the deal didn't seem to increase the Company's financial risk significantly. As a result, Mike reasoned that Buyerco's P/E ratio would go up if the merger were consummated at the $400 million price. Sure, the higher P/E would be applied against a slightly small EPS initially, but after a short transition period, Buyerco's shareholders would realize a substantial increase in their share values. To confirm this conclusion, Mike called a couple of stock analysts with a hypothetical question. How much were 3 percentage points in added growth rate worth in terms of a P/E multiple? The answer came back with many caveats, but he interpreted them to mean at least two or three multiples, and no one seemed concerned about increased leverage. Accordingly, in developing pro forma per share values, Mike added two multiples to Buyerco's 18 P/E to arrive at a 20 P/E multiple with the Quality deal. He used the existing 18 P/E multiple in his "deal-free" calculations. The end result was a higher share price with the deal than without it (Exhibit 16-10).

His numerical results were unmistakable. The deal could increase Buyerco's share value. Knowing that Ann Insalaco and Phil Petrowski

EXHIBIT 16-10 Mike Paul's Buyerco share price forecasts ($)

	1996	2000
Acquisition and 20 P/E	$46.40	$84.80
No acquisition and 18 P/E	43.20	70.20

planned to visit Quality Products shortly, Mike finished his report and forwarded it to them. This report became known at Buyerco as the "Base Case."

BEGINNING DUE DILIGENCE

A review of the Quality Products offering memorandum uncovered no Deal Killers or Probable Deal Killers, and the Buyerco acquisition team concluded that the deal was a good fit from an strategic point of view. Confirming this positive outlook required thorough investigation, however, and the team prepared an information request, which was sent to Gordon Hull in advance of Buyerco's on-site visit. Lastly, the team designed an agenda for their initial meeting with Quality Product's management.

Realizing that they only had one day to spend with the seller, the Buyerco executives limited their due diligence list to a few key issues. Money topped the list and the team was anxious to learn if the $8 million per year synergy estimate was realistic. Also, the audited balance sheet didn't reveal possible "big ticket" items left out of the offering memorandum, such as real estate values, environmental liabilities, and long-term leases. The team wanted to learn if these items existed and if they affected Quality's valuation. Corporate culture and personnel policies were also high on Buyerco's list, as Phil Petrowski was anxious to see a smooth transition if the deal took place. Everyone on the buyer's side realized that they had at most 4 to 5 hours to question Quality's executives. The rest of the day was dedicated to romancing the owner, Stewart Jones. It was important that he know that Buyerco was a good corporate parent to its prior acquisitions; that it could be a perfect caretaker for Quality Products going forward.

The day at Quality Products went well. Its corporate culture was similar in many respects to Buyerco's and the top management seemed genuinely interested in an alliance. The discussion about the company's prospects was frank and management provided additional data that augmented Buyerco's initial financial analysis. From the visit and follow-up communications, the Buyerco team decided on the following four adjustments to their merger analysis:

Future Earnings Adjustments	Dollar Impact versus First M&A Analysis
1. *Cost Reduction.* Retain $8 million estimate of cost cuts.	No change from first analysis.
2. *Revenue Increase.* Buyerco's extensive marketing network will increase Quality sales by 5% annually.	Use a more optimistic sales scenario.
3. *Excess Inventory.* By using Buyerco's systems, Quality will reduce inventories by $5 million.	$5 million in extra cash will be available to Buyerco shortly after closing.
4. *Environmental Cleanup.* Confidential environmental audit commissioned by Quality shows expected $15 million clean-up.	$15 million cash expense at closing.

The adjustments increased Buyerco's pro forma EBIT projections going forward, but the effective purchase price rose due to the environmental cleanup costs. With higher EBIT outweighing the increased acquisition cost, the balance tilted in favor of the transaction. As illustrated in Exhibit 16-11, the revised data showed even more EPS from the acquisition than the first base case. The balance sheet projections also continued to look favorable. On a pro forma basis, Buyerco's initial debt/equity ratio of 35:65 in 1996 declined to 21:89 by 2000, and the Company's working capital position stayed healthy over the forecast period. Sensing a good financial and operating fit, the team recommended to Jack Wilson that Buyerco make an offer to buy Quality Products.

EXHIBIT 16-11 Buyerco acquisition of Quality Products, revised pro forma earnings per share forecast ($)

	1996	1997	1998	1999	2000
Revised base case	$2.32	$2.91	$3.33	$3.81	$4.36
First base case	2.32	2.90	3.31	3.77	4.24
No acquisition	2.40	2.80	3.20	3.50	3.90

While awaiting the result of Buyerco's preliminary evaluation, Tim Smith, the Gordon Hull investment banker, was busy working the phones. Gordon Hull had identified 30 operating companies with businesses that were complementary to Quality Products. For various reasons, Stewart Jones had eliminated 12 of these companies, leaving Gordon Hull with a "first contact" group of eighteen. As solicitation lists went, 18 was skimpy, but Tim knew he could convince Mr. Jones to cast a broader net if none of the 18 offered a fair price. After two weeks of calling, Tim had sent out eight memoranda to interested parties. From the remaining 10 companies on his list, he had received the following responses: Six firms told him that Quality was not a good strategic fit; two competitors indicated that they did not wish to add to their fastener portfolio; and two other companies rejected the deal due to the seller's price expectations. Of the eight firms receiving the memorandum, four had visited Quality, but the remaining four were taking their time in arranging on-site meetings. Based on his discussions to date, Tim thought Gordon Hull was working with 3 Window Shoppers, 2 lukewarm candidates, and 3 *real* buyers.

BRINGING IN BUYERCO'S INVESTMENT BANKER

Buyerco was one of the real buyers and its chief executive, Jack Wilson, was making a decision. He agreed with his internal team's recommendations and their analysis, but with a potential $400 million deal at hand, he knew they needed help. Buyerco was equipped to close smaller transactions in-house, but its resources were stretched for large transactions. The Company needed an investment banking firm, experienced in dozens of transactions, to assist Buyerco in meeting its three key objectives: (1) paying a price that wouldn't damage Buyerco's overall shareholder value; (2) obtaining optimal terms on the contemplated debt and equity financings; and (3) closing the deal in a smooth, professional manner with a minimum of postclosing contingencies. Reflecting on these needs, Mr. Wilson remembered Buyerco's recent experiences with Wall Street bankers.

Like many growing businesses, Buyerco did not have a traditional investment banker. The Company played the field, soliciting investment bankers for their specialized skills in certain transactional fields.

Over the preceding three years, the firm had employed four different investment banking firms in five transactions: a public equity offering, a public bond offering, two acquisitions, and a privately placed lease financing. Two of the deals had been handled by medium-sized investment banking firms, one of which, Picot Suez & Company, had impressed Jack Wilson. While he leaned toward using Picot Suez, he knew his board would need to see a large deal, like Quality Services, arranged with the help of a "name" Wall Street firm. That way the board could try to pin any subsequent problems related to the acquisition on the prestige of the adviser. Accordingly, he considered two large investment banks: Stein Schultz & Company and Largent Securities, Inc. Both firms knew Buyerco's industry reasonably well from a financial point of view, covered Buyerco's stock in their research departments, and employed large M&A staffs with the requisite expertise. After consulting with Buyerco's chief financial officer, he placed a call to Steve O'Connor, a Managing Director of Largent, who was Buyerco's contact person for all of Largent's corporate finance services.

Steve had heard rumors that Quality Products was on the market, but he had been unable to substantiate them. Wilson's call was the first concrete evidence to date. He and Wilson reviewed the scope of Largent Securities' potential responsibilities and the progress of Buyerco's evaluation. Wilson emphasized that Buyerco was interested in the Quality deal, but it wasn't willing to pay an unreasonable price. Agreeing with this sensible philosophy, O'Connor indicated a likely fee schedule of $200,000 up-front, with a ¾% success fee. He also suggested that Buyerco provide Largent with assurances that his firm would have a role in raising acquisition-related financing, providing it with the potential for additional fees. At first glance, O'Connor believed Largent Securities had no apparent conflict of interest with respect to representing Buyerco in a Quality Products acquisition, but he wanted to double-check with his management before agreeing to the assignment. In the meantime, O'Connor said he would assemble a team of professionals to advise Buyerco, put together relevant information for the deal, and send Wilson a standard advisory agreement. A face-to-face meeting was scheduled in Buyerco's office for two days hence.

As he hung up the phone, Wilson wondered if Largent, or any other investment bank, could really advise a client company with the client's best interests at heart. Neither the clients nor the banks had much loyalty to each other these days, and the small retainer fees hardly justified the bank's efforts in a deal that didn't close. Thus, Steve was under a lot of pressure to close a transaction and collect his success fee, whether or not the deal was really beneficial to Buyerco's long-term shareholder values. Despite this built-in conflict of interest, Wilson knew Largent was going to play an important role in a Buyerco/Quality merger. Its M&A market intelligence, resulting from a constant flow of advisory assignments, gave it a leg up on Buyerco's valuation analysis, and its keen understanding of the mechanics of transactions enabled the firm to develop financial innovations tailored to specific situations. Moreover, the firm's extensive knowledge of Buyerco's institutional investor base was going to be helpful in gauging the market's reaction to a Buyerco purchase and the resultant impact on Buyerco's share price. Finally, Largent Securities was better equipped to talk frankly to Gordon Hull. The two investment banks interacted frequently on different transactions, and Wilson imagined that a number of their senior executives had developed a "banker to banker" rapport that would make Buyerco's negotiations go smoother.

The initial meeting between Buyerco and Largent Securities focused on two topics: How much was Quality Products worth in the marketplace and how was the deal going to affect Buyerco's income statement, balance sheet, and stock price? The Largent team had analyzed data on many comparable companies and transactions, and it had started to prepare projected data on the combined entity. Its work to date was contrasted with the findings of the Buyerco internal acquisition team. Following some discussion, the two groups consolidated various assumptions for use in future financial analyses. After agreeing to a schedule of work and a division of responsibility, the two groups scheduled another meeting two days later, at which time Largent expected to have recommendations regarding a proposed offering price.

HOW MUCH TO PAY?

The Largent team quickly synthesized the historical operating performance of Quality Products, its current financial condition, and its future prospects within the industrial fastener industry. The firm's view of the acquisition candidate was then reflected in a series of numerical analyses designed to provide a range of likely values for Quality.

DISCOUNTED CASH FLOW (DCF) ANALYSIS

Largent calculated the present value of the future streams of unleveraged after-tax cash flow that Quality Products could be expected to
produce, as an independent business, over a five-year period (net income plus depreciation minus working capital increases minus capital
expenditures). To the present value of these cash flows was added the
present value of Quality's assumed sale in the fifth year, based on different EBITDA multipliers.

Largent used Sale Price Multiples of 8×–10× EBIDTA, less the
company's projected net debt and contingent liabilities. Because Quality was privately-held and had no defined cost of capital, Largent
applied discount rates reflecting an estimated cost of capital of 12% to
14%, which were based on capital costs of similar publicly traded companies. The resulting valuation matrix, shown in Exhibit 16-12, provided equity value of Quality ranging from $311 million to $409
million.

The wide range between the lowest and highest values, almost
$100 million in this case, was typical of DCF valuations. Largent's an-
alysts believed the $350 to $370 million range was appropriate for
Quality's situation.

Like most investment banks, Largent did not contemplate a future recession in its projections, despite the tendency of the U.S.
economy to experience a recession every five to six years. This cus-
tom was particularly inappropriate in this case because, as an industrial manufacturer, Quality Products was susceptible to sharp
earning declines during recessions. In the 1990–1991 recession, for

**EXHIBIT 16-12 Quality Products, Inc.,
valuation—Largent Securities
DCF analysis (in millions)**

Discount Rate (%)	EBITDA Multiple for 2001 Sale Price		
	8×	9×	10×
12	338	373	409
13	325	358	392
14	311	343	376

example, the company's earnings had dropped 20%. Any Largent assumption of a future earnings decline would have dropped Quality's present value accordingly.

Leveraged Buyout Analysis

Because of the prominence of the buyout firms in the M&A business, and the potential attractiveness of Quality as an LBO, Largent Securities estimated the purchase price by an LBO firm seeking a target return on its investment of 30%–35% through a resale of the business after five years. This analysis used the same operating assumptions for Quality that were used in the DCF Analysis. The LBO analysis satisfied a number of parameters that represented current market conditions, including (1) an LBO capital structure of at least 20% equity; (2) the repayment of LBO debt in 10 to 12 years; and (3) targeted interest coverage ratios, particularly EBIT to total interest expense, of at least 1.3×. Based on these hypothetical LBO calculations, Largent arrived at a range of value for Quality of $320 million to $360 million.

Going Concern Analysis

Using the dividend discount model found in textbooks and the dividend estimates prepared in the DCF Analysis, Largent completed a going concern analysis that calculated the current value of Quality Products' equity based on the expected return over time to a hypothetical individual shareholder. The range of these values was between $290 million and $350 million, depending on the long-range growth rate utilized in the calculation.

Comparable Company Analysis

Largent compared the historical performance of Quality to a group of publicly traded comparable companies, which included all of Ann Insalaco's earlier selections. The analysis looked at key operating, balance sheet, growth and valuation ratios and focused on smaller firms with a market value of less than $1 billion. Overall, Quality's operating margins and efficiencies were on par, but its growth rate for the preceding five years was low relative to the peer group. As a result,

Largent believed Quality's theoretical public trading value would be slightly below the multiples of its comparables. It also considered the inherent differences between Quality's business and prospects and those in the comparable group. The resulting estimated multiples were applied to the corresponding results of Quality on a stand-alone basis. Applying the two most relevant multiples, EBIT and EBITDA, implied a range of value of $280 million to $340 million.

These theoretical public-trading values assumed no large acquisition premiums, which were typically the case when a publicly traded company sold out entirely. As such, it understated Quality's worth in a takeover.

Comparable Transactions Analysis

In the final step of its valuation estimate, Largent Securities reviewed the financial terms of 12 acquisitions transactions that were similar to the would-be Quality deal. To the list of seven comparable deals suggested by Ann Insalaco, Largent's M&A department added five private transactions, the details of which were widely available in the practitioner community. Several of Ann's calculations were modified to reflect specific financial attributes that Largent knew about through its advisory work. For example, one acquisition had received an above-average multiple because of substantial underutilized real estate values that raised the purchase price beyond that which would have been achieved through the acquisition's operating prospects. Likewise, another seller with a premium growth rate had received only an average EBITDA multiple because of its significant undisclosed liabilities.

For each transaction, Largent not only calculated the equity purchase price as a multiple of net income and book value but also the enterprise value as a multiple of sales, EBITDA, and EBIT. Medians and averages were determined for each multiple category, and they were applied to the corresponding information for Quality. The corresponding range of values was then adjusted based on Largent Securities' judgment and expertise in the M&A field. Given this methodical process, Largent arrived at the implied enterprise value for the business of $380 million to $450 million,. These figures were slightly higher than the range suggested by Quality's investment banker, although Largent pointed out in its report that a limiting factor for Quality might be the firm's relatively high price/book value ratio. Any excess of purchase price over book value would have to be amortized through higher depreciation or amortization charges, decreasing net earnings if the buyer followed U.S. accounting rules. Certain foreign players had more flexibility in this respect and might pay more.

SUMMARY ANALYSIS

In general, Largent thought Quality Products was an attractive acquisition candidate with appeal to a variety of industrial and financial buyers. With interest rates relatively low and financing easy to come by, the deal was hitting the market at a good time. About 15 large companies were obvious Market Share/Product Line Extenders in Largent's view. At least half of these firms refused to pay over 8× EBIT for any business and several rejected any deal involving even the smallest amount of EPS dilution. This limited the field of likely buyers to a select group of operating corporations that could realize significant synergies and therefore pay a premium price, such as the $400 million suggested by Gordon Hull. LBO firms, for the most part, wouldn't pay more than $320 million for the business because its growth prospects were mediocre relative to other available companies. The only wildcard in the valuation equation would be a foreign buyer, such as a European fastener company seeking a beachhead in the large U.S. market. Foreign buyers, however, were unpredictable, and after conversations with Buyerco's in-house team, Largent's gut feel was that Quality's owner, Stewart Jones, preferred an American buyer that wouldn't need him to run the company for another three to five years. Largent included a table (presented here as Exhibit 16-13) incorporating Largent's findings in the first part of its Buyerco presentation.

Because the going concern and comparable company methodologies excluded a control premium, Largent believed these values were understated and it relied more on its comparable transaction. As such, the firm settled on an Enterprise Value of $360 to $420 million, which corresponded to an equity value of $325 to $385 million. Having settled on its opinion of how much Buyerco would have to pay to acquire Quality Products, Largent's analysts turned to the next big question. Would the deal increase Buyerco's shareholder's value?

EXHIBIT 16-13 Largent Securities, Inc., preliminary valuation estimate, Quality Products, Inc. (in millions)

Methodology	Range		
	Low		High
Discounted cash flow	$350	—	$370
Leveraged buyout	320	—	360
Going concern[1]	290	—	350
Comparable company[1]	280	—	340
Comparable transactions	380	—	450
Likely enterprise value	360	—	420
Add: Extra cash		+10	
Subtract: Environmental costs		−15	
Subtract: Outstanding debt		−30	
Net equity value	$325	—	$385

[1] Going concern and comparable company ranges exclude control premium.

DOES THE DEAL INCREASE BUYERCO'S VALUE?

In estimating the pro forma effects of the prospective merger on Buyerco's shareholder value, Largent had to evaluate two disparate sides of the way in which stocks are priced. On the one hand, the market could be reasonably rational in analyzing a transaction. The combination's pro forma financial results would be studied and Wall Street would price the Buyerco's shares using traditional methods of security analysis. On the other hand, each of these methods gave the average stock analyst a lot of flexibility in choosing growth rates, discount rates, and comparable company criteria. As a result, the Street's opinion on the expected results of the deal would be subject to the vagaries of the analysts' perceptions, rather than that of management. Accordingly, after preparing its fundamental analysis of the prospective transaction, Largent intended to assert the probable market reaction of a deal announcement on Buyerco's stock price. A lofty acquisition price, such as $400 million, and the attendant EPS dilution might make Buyerco's shareholders jittery, prompting the sale of their shares, no matter what the deal's long-term benefits. A flood of share sales would mean lower stock prices and potential problems in raising the required equity financing. As a result, in addition to calculating the hypothetical shareholder value of Buyerco on a pro forma basis, Largent's team needed to consider a public relations "spin" that promoted the acquisition. "Perception," thought Steve O'Connor, "*was* reality on Wall Street."

Buyerco's existing $36 share price seemed reasonable in the view of Largent Securities. The firm's diversified industry analyst rated the stock a "long-term buy," which was another way of saying she was neutral on the prospects of the share price advancing faster than the broad market. The stock's 18× P/E multiple was higher than most of the comparables, because of Buyerco's premium growth rate. About half the growth rate resulted from acquisitions rather than internal expansion, and this fact made Largent's analyst nervous since Buyerco's increasing size—annual sales were now $1.5 billion—made finding good deals more difficult. Thus, she assigned the stock a neutral rating because of her doubts on the Company sustaining its above-average growth through acquisitions.

Discounted cash flow and comparable company analysis prepared by the analyst on a regular basis supported her assertion. Buyerco's share price was fairly valued within a range of $34–$39, assuming the analysis reflected its "going concern" value to a public shareholder. At a price above $39, Buyerco's shares were a likely "sell" recommendation. At prices below $34, the investment bank would probably change its rating to a "Strong Buy." Furthermore, Largent saw no technical or momentum factors that affected the stock price in a significant way. In fact, Buyerco's $36 price was in the middle of a tight trading range of $32–$40 that had been in place over the past six months.

As shown in Exhibit 16-14, using the analyst's reports and Buyerco's business plans, Largent's M&A department developed a number

**EXHIBIT 16-14   Largent Securities
                 summary deal analysis**

1. Determine likely price of acquisition.
2. Project buyer's stand-alone results.
3. Project seller's stand-alone results.
4. Include synergies.
5. Perform various scenarios for combination.
6. Reach conclusion.

of future earnings scenarios for Buyerco on a "stand-alone basis." It then examined the impact of a Quality acquisition on Buyerco's forecast earnings per share, given a range of possible synergies. The Company's performance in achieving targeted synergies in previous acquisitions had been favorable and the deal seemed to involve minimal operating risk since Buyerco would, in fact, be buying a competitor that shared much of Buyerco's corporate philosophy and culture. Largent was confident of the $8 million figure provided by Buyerco management in the cost savings area, and it used this assumption in its projections. Largent also ran several scenarios that included revenue enhancements derived from Buyerco's superior marketing and distribution network. Using a $400 million enterprise value for Quality Products, most of Largent's initial projections showed higher EPS with the deal than without it. Plus the Debt/Equity ratio remained within a promising safety zone, implying that financial risk of Buyerco would be little changed (see Exhibit 16-15).

Given the favorable results of its Base Case calculations, Largent examined the financial impact of the deal under numerous other conditions, including those shown in Exhibit 16-16.

DISCOUNTED CASH FLOW ANALYSIS SUMMARY

Under the majority of scenarios that Largent Securities considered likely, the prospective acquisition augmented future EBITDA, EBIT,

EXHIBIT 16-15 Largent Securities, Inc., pro forma merger analysis for Buyerco earnings per share ($)

	1996	1997	1998	1999	2000
Base case—No acquisition	$2.40	$2.77	$3.15	$3.41	$3.78
Acquisition—Base case with $8MM synergies	2.31	2.85	3.24	3.65	4.11
Acquisition optimistic case with $12MM synergies	2.36	2.90	3.29	3.70	4.16
Acquisition pessimistic case with $4MM synergies	2.26	2.80	3.19	3.60	4.06

EXHIBIT 16-16   Largent Securities, Inc., Buyerco acquisition of Quality Products, pro forma merger analysis under alternative scenarios

Scenarios	Results
Quality purchase prices ranging from $360 million to $440 million.	Higher prices decreased EPS and postponed the merger's financial benefits.
Variety of financing alternatives, from 100% debt financing to 100% equity.	100% debt financing of the acquisition resulted in fastest EPS growth and the highest shareholder value, but increased risk and reduced financial flexibility were negatives. The full-equity option eliminated Largent's purchase accounting adjustments, but led to higher EPS dilution.
Changes in the forecast growth rates of Quality.	If Quality grew at its historical rate, the deal was of marginal value to Buyerco.
Reduction in amortization period of goodwill from 40 years to 20 years and a commensurate increase in amortization expense.	A 20-year amortization period reduced EPS by $.09 per year. Cash flow was unaffected but most investors relied on EPS as a measurement of success.
Changes in the amounts and times of projected synergies.	Larger synergy amounts, arriving sooner, boosted shareholder values.

EPS, and dividends. Most involved limited increases in Buyerco's cost of capital. Buyerco's per share value would increase if the deal was consummated.

GOING CONCERN REVIEW

Having finished its DCF review, Largent next looked at Buyerco's share price on a stand-alone basis for the next five years, 1996–2000, by multiplying projected EPS, without the deal, by the existing P/E of 18×. Given identical Buyerco operating assumptions for the time period, the share price forecasts were made for a Buyerco/Quality

EXHIBIT 16-17   Largent Securities, Inc., pro forma merger analysis of Buyerco/Quality Products

	Projected Share Prices and Dividends				
	1996	1997	1998	1999	2000
Share price—No deal	$43	$50	$57	$61	$68
Share price with acquisition	44	54	62	69	78
Dividends—No deal	0.10	0.11	0.12	0.14	0.16
Dividends with acquisition	0.10	0.11	0.13	0.15	0.17

combination. The higher growth rates under the merger prompted Largent to use a 19× P/E ratio instead of the present 18×. In each year, the stock price increased and the cash dividends were higher (see Exhibit 16-17).

The DCF and Going Concern analyses had many subjective elements that permitted Largent to exercise a lot of judgment about the future. Steve O'Connor and others in the firm knew that shading a few assumptions regarding the operating forecasts of Quality could easily upset the deal's economics. On the whole, however, the prospective acquisition looked reasonable from a financial point of view if the price didn't exceed $400 million and the expected synergies were realized quickly. Moreover, the Market Share/Product Line Extension character of the deal was a positive as were certain other qualitative factors regarding management culture and philosophy. Accordingly, Largent was prepared to recommend that Buyerco continue pursuing the acquisition.

A DISSENTING VOICE

As the stream of Largent bankers hurried to finish its report for the next Buyerco meeting, a junior M&A banker, recently graduated from the University of Maryland's Business School, mentioned to O'Connor that the Quality purchase was marginally attractive under two scenarios. One, if the economy went through another cyclical recession as it had in 1990–1991, the EBITDA of the acquisition would probably drop 20%–30%. During those recessionary years, the deal wouldn't cover its capital costs, thus irreparably hurting the net present value of Buyerco's shares. Two, at the University of Maryland, the junior banker had been taught to evaluate large acquisitions against a substitute strategy of corporate share repurchases. If Buyerco spent $400 million buying its shares in the open market instead of purchasing Quality, its shares outstanding would decline and EPS growth would increase faster than under the Quality scenario. And while the added leverage from share repurchases increased the financial risk of Buyerco relative to the acquisition strategy, the operating risk would be less because the repurchase alternative had fewer unknowns regarding synergies and Quality's actual growth prospects. Complimenting the young banker on his thoroughness, O'Connor explained, "First, there's no guarantee of a future recession. Second, your repurchase scenario might well mean a sharp decline in Buyerco's P/E as investors turned away from its diminished growth prospects." Walking away from his charge, O'Connor thought to himself, "And, my young friend, Largent Securities doesn't receive large fees when deals don't happen!"

Despite Largent's view of the probable long-term positive effects of the merger, the firm knew that the potential short-term effect of the deal on Buyerco's stock price might be negative, primarily due to the 4% dilutive impact on 1996 estimated EPS (see Exhibit 16-15). And, if cost savings and revenue enhancements weren't achieved on a timely basis, the dilution would continue to be a drag on Buyerco's stock price. A lower acquisition price served to mitigate these concerns, but Largent's M&A department was wary of counseling its client that Quality was available for less than $400 million of total enterprise value. There was simply too much competition for good businesses in the marketplace.

TACTICS

Steve O'Connor, Buyerco's investment banker, knew Tim Smith, Quality's investment banker, reasonably well. Both men had been in the business for about 15 years and they had worked together on three transactions over that time period—two M&A deals and one public offering. Soon after receiving the Buyerco assignment, O'Connor called Smith on a fact-finding mission. They covered Quality's price objectives first and then advanced to the company's "pros" and "cons" relative to recent diversified industry transactions. As a brief prelude to possible negotiations, O'Connor pointed out Quality's low growth rate relative to recent acquisitions and he inquired about the owner's ability to accept Buyerco stock in lieu of cash. An "all stock" deal relieved Buyerco of the need to use purchasing accounting in the acquisition; it thus eliminated the need for Buyerco to write-up Quality's assets and incur added depreciation and amortization costs. An all-stock transaction also enabled Quality's owner to defer capital gains taxes on the deal until he sold his Buyerco shares. In response, Smith stressed the seller's desire for cash but he didn't rule out an all-stock transaction. In a final note, O'Connor asked for details on competing buyers and on Gordon Hull's sales process. Smith replied that the company was presently being sold under the "modified auction" method. Exaggerating a little, he said he was authorized to contact 15 companies and 5, including Buyerco, showed real interest. This being said, Smith told O'Connor that Buyerco impressed Stewart Jones (Quality's owner), was a logical fit, and had the financial capacity to get the deal done.

In the follow-up meeting with Buyerco, Largent Securities presented the results of its analysis:

> *Pricing:* Quality Products' total enterprises value fell into a range of $360 million to $420 million.

> *Impact of Buyerco:* At a price of $400 million or less, the deal would contribute positively to shareholder value.

> *Tactics:* Quality was being sold via a modified auction. Buyerco was a leading candidate among a handful of interested corporate buyers. A first bid should be in the high 300's, underscoring our serious intentions, and Buyerco's managers should make every effort to romance owner Stewart Jones, who had a high regard for Buyerco.

> *Financing:* Largent Securities noted that Buyerco could easily raise $400 million of debt financing for the proposed transaction. The company's objective of paying down $150 million of this debt through a subsequent common share offering was readily achievable under existing market conditions. (Jerry White, Buyerco's chief financial officer, observed that his preliminary contacts with the company's lead lenders confirmed the availability of debt finance.)

Buyerco's acquisition team had reached similar conclusions with respect to the issues addressed by Largent Securities. In fact, Buyerco's outside counsel, Cohen & Berg, which was attending the meeting, had commenced the preparation of a formal offer letter. Together, Buyerco, Largent, and the law firm thrashed out an offer tailored to the deal's unique aspects. Afterward, Jack Wilson, Buyerco's Chairman, arranged a telephonic Board of Directors meeting for the next morning. The topic: approval for an offer of $335 million for the equity of Quality Products. Adding the net effect of liabilities, Buyerco was going to offer Stewart Jones a total enterprise value of $370 million.

SUMMARY

With the assistance of its investment banker, Buyerco methodically analyzed the likely financial effects of a Quality Products acquisition. The prospective deal passed Buyerco's many Deal Killer and Probable Deal Killer hurdles, and it advanced to the next steps in Buyerco's acquisition evaluation process. But it wasn't time to pop the champagne corks. Quality had to agree to Buyerco's offer and its associated conditions. There was sure to be a lot of extensive negotiations before that happened. At the same time, Buyerco needed to undertake its accounting, legal, and operational due diligence efforts, find $400 million in financing, plan the merger's integration, and sell the deal to Buyerco's various constituencies. No doubt, everyone was going to be busy for the next few weeks.

17 THE BASICS OF NEGOTIATING, DUE DILIGENCE, AND STRUCTURING

This chapter continues the hypothetical case of Buyerco, which is considering a Market Share/Product Line Extension. As we follow Buyerco, we learn the typical process of making a significant acquisition.

As shown in the previous chapter, Buyerco was on the verge of making a purchase offer involving a sizable amount of money. In most of its smaller deals, Buyerco had avoided the use of formal letters of intent, outside attorneys, and investment bankers, but the larger M&A battlefield was full of expensive pitfalls. As a result, management believed it needed assistance from the external M&A community to negotiate and structure the deal properly. With the hiring of Largent Securities and Cohen & Berg, Buyerco began to assemble its team of outside experts for the remainder of the acquisition process. The next step was providing Quality Products with a real offer. Without a formal indication of interest, Quality Products, on the advice of its own financial advisor, was unwilling to let Buyerco proceed with further due diligence.

Waiting to see the first draft of the letter of intent (LOI), Ann Insalaco wrote an outline of tasks and responsibilities for the upcoming transaction, as shown in Exhibit 17-1.

EXHIBIT 17-1   Buyerco acquisition of Quality Products, outline of key tasks

Task	In-House Responsibility	Outside Assistance
Negotiating terms and conditions through LOI.	Chairman's Office, Corporate Development Department.	Largent Securities, Cohen & Berg.
Completing accounting, tax, legal, and operational due diligence.	Finance, Fastener Division, Legal and Corporate Development.	Buyerco's outside accounting firm; Cohen & Berg; pension, environmental, human resources, and real estate consultants.
Receiving regulatory clearances.	Legal, Corporate Development.	Cohen & Berg.
Raising acquisition finance.	Finance, Legal.	Largent Securities.
Preparing the postclosing integration plan.	Fastener Division.	Pension, environmental, and human resources consultants.
Executing and negotiating merger legal documentation.	Corporate Development, Legal, Finance.	Cohen & Berg, Largent Securities.

THE LETTER OF INTENT

Referred to as a letter of intent by the trade, the offer was a three-page letter outlining the terms of Buyerco's initial bid, providing the key conditions to the deal's completion and summarizing the proposed schedule for closing the transaction. With the exception of "no-shop" and confidentiality provisions, the LOI was more a good faith expression between buyer and seller than a binding legal document. For the seller, however, the LOI was a critical step in the process. It established Buyerco's definitive interest and set a time schedule for things to get done. But, at the same time, it limited Quality's flexibility in seeking better offers through a "no shop" clause.

EXHIBIT 17-2   Buyerco acquisition of Quality Products

Letter of Intent Key Items	Commentary
Structure. Cash purchase of all of Quality's assets and the assumption of stated liabilities (i.e., an "asset deal").	By doing an asset deal instead of a stock acquisition, Buyerco avoids the potential problem of undisclosed liabilities that can arise from purchasing a seller's stock. Most undisclosed liabilities would remain with the seller's surviving corporation. From the seller's viewpoint, the asset deal may result in more capital gains taxes in addition to those potential liabilities.
Price. $335 million in cash. $10 million of this amount allocated to a 5-year noncompete agreement for Mr. Jones. 15% of this price will be held in escrow for three years. (Equivalent to $370 million Enterprise Value.)	With a noncompete, Stewart Jones can't start a new fastener company. Also, the noncompete is a tax-deductible expense for Buyerco, but it represents current income for Mr. Jones. The escrow account provides Buyerco with immediate recourse to Mr. Jones for misstatements of fact.
No Shop. For the next 60 days, Quality is prohibited from engaging in merger discussions with other companies.	Buyerco intends to complete its due diligence and legal documentation in 60 days. Quality will suggest 30 days to move things along.
Confidentiality. Except for public disclosures required by law and Buyerco's status as a public company, the results of Buyerco's due diligence and merger negotiations will be kept confidential.	Neither company gains from unwarranted publicity.
Time Limit. Buyerco's intentions expressed in this LOI expire in five days unless the LOI is countersigned by Quality Products.	If Buyerco doesn't threaten to withdraw its offer, Quality will shop the offer and try to obtain a higher bid.
Fees. Jones pays all of Quality's transaction fees.	Money issue.

EXHIBIT 17-2 *(Continued)*

Letter of Intent Key Items	Commentary
Key Conditions to Closing the Transaction:	

1. *Disclosure.* Buyerco will have full access to Quality books and records.
2. *Approvals.* Buyerco will have received all regulatory approvals.
3. *Due Diligence.* Buyerco's due diligence results are satisfactory.
4. *Employment Contracts.* Selected Quality executives have signed Buyerco employment contracts.
5. *Legal Documents.* All M&A legal documents have been executed.
6. *Financing.* Buyerco has obtained the necessary financing.

These six closing conditions are standard and give Buyerco latitude, particularly in defining its "satisfactory" due diligence. Of possible concern to Quality are the regulatory approvals since Buyerco's acquisition of a competitor may raise antitrust issues within the federal government. With a less qualified buyer, the financing contingency might be a seller concern, but Buyerco can easily raise the acquisition financing.

Buyerco would have preferred to go straight to an acquisition contract, as a means of avoiding potential LOI legal liability, but it understood the seller's need to have a written offer. Buyerco's letter of intent provided the following items (Exhibit 17-2), including all key business terms and conditions. Related commentary appears alongside the LOI.

Alerted to the impending arrival of the LOI by Steve O'Connor, Buyerco's investment banker, Tim Smith of Gordon Hull & Co. redoubled his efforts to encourage the remaining suitors of Quality Products to make a bid. At most, Tim figured he had one week to find a competing offer. He and Quality's lawyers couldn't stall Buyerco and Largent Securities for much longer than that. The offer price was fair, Buyerco was bankable, and the terms were reasonable, but Tim needed to make sure that his client was obtaining the top price. Only one potential acquirer, Martin Industries, accelerated its evaluation efforts on hearing of the prospective competing offer. The remaining candidates that had investigated the deal seemed hesitant because of Quality's price objectives.

Martin Industries was sincerely interested in buying Quality and it was willing to pay a fair price, but it had just finished absorbing a

$200 million company that it had purchased eight months earlier. Martin was in the process of refinancing the related acquisition debt, and it needed to address delicately the possibility of another, larger deal to its lending group. To perform its financial analysis and to review the deal with its financing sources required some time.

NEGOTIATING THE TERMS OF BUYERCO'S OFFER

Privately, Tim Smith was delighted with Buyerco's LOI. He knew a deal was within his client's grasp. Although the $370 million enterprise price was slightly below the proposed value range of $380–$400 million, Tim rightly assumed that Buyerco had the ability to increase its price by 5% to 10%. He thought the 60-day exclusivity period was too long and questioned Buyerco's need for public disclosures until the deal was further along. Without a competing offer, however, he realized his negotiating leverage was limited. To review these and other matters he scheduled a meeting with Stewart Jones and Quality's outside counsel for the next day.

At the meeting, Mr. Jones expressed his reluctance to take the first offer on the table. What if there was a better deal available? He also complained about the noncompete agreement, his personal obligation to pay Quality's investment banking and legal fees, and the 15% escrow. Tim Smith pointed out: (1) the proposed price could probably be increased; and (2) the offer was from a buyer that would have no problems raising the financing. Furthermore, he thought Gordon Hull could negotiate away the fee obligation, shorten the noncompete to three years and lower the escrow amount. Encouraged by these comments, Jones authorized Smith to proceed on this basis, but suggested he try to stretch out the discussions to allow for their other potential buyers to come forward. At no point, however, did Jones permit Smith to broaden his search list past the original 18 companies.

By claiming a cluttered travel schedule while at the same time demanding a face-to-face meeting with Largent Securities, Tim Smith was able to delay any serious negotiations for four days. Once the bankers met, the exclusivity period, noncompete contract, and fee responsibility issues were settled quickly, but negotiations bogged down on price. Tim argued that a $400 million value was the minimum amount acceptable to his client and he insisted that he had competing offers in the wings. Referring to the Elco/Textron transaction in October, he mentioned the relevance of an 11× EBIT multiple and the superior growth prospects of Quality. In countering Smith's suggestions, Steve O'Connor recommended, with raised eyebrow, that Quality Services should accept immediately any of Tim's alleged offers exceeding $400 million, because Buyerco was unwilling to pay this amount. And in response to the time-honored assertions of Quality's good prospects, O'Connor offered an equally time-honored counteroffer—a low upfront price combined with an "earn-out" through which Jones could participate in the future earnings growth of his company. In exchange for the earn-out, Buyerco would lower its cash price to only $300 million. The "banker to banker" posturing and negotiating continued for several days, with the principals being consulted behind the scenes.

It was important for Buyerco to have Largent Securities as its foil for keeping the price down. Any implied criticism of Quality Products' prospects reflected on Stewart Jones, the owner and the same person that Buyerco was trying to romance into a merger. Thus, any negative remarks made by Steve O'Connor in the heat of negotiations could be disowned by Buyerco's management. Likewise, Tim Smith's exaggerations regarding Quality's asset value or its auction process could be discounted by Stewart Jones in subsequent conversations with Buyerco. Lawyers on both sides would serve a similar buffer function during the drafting of the legal documents.

As the negotiations proceeded, Largent used its contacts in the practitioner community to determine the market's true interest in Quality. The team concluded that Gordon Hull really was conducting a limited auction. Neither LBO firms nor diversification-type acquirers had seen the deal. Two competing investment banks, acting without specific client requests, were trying to interest several foreign industrial firms in the transaction on a speculative basis, but so far the foreigners were waiting to see the offering memorandum. Only a handful of potential buyers had made the trip to Quality's headquarters and Largent's bankers knew from experience that at least two of the visitors were certifiable Window Shoppers at any price above 8× EBIT. This iterative process left two to three potential bidders in the eyes of Largent's M&A department, and Buyerco could compete with any of them in terms of operating synergies and price considerations. In sum, Buyerco's bid was close to what the other logical players could reasonably afford, and Largent didn't see a need to increase the offer price more than $5 million or $10 million. By the end of five days of off-and-on negotiations, Largent extended Buyerco's final offer to Quality Products. This offer represented a compromise on several points (see Exhibit 17-3).

Gordon Hull was inclined to recommend the offer to Stewart Jones. One week of urging the seven other potential acquirers to submit bids had resulted in one lowball offer of $315 million from a Window Shopper and a semioffer of $350 million from Martin Industries. The latter, while $5 million higher than Buyerco's proposal, was highly

EXHIBIT 17-3   Buyerco acquisition of Quality Products, revised letter of intent

First Offer	Revised Terms
Structure. Cash purchase of all of Quality's assets and the assumption of stated liabilities (i.e., "an asset deal").	Same.
Price. $335 million in cash. $10 million of this amount allocated to 5-year noncompete agreement for Mr. Jones. 15% of this amount held in escrow for three years.	$345 million in cash. Noncompete portion reduced to $6 million and three years. Escrow to be 10% (i.e., $380 million in enterprise value).
No Shop. For the next 60 days, Quality is prohibited from engaging in merger discussions with any other company.	45 days.
Confidentiality. Except for public disclosures by law and Buyerco's status as a public company, the results of Buyerco's due diligence and merger negotiations will be kept confidential.	Same.
Time Limit. Buyerco's intentions expressed in this LOI expire in five days unless the LOI is countersigned by Quality Products.	No longer relevant with final LOI.
Fees. Jones pays all of Quality's transaction fees.	Buyerco pays all fees.
Conditions.	Same.

conditional and Gordon Hull preferred a bird in the hand to two in the bush. The investment bank had received also a dozen or so unsolicited calls, mostly from LBO firms, but they could hardly afford the same price as Buyerco. Accordingly, in a four-way conference call between Buyerco, Quality, Gordon Hull, and Largent Securities, an agreement was made to go ahead with the merger. Buyerco's final diligence commenced immediately.

ACCOUNTING, TAX, LEGAL, AND OPERATIONS DUE DILIGENCE

Every seller has undisclosed problems at the final due diligence stage. For reasons of confidentiality, information flow to the prospective purchasers has been limited up to this point, and for reasons of marketing, the seller's agent has emphasized the most attractive elements of the seller's business. As a result, a prospective buyer has been shielded from negative factors that might have deterred it from pursuing the deal. Occasionally, the buyer's final due diligence effort uncovers a golden nugget of value, but in my experience, the opposite generally occurs. Final, intensive due diligence inevitably reveals negative items that diminish the seller's value by a considerable amount. Once this becomes apparent, the would-be buyer is left with two alternatives: (1) renegotiate the purchase price; or (2) walk away from the deal. Most choose the former alternative.

In the offering memorandum and in subsequent on-site visits, Quality's management made certain representations regarding its financial condition and future profitability. While this furthered Buyerco's preliminary analysis and led to its LOI, the twin goals of the final due diligence remained: (1) to confirm management's depiction of Quality's business; and (2) to pin down a better estimate of likely synergies. Unlike many of Buyerco's transactions, this deal featured a well-prepared offering memorandum, a company with audited financial statements and a knowledgeable seller's agent. While all these attributes made the process easier and faster, Buyerco was obligated to conduct as thorough a due diligence as possible. To accomplish these tasks in the 45-day exclusivity period, Buyerco contracted for the services of several new additions to its practitioner team:

Existing Members

Buyerco investment bank.

Outside law firm.

New Members

Existing Buyerco accounting firm (audit and tax sections).

Human resources, pension, and benefits consultant.

Environmental consulting firm.

Systems/electronic data processing (EDP) consultant.

Real estate consultant.

Each of these team members had employees skilled in evaluating acquisitions and used to working around the clock to get a deal done. Ann Insalaco, Buyerco's corporate development chief, and Jerry White, Fastener Division President, coordinated the efforts of the due diligence team, which included seven additional Buyerco employees. They had one month to complete their work.

The purpose of the due diligence investigation was to verify that Buyerco was getting its moneys worth. In its review of the offering memorandum, conversations with Quality management, and discussions with Gordon Hull, the would-be acquirer had been presented with an image of Quality as a good business with promising prospects and a strong balance sheet. While this image complemented Buyerco's research from other sources, the company was planning on spending a huge sum of money—almost $400 million—to buy the business, and management had to make doubly sure that its expectations were going to be met. In working with other sellers over the years, Buyerco had learned that most sellers didn't deliberately misinform prospective buyers. They might shade the truth to place their business in an optimistic light or commit an error of omission, but outright lying or fraud was rare. In several prior cases, Buyerco's due diligence uncovered negative attributes about which the seller was honestly unaware, such as environmental problems or multiemployer pension liabilities. In the Quality investigation, Buyerco didn't quite know what to expect, but the M&A team knew something bad was going to pop up. It always did.

Over the next month, Buyerco's M&A team completed the necessary due diligence efforts.

ACCOUNTING AUDIT

Buyerco's controller section and the company's outside accounting firm performed an independent verification of Quality's financial statements. They checked the work papers of Quality's accounting firm in a number of areas and did a physical audit of certain items that were important to Quality's value. Additionally, the electronic accounting systems of the proposed acquisition were tested. The results of the audit were generally favorable, although it revealed several items of some importance. First, about $5 million of Quality's finished products were over 18 months old and therefore obsolete. Rather than writing the inventories down to realizable value and selling them at a loss, Quality's management had simply ignored the problem. Second, Quality's owner had been running $300,000 of personal expenses through the company's books every year. This was a positive from Buyerco's point of view since these unforeseen personal expenses wouldn't be incurred under new ownership. Third, the company's loss reserves on receivables were substantially lower than Buyerco's. Conforming them to Buyerco's standards would result in a pro forma decrease in the acquisition's income of about $400,000 annually. Buyerco intended to request a $5 million decease in the purchase price as a result of the inventory problem; the other issues would go unmentioned.

OPERATIONS AUDIT

Buyerco's Fastener Division sent several teams of operating executives to conduct an operations audit. The work was multifaceted and covered the following tasks:

- Visit Quality's manufacturing plants and distribution facilities.
- Interview the acquisition's key executives, including those in production, marketing, distribution, personnel, and purchasing.
- Check production records, costing procedures, EDP systems, and customer lists.
- Confirm the acquisition's ability to sustain sales and earnings growth.
- Evaluate management.

- Identify specific areas for cost reduction and revenue enhancement ("synergies").

With the information from the operation audit in hand, Buyerco's operating teams prepared a postacquisition plan of integration for the future Buyerco/Quality entity, and submitted it to Buyerco's chairman for consideration.

Among the findings of the operational audit were that annual cost savings synergies would likely be about $10 million, instead of the $8 million originally anticipated. Quality's purchasing department and insurance coverage were relatively inefficient for a sizable firm, and the Buyerco's Fastener Division executives saw substantial extra savings in these areas. A negative feature was an estimated $1 million overhaul of the Quality's EDP capacity. Revenue enhancements were more difficult to predict, but Buyerco's team thought the Corporate Development Department's 5% growth target was achievable.

The human resources consulting firm examined Quality's personnel policies, wage scales, and benefits packages. Many facets of Quality's personnel operations were similar to Buyerco. A few benefit packages, particularly in health insurance, fell below Buyerco's minimums and required upgrading at Buyerco's expense. The consultant estimated an annual incremental cost of $0.3 million to $0.5 million per year.

Reviewing the Fastener Division's postintegration plan, the consultants noted the unfortunate human consequences of the acquisition. About 120 Quality Products' employee were facing downsizing after the deal's completion. Applying Buyerco's standard severance formulas and outplacement assistance costs, the consultants projected a one-time charge of $6 million for the transition. This number was in-line with the Corporate Development Department's prior calculations.

As part of the closing conditions, Buyerco required employment contracts with five key Quality managers. Preliminary discussions with these individuals were initiated by Phil Petrowski. All were offered incentives to stay.

LEGAL AUDIT

While two of Cohen & Berg's attorneys drafted the legal documentation and applied for Buyerco's regulatory clearances, three other lawyers, accompanied by Buyerco's in-house counsel, went through the laborious task of verifying Quality's legal standing, reading key operating contracts and going through the Board of Directors' meeting minutes. Afterward, they examined the proposed acquisition's pending lawsuits, patent filings, and trademarks. Finally, the firm's tax situation and product liability potential were considered. The legal audit uncovered no serious issues.

ENVIRONMENTAL AUDIT

Because of the extensive liability surrounding environmental pollution and its own desire to be a good corporate citizen, Buyerco ordered a professional environmental audit of each prospective acquisition. Not only did these audits reveal potential costly problems, but they also provided Buyerco with advice on how to improve the environmental behavior of its acquisitions. Fastener production was not a dirty business, but Buyerco wanted assurances. The environmental consultants tested the noise, air, and water emissions of Quality's plants and conducted an examination of the soil near where Quality stored solvents and fuels. The $15 million that Quality had projected for a cleanup at its major manufacturing facility was adequate, but the consultants' review had located contaminated soil near a second smaller plant. Remediation of the problem would cost an estimated $2 million. The consulting firm also suggested a number of nonmandatory noise and emission reduction measures involving an additional $2 million in capital improvements.

REAL ESTATE AUDIT

The real estate consulting firm reviewed the value of Quality's owned real estate, the terms of its building leases and the titles of its properties. The few significant "premium value properties" had been disclosed in the offering memorandum, and Buyerco had factored this information into its bid. The audit revealed that two of the sellers's warehouses were leased from Stewart Jones, Quality's chairman. Since the leases had market rates, this wasn't an issue for the would-be buyer.

NEGOTIATING DUE DILIGENCE ISSUES

As was the case with most due diligence efforts, Buyerco's investigation uncovered a number of undisclosed problems that would cost it money. None of Buyerco's discoveries was deal threatening; in fact, the most prominent of these items was the $5 million of obsolete inventory, which was only 1.3% of the proposed acquisition cost. In several earlier deals, the due diligence study revealed sufficient accounting irregularities to require 20% to 30% purchase price adjustments, which the respective sellers failed to agree on. As a result, Buyerco walked away from each of these prospective mergers. The Quality Products business, in contrast, was "clean" by practitioner standards. Only two negatives were important:

Obsolete inventory	$5 million
Additional environmental remediation	$2 million
Total cost to Buyerco	$7 million

To some degree, these two negatives were offset by the $2 million in extra synergies found by Buyerco's operations team, but the would-be acquirer kept these "extras" a secret from Quality and its advisors.

In a follow-up meeting with Quality and Gordon Hull, Largent Securities and Buyerco laid out Buyerco's request for a $9 million reduction in the purchase price. Acknowledging that Quality was a fine business with outstanding prospects, Largent Securities' Steve O'Connor pointed out that inventory and environment were two "hard money" issues that had to be made right. Rather than denying the problem, Tim Smith sought the middle ground by disputing Buyerco's bad inventory estimate and the consulting firm's projected remediation expense. After prolonged haggling that lasted one week, the parties settled on a $5.5 million decrease in the purchase price.

This price adjustment, the added synergies, and the other earnings changes suggested by the due diligence review were then incorporated by Ann Insalaco into Buyerco's financial merger model, which indicated no material adverse impacts on the acquisition's projected rate of return. She called Cohen & Berg to inquire about its progress on the legal documentation.

LEGAL DOCUMENTATION

An in-depth discussion of the legal documentation involved in an deal such as Buyerco/Quality is better left to lawyers, several of whom have written entire books on the subject of merger law. The primary legal document for a straightforward transaction such as Buyerco's acquisition of Quality is an "Agreement and Plan of Merger." This agreement is supplemented by the attendant regulatory filings and the necessary financing documentation. Many merger agreements are signed concurrently with the purchase money changing hands from buyer to seller. Others are signed by both parties, but the actual closing waits until regulatory clearances and other conditions are fulfilled. This interim period can cover weeks or months, depending on the circumstances involved.

The Buyerco/Quality Agreement had all the standard provisions of an M&A agreement, including the following key items.

Buyerco/Quality Merger Agreement, Key Legal Provisions

Structure/Timing/Objective

The document described the all-cash, asset-purchase structure of the offer, the proposed closing schedule and Buyerco's objective of acquiring all assets relevant to Quality's business.

Representations and Warranties

Through the section on representations and warranties, Buyerco sought to have Quality's owner make a series of statements confirming that Quality had disclosed all important financial, operating, and legal aspects of its business to Buyerco. Although the would-be purchaser had conducted its own extensive due diligence, it wanted added legal protections if an unknown problem arose after the deal closed. Thus, these stipulations served to reduce Buyerco's risks in the transaction. For example, in the first drafts of the agreement, Buyerco proposed that Quality's owners and managers assert the following:

- All Quality financial statements were true in every material respect, except for inventories.
- There was no pending or possible serious litigation against Quality.
- Quality had no material lability that had not been disclosed to Buyerco.
- Quality's patents were wholly enforceable.
- All of Quality's production machinery was in good working order.

Any damages incurred by Buyerco as a result of a misstatement would be paid out of the 10% escrow amount, without regard to the protestations of Quality's former owner, who was counting on eventually receiving the escrow money. If a production line broke down at a cost of $5 million and Quality had warranted that all machinery was in good condition, Buyerco might have a justifiable reason to remove $5 million in cash from the escrow amount, thus reducing the ultimate purchase price by $5 million. If cost of such warranty breaches exceeded the total value of the escrow (i.e., $33.5 million), Buyerco would have the right to sue Stewart Jones to recover its expenses.

Mr. Jones was highly motivated to reduce Buyerco's ability to take money out of the escrow and to sue him years after the closing. Accordingly, the broad representations and warranties requested by Buyerco were narrowed through negotiations by the parties' attorneys. With respect to certain risky areas in environment and litigation, the lawyers settled on adding detailed disclosure schedules to the agreement.

As was typical in such arrangements, Quality agreed to a series of covenants stipulating that it would operate in the "normal course of business" between the agreement's signing date and the closing date. Although the parties expected to sign and close on the same day, regulatory approvals could be delayed and the attorneys wanted to anticipate the likelihood of three to four weeks between signing and closing. The no-shop and confidentiality points covered in the letter of intent were repeated here.

Closing Conditions

Regulatory approvals were among a number of closing conditions contained in the agreement. Several conditions such as full disclosure, satisfactory due diligence and employment contracts, had been fulfilled. Others were legal housekeeping matters. A key business condition was Buyerco obtaining the requisite $385 million financing for the transaction.

STRUCTURING THE FINANCING

While the due diligence effort and legal documentation were being completed, Buyerco's chief financial officer was seeking an optimal financing structure for the deal. Unlike many acquirers, Buyerco was in a favorable position to obtain funds; it had an investment-grade credit rating, so it had the flexibility to tap a large variety of debt-financing sources to find the most attractive package. In fact, on hearing of the proposed transaction, many lenders approached Buyerco and its investment bank with debt-financing suggestions. At the same time, Buyerco was besieged by securities firms hoping to act as a lead or as a comanager of any public offering contemplated by the company.

In the beginning of the Quality evaluation process, Jerry White had insisted that Buyerco's acquisition-financing scheme include a substantial equity component. An all-debt transaction, he feared, might jeopardize Buyerco's prized investment-grade credit rating. Largent Securities' analysis of the merger's financial effects seconded his views, and the financing plan for the deal became a two-step venture.

Financing Plan, Buyerco Acquisition of Quality Products

Step 1. $375 Million Bridge Loan

Buyerco would borrow $375 million from a syndicate of commercial banks on a short-term basis to fund the acquisition's closing. After a brief interim period for filing the appropriate SEC documents, the Company intended to offer bonds and common shares to the public. The proceeds of the offerings would repay the debt needed to "bridge" the deal.

Step 2. Public Offering of $225 Million of 15-Year Bonds and $150 Million of Common Shares

Using Largent Securities as lead underwriter, Buyerco intended to sell publicly bonds and common shares to institutional and individual investors. The market knew a financing was in the works because SEC regulations had already required Buyerco to publicly disclose the letter of intent. Even before this disclosure, Buyerco, its financial relations firm, and Largent Securities had developed a collective spin on the acquisition to heighten its attractiveness to the Wall Street security analysts and reporters who covered the Company's activities. The fundamental story behind the deal: *minimal EPS dilution in 1996 and higher EPS growth thereafter from a low-risk acquisition representing a perfect operating fit.* The strategy seemed to work; Buyerco's shares had climbed $1 in price since the LOI had been announced.

SEEKING A BRIDGE LOAN

To approach commercial banks, Jerry White and Largent Securities prepared a brief financing memorandum, outlining the terms of the acquisition, describing the two companies, and summarizing historical, pro forma, and projected financial data of the combined entity. After reaching a preliminary business agreement with National Bank of New York, which would function as lead lender and loan syndication agent, Buyerco invited National to perform its lender's due diligence investigation of Buyerco and Quality Products. The lender's review was considerably less detailed than the acquisition due diligence, and the parties were able to start legal documentation for the financing in short order.

PUBLIC OFFERING OF BONDS AND COMMON SHARES

The public offering of the Company's securities was to take place after the deal's closing. Based on the market's favorable reaction to the proposed acquisition, Buyerco was forecasting a lower interest rate on the bonds and higher price on the shares, compared with its Base Case scenario.

These positive changes were added to Buyerco's merger financial model, providing a better return on the acquisition and less EPS dilution.

Subsequent to the closing, Buyerco intended to prepare two offering prospectuses—one for the bond offering and one for the common-share offering. Running 80 to 100 pages in length, respectively, the documents were going to be crammed with detailed descriptive information on the transaction, the financing, the businesses of Buyerco and Quality, and the historical and pro forma financial statements of Buyerco and Quality.

As the investment bank advising on the merger, Largent Securities was the logical choice to lead-manage both offerings. To reward other investment banks that had helped Buyerco in the past, Jerry White hoped to select several comanagers following the acquisition's closing.

CLOSING AND POSTMERGER INTEGRATION

With the merger negotiations and legal documents essentially complete, Buyerco took the merger agreement, its amended business plan, and the acquisition financing arrangement to its board of directors, which approved the deal unanimously. The next day, Buyerco and the seller signed the agreement and waited two weeks for final regulatory approvals to arrive. Then, the transaction closed and Stewart Jones had a lot of cash in the bank.

Buyerco's Fastener Division was primarily responsible for integrating Quality Products into the Buyerco fold. Workforce reductions were made quickly and the Fastener Division communicated these actions to Quality's employees, who, like many employees of acquired businesses, feared the uncertainty associated with the merger. The communication program instituted by Division management was effective in boosting the low morale of Quality's workforce, but the acquisition suffered from postclosing productivity losses. Several of Quality's younger managers opted to take positions with other companies after the closing, and Buyerco redoubled its efforts to retain that portion of Quality's employee base not scheduled for layoff.

Significant Quality customers and suppliers were individually visited by Fastener Division executives. New purchasing, marketing, and distribution arrangements were explained to them and most agreed to take a wait-and-see attitude. Buyerco's experience in integrating earlier acquisitions was a reassuring sign.

Six months after the closing, the deal was performing well. Quality's sales had increased according to plan and the bulk of the expected synergies were being realized. Pleased with the success, Ann Insalaco and the Corporate Development Department returned to hunting for new acquisitions.

APPLICABILITY OF THE BUYERCO CASE

The Buyerco/Quality Products case illustrated the key steps in the acquisition process: screening the deal, valuing the business, considering the merger's financial and operations effects, performing due diligence, negotiating legal documents, finding the financing, planning the postmerger integration, and closing the transaction. From a practitioner's viewpoint the Quality purchase went smoothly. There was a limited auction, the owner's price expectations were realistic, the target's operating and financial condition was relatively clean, the buyer obtained financing easily, and the legal documentation proceeded in an efficient manner. In most of my merger deals, the buyer and the seller confronted more roadblocks along the way to closing. A level head and experienced hand resolved many problems which, in the heat of battle, often get blown out of proportion, In the Buyerco deal, for example, the $5 million inventory issue represented less than 1% of the deal's cost. If there was a specific problem preventing a compromise there, it could have been horse-traded for concessions in other areas.

As a rule, small transactions involving family owners tend to have a complicated due diligence effort. Many times, the seller's data on finances, operations, or legal matters are poorly organized or simply unavailable. The buyer may also be confronted with a host of insider transactions and tax issues that are typically not present in a large corporate sale. Fortunately, the documentation phase tends to move faster since family owners generally are less interested in the arcane aspects of legal documentation that absorb many hours of time in larger deals.

Large Fortune 1000 type acquisitions tend to involve less "hands on" due diligence compared with medium-sized, private deals. This is an interesting paradox from the buyer's standpoint. *More* purchase price should equal *more* due diligence because the buyer has so much more to lose. Nevertheless, big public transactions have a lower due diligence threshold for two reasons. One, the competition is stiffer for large, marquee deals so that buyers are forced to drop their standards to play in the bidding. Two, the terms of many public company auctions limit the buyer's investigation to a timespan that is less than optimal. In virtually any large hostile takeover, for example, the buyer's due diligence is by definition severely limited, since it has had no access to the target's managers, plant locations, and internal records.

The legal side of the larger deals tends to be more complex. Both buyer and seller can afford to hire the most expert, and the most expensive, M&A law firms. In protecting their clients' interests, these law firms spend countless hours splitting legal hairs over the merger's many facets, while ensuring that each party follows the corporate mating ritual to the letter of the law. At times, the legal expenses on such transactions run into the millions of dollars.

SUMMARY

Chapters 16 and 17 provided a distillation of the acquisition process through the Buyerco case. Valuation, negotiation, and structuring tactics were covered, along with the use of selected practitioners to assist the buyer's in-house staff. As the business terms of the deal were altered or as the acquisition's prospects were modified, the buyer carefully amended its financial model to ensure that the deal was economically viable. "Stroking the seller" was revealed to be an important element of the buyer's strategy, and its investment banker was often relegated to being the "black hat" at the negotiating table. Six months after closing, the Quality Services deal was headed for a happy ending. Sales were up and synergies were being realized. Buyerco was last seen heading for the next acquisition opportunity.

18 LEVERAGED BUYOUTS

Most mergers involve one operating company buying another operating company. The buyer's return on investment is primarily derived from the long-run benefits associated with combining the businesses. Profits are increased through the merged companies' higher operating efficiencies, new product lines, added revenue growth and, in certain instances, enhanced pricing through reduced competition. In such transactions, the buyer's ultimate objective in acquisitions is to augment its shareholder value by grafting onto itself new product lines and complementary businesses. Of 1995's 20 largest acquisitions, 80% fell into this category.

The dominance of operating company/operating company mergers notwithstanding, a tremendous amount of acquisition activity is originated by what the trade calls "financial buyers." The acquirers in this category do not consider themselves in the business of manufacturing products or providing services like an operating company. Rather, their business *is* the purchase and sale of businesses. For them, the basic idea is to (1) buy an operating company at a reasonable price; (2) improve its performance and image; and (3) sell it at a price that provides a handsome time-adjusted rate of return. Relegated to the sidelines of the business world 20 years ago, financial buyers are now broadly accepted in corporate America. In fact, some of America's largest firms have spun off divisions to financial buyers, and many established corporate, state, and union pension funds have placed billions of dollars in the hands of investment pools run by such investors.

The next three chapters will cover several variants on the "financial buyer" theme. In this chapter, we will review leveraged buyouts, the most famous of these strategies. In Chapter 19, we will discuss asset deals, bust-up transactions, and bottom fishing. Chapter 20 will provide a summary of the popular strategy of "buying companies wholesale" and "selling them retail."

UNDERSTANDING LEVERAGED BUYOUTS

The basic principle behind the leveraged buyout is simple: "OPM," or "Other People's Money." The leveraged buyout firm attempts to acquire companies while investing as little as possible of its own money. The bulk of the purchase price is borrowed from banks or other knowledgeable lenders engaged in the field of highly leveraged transactions. The LBO firm does not guarantee the related debt financing, which is secured solely by the assets and future cash flows of the target company. Nor does the LBO firm promise the lenders much in the way of operating expertise, since it is typically staffed with financial professionals who know little about how to run a large manufacturing or service business. The LBO firm is basically a transaction promoter, which is a full-time job in and of itself. Finding a acquisition candidate, pricing the deal, performing due diligence, finding financing, and negotiating legal documents is a lengthy and complex process, requiring combinations of contacts and skills that are not easily duplicated.

Since the LBO business emerged from obscurity in the early 1980s, it has become institutionalized. Today, about 150 investment firms specialize in arranging leveraged buyouts. Another 50 to 100 investment banks, venture capital firms, and general investment funds dabble in the field, closing one or two deals per year. Collectively, these buyers work with many of the Fortune 500 companies, and in some cases are significant corporate shareholders, having bought some of these large companies in the frenetic late 1980s, when the LBO market hit its peak. The success of many LBO investments has attracted many blue-chip state, corporate, and employee pension plans to the field and they are now the primary funding sources behind the vast equity pools commanded by the buyout firms. According to the March 1995 *The Private Equity Analyst,* in 1994 LBO funds raised $8.5 billion in new equity "which could, if leveraged at 4:1, acquire corporate assets worth $34 billion."

By using large amounts of leverage, the LBO firm enhances its investment returns because lenders share little or none of the increase in value of the corporate assets. As shown in Chapter 6, high leverage also magnifies the negative impact of downward movements in corporate values. However, even in the worst case, the LBO investor's downside is limited. He can only lose his initial investment, perhaps 20% of the deal's purchase price, while he enjoys practically 100% of the upside. Since corporate earnings tend to have upward tendencies because of inflation and economic growth, the LBO tactic of using lots of borrowed money to buy corporate assets is sensible, particularly if the related acquisition prices are reasonably in line with historical standards.

"Buying right" is the second linchpin of the LBO artist because a premium price can spell failure quickly. Overpaying for a business is costly for two key reasons. First, like any other corporate acquirer, an LBO firm faces smaller returns with each extra dollar it pays for a deal. Second, an LBO firm operates with a small margin for error, even when it buys a deal "right." When it overpays, the acquisition is loaded up with even more debt than would normally be the case. If the deal's operating earnings come in even slightly lower than forecast, its ability to pay debt service is in jeopardy with the higher debt load. Consistent debt service problems lead to a restructuring of the premium-priced LBO's obligations, and this circumstance inevitably requires the LBO firm to offer the creditors concessions in exchange for deferring debt payments or reducing them altogether. Usually, such concessions include giving the lenders "a piece of the action," and any own participation extended to the lenders reduces the LBO firm's own returns. In the extreme case, where the parties cannot reach a compromise, a bankruptcy filing is in order. Many times, a bankruptcy wipes out the value of the LBO firm's investment. Accordingly, LBO investors scour the M&A landscape, searching for transactions that they can buy cheap. Connections, experience, and patience are valuable commodities in this endeavor.

A third leg of the LBO table is enhancing the operating performance of the acquisition. LBO firms seek above-average efficiencies from their operating management teams. Top managers are provided with a meaningful equity participation and they are expected to run the business like owners instead of employees. Many respond by cutting expenses that otherwise would be tolerated under the public ownership model. The result for the LBO firm is a more profitable acquisition that can exceed its projections.

Because many large companies and corporate divisions are sold off through an auction process, LBO firms have a hard time finding relative bargains. In many cases, they turn to out-of-fashion industries that corporate America is avoiding. The auctions for businesses in these unpopular industries draw little interest from synergy players and asking prices are low compared with the popular industries. In other instances, LBO buyers turn to situations in which they may have an advantage in getting the deal at a favorable price. Certain LBO firms have an industry specialty that gives them a leg up on the competition. The Carlyle Group in Washington, DC, for example, invests heavily in defense industries. Thomas H. Lee Company in Boston has a large portfolio of consumer companies. When industry knowledge and out-of-fashion don't help, LBO firms rely on insider contacts. Whom do they know? Who can help them obtain a business at a price that is less than its fair value in an orderly auction?

Insider deals can take many forms. One model is the LBO firm buying a corporate division on the cheap. If the top managers of a division have a good relationship with an LBO firm, they may be able to persuade their parent company to steer the deal to that particular firm. The parent company may be willing to accept less than top dollar for the division to ensure a quick and smooth transaction. In other circumstances the parent company's chief executive may simply be giving the division management a payoff for services rendered. Another commonly-used tactic seen in LBO's is the leveraging-up of the family business at less than full value. In certain situations which I have observed, the older generation is retiring and wants "out" of the business. Like many corporate owners they want to sell their ownership for a lot of money, but they are also thoughtful parents, not wishing to disenfranchise their children by handing the business over to a large corporation that might reorganize the company and install its own executives. The logical compromise for the owners is selling to a financial buyer, who leaves operating control with the younger generation allowing them to retain a significant equity interest. To help the kids, the older generation accepts a lower than market price, because this means less LBO debt. Reduced leverage allows the recapitalized business to start off with a good chance of surviving any unforeseen downturn.

For the most part, privately owned companies and family-operated businesses are under no obligation to search for "top dollar." In some cases where the firm has a large loan outstanding, the lender may require asset sales to be conducted on an arm's length basis, but this standard is difficult to nail down, particularly in a subjective area like corporate valuation. Publicly traded companies face regulatory requirements regarding fair dealing to protect public shareholders against insider enrichment. For many divestures, publicly traded sellers obtain opinions from investment banks, stating that the transaction is fair, from a financial point of view, to the company's shareholders. Designed as an insurance policy against disgruntled shareholders, the fairness opinion is usually delivered by the same investment bank that is handling the deal and thus receiving a fee on the transaction's completion.

The bank's built-in conflict of interest renders its opinion suspect in marginal situations but the practice continues. Because they are client-driven concerns, investment banks demonstrate a tendency to conform their opinions to their clients' requirements. Witness the 1995 brouhaha between AT&T and the public shareholders of LIN Broadcasting. AT&T, which owned 52% of LIN, was trying to buy the remaining 48%. Preferring to pay a low price, it offered the minority shareholders $105 per share for their equity interests and brandished an opinion from Morgan Stanley & Company indicating the price was fair. The LIN minority shareholders, desiring the highest possible figure, countered with a Merrill Lynch letter opining that a fair price was really $155 per share. After much squabbling, the two principals agreed to hire a third investment banker to set the definitive "fair value." Wasserstein Perella & Company split the baby in half by concluding that the "fairest" price was $127.50 per share, or a total of $3.3 billion. With buyer and seller 50% apart, the AT&T/Lin Broadcasting deal highlighted the range of potentially acceptable fair values. It also illustrated the room in which LBO investors and their friends can operate with regard to price.

LBO MECHANICS

The mechanics of implementing an LBO are well known and center around finding a business that can support the debt needed to finance about 80% of its purchase price. While this degree of leverage is typical in real estate, autos, and airplanes—to name a few asset categories—it is uncommon in operating companies that manufacture a product or provide a service. Why? Because operating company values fluctuate widely from year to year. Even the values of big-name corporations exhibit wide ranges. In 1995, the price of B.F. Goodrich stock traded between $41 and $72, a 75% difference in just 12 months. Caterpillar shares moved within a $48 to $75 range, a 56% difference. To justify taking the risk of a significant valuation drop, LBO lenders look for borrowers with a few key characteristics:

- *Low-Tech.* LBO lenders prefer businesses relying on technology that is not subject to rapid change.
- *Solid Track Record.* LBO lenders prefer low-tech businesses with a history of consistent profitability and a pro forma ability to cover LBO debt service.
- *Hard Assets.* As an insurance policy against potential operating problems, LBO lenders prefer borrowers with lots of tangible assets, such as real estate, plant and equipment, inventory, and receivables. When the competition for LBO financing heats up, lenders relax this requirement.
- *Low Indebtedness.* To support acquisition debt, the target company needs to have low leverage in the first place.

In reviewing potential buyout candidates, LBO firms balance these lender preferences against likely purchase prices. Basic calculations are performed to determine a would-be acquisition's attractiveness to the lending community.

Consider an LBO firm's likely consideration of the acquisition of Medrad, Inc., a medical equipment manufacturer which was sold

EXHIBIT 18-1   Medrad, Inc., selected financial information (in millions except for share data)

	Year Ended January 31		
	1993	**1994**	**1995**
Income Statement Data			
Net revenue	$67.4	$71.7	$78.3
EBIT	8.2	7.8	10.8
Net earnings	5.3	5.7	7.3
Earnings per share	$ 0.88	$ 0.92	$ 1.17

	At January 31, 1995
Balance Sheet Data	
Current assets	$45.0
Total assets	66.5
Current liabilities	11.9
Long-term debt	4.6
Shareholders' equity	49.1
Share Data	
Price range Oct. 94–Jan. 95	13¼ to 16¼
Shares outstanding	6.2 million

in September 1995 to a Product Line Extender. Medrad had a consistent record of profitability and was engaged in a medium-tech business. When Medrad decided to consider selling out in early 1995, its share price was in the mid-teens and the company had ample LBO debt servicing capabilities. Exhibit 18-1 sets forth selected financial information.

HOW MUCH CAN THE LBO FIRM PAY?

Medrad is a good LBO candidate, but how much can an LBO firm pay? The $10.8 million EBIT number is the first place to start. Using a 1.3 EBIT/Interest ratio as a "rule of thumb" for lenders, Medrad can support $8.3 million per year of interest payments (i.e., 10.8 ÷ 1.3 = 8.3). Figuring an 8% interest rate on LBO debt (2.25% over the 10-year

EXHIBIT 18-2   Medrad LBO enterprise value

	Millions	%
LBO debt	$104	80
Equity	26	20
LBO enterprise value	$130	100

U.S. Treasury Bond), Medrad can shoulder about $104 million of debt (i.e., $8.3 \div 0.08 = 104$). Applying a debt-equity ratio of 80/20 to the transaction means the LBO firm can give Medrad a total price of $130 value, including $26 million of new equity and the assumption of any outstanding debts (see Exhibit 18-2).

Medrad's long-term debt in early 1995 totaled $4.6 million. Since this debt must be either assumed or repaid by the LBO buyer, it is subtracted from the enterprise value. The net amount is Medrad's equity acquisition value, which is divided by the number of shares outstanding to provide a maximum LBO per share value (see Exhibit 18-3).

This $20.23 per share value is a guide to LBO affordability. Given that it is higher than the market trading range of $13¼ to 16¼, it holds open the possibility of Medrad selling out to an LBO firm. The number, however, is a rough estimate. Further due diligence might uncover hidden assets or liabilities that could increase or decrease the value.

Projections prepared by the Company and made publicly available in SEC filings indicated that Medrad was in a position both to support an LBO-type debt load and to provide lenders with an appropriate LBO safety margin. Exhibit 18-4 provides summary projected data for a $130 million deal.

EXHIBIT 18-3   Medrad LBO per share value
(in millions, except per share)

Enterprise value	$130.0
Less: Existing debt	(4.6)
Adjusted enterprise value	125.4
Divided by outstanding	
Medrad shares	÷6.2
LBO per share value	$ 20.23

EXHIBIT 18-4   Medrad, Inc., hypothetical $130 million LBO summary projections (in millions)

		Year Ended January 31				
	Actual		**Projected**			
	1995	**1996**	**1997**	**1998**	**1999**	**2000**
Income Statement Data						
Net revenue	78.3	89.4	107.8	122.1	143.6	170.3
EBIT	10.8	13.0	16.1	19.3	23.4	28.7
Assumed LBO interest	8.3	8.3	8.3	8.3	8.3	8.3
EBIT/Interest ratio[1]	1.3	1.6	1.9	2.3	2.8	3.5

[1] Minimum acceptable ratio is 1.3×.

The projections reflect the usual seller's optimism with respect to future results, and Medrad's EBIT is forecast to increase at a compound annual rate of 22%, significantly higher than recent historical performance. Nevertheless, even if management's projections are trimmed, Medrad still covers its debt service easily on a pro forma basis.

HOW HIGH IS THE MEDRAD LBO'S RETURN?

LBO firms invest in transactions that have the potential to provide equity returns of 25% to 35% on a compound annual basis. Using the $20.43 per share purchase price and leverage scheme outlined earlier, the Medrad LBO example passes this rate of return hurdle with an estimated IRR of 59%.

The rate of return calculation shown in Exhibit 18-5 is typical for a buyout. It assumes no dividends over the five-year holding period, 20% debt repayment, and a final sale price that is equivalent to the 1995 purchase price in terms of the EBIT multiple. In this exhibit, the IRR incorporates management's optimistic 22% annual growth forecast for sales and EBIT. Even if this aggressive growth rate is cut in half, the LBO shows an excellent IRR, raising the likelihood that the company's price will go higher as investors increase their bids. When the purchase price increases, the corresponding IRR declines. Exhibit 18-6 shows IRRs under several purchase price and future growth scenarios.

EXHIBIT 18-5   Medrad LBO rate of return calculation

1995 Start		2000 Finish	
Buy Medrad at 12 × EBIT	$130 million	Sell Medrad at 12 × EBIT	$345 million
Incur debt	$104 million	Repay debt	(84)
Invest equity	26	Proceeds to LBO investors	$261 million
Total financing	$130 million	Less beginning equity	(26)
		Capital gain	$235 million

Rate of Return Calculation
—$235 million capital gain, before taxes ($261 million profit less $26 million original equity investment).
—IRR = 59% on $26 million original equity investment, compounded annually over five years.

A potential Medrad LBO buyer would run numerous other financial sensitivities on a personal computer. For example, to determine downside protections in the deal, the sale price in the year 2000 might be reduced, future growth rates might be further decreased, or the purchase price might be raised another $1 or $2 per share. Under many of these scenarios, Medrad is an attractive LBO candidate at a purchase price in the low 20s per share.

In the actual Medrad deal, LBO firms competed with operating companies. The latter had the potential to achieve operating synergies and some had strategic objectives in which price was a secondary consideration. Including synergies, several of these operating companies

EXHIBIT 18-6   IRR matrix hypothetical Medrad LBO (% IRR)

Medrad per Share Purchase Price	Medrad Growth Rates (%)	
	11	22
$20	39	59
$22	28	47

could have paid a higher price and still obtained favorable returns on investment. Furthermore, Medrad participated in a fashionable industry—medical products—and had a leading market share in its special segment of this market. The ultimate outcome of the Medrad sales process was its acquisition by a Product Line Extender, Schering AG Germany, at a price of $28 per share in October 1995. Schering AG Germany is a multinational medical products company, with annual sales in excess of $3 billion.

SUCCESSFUL LBOs

Putting together leveraged buyouts is not the intellectual equivalent of rocket science. LBO technology is well established and broadly accepted by institutional lenders and equity investors of every stripe. The field has many players. Some LBO firms, like Kohlberg Kravis, are a constant market presence and control many operating businesses. Others are niche participants, perhaps only closing a small deal every year or two. Based on current equity fund balances of $10 to $15 billion, LBO firms collectively have a buying power of $50 to $60 billion. This large cash kitty keeps them on the lookout for any acquisition, large or small.

Although every deal has unique aspects, the LBO firms try to follow a well-worn path that has resulted in large profits. The road has five major steps and usually covers several years. The following brief chronology sets forth the typical deal:

1. *Closing the Transaction.* The first step is buying the deal "right," and obtaining enough debt to enhance prospective equity returns.
2. *Realizing Operating Efficiencies.* With a well-motivated management team, the LBO sets out to reduce expenses below the levels tolerated in the LBO's prior life. Formerly a publicly traded company, corporate division, or family business, the LBO incurred many expenses that were not totally necessary.
3. *Selling Equity to the Public.* With a short, but adequate, track record of LBO operation, the owners wait for a favorable stock market into which they can sell a portion of the LBO's equity to the public. A favorable market and a stockbroker's hype result in

a premium price for the LBO equity. Proceeds of the offering are used to repay debt, thereby reducing the LBO's financial risk. The Wall Street slang for Step 3 is "flipping the equity." Many LBOs attempt to go public shortly after going private, almost in the same time as it takes to flip a hamburger on a grill.

4. *Secondary Equity Offerings.* Once the LBO's public shares are seasoned from a few months of trading, the LBO investors are free to start selling their own shares through additional stock offerings. While this frees up cash and leaves the existing management group in control, it does not provide the maximum price for the investors' shares. Top dollar can only be achieved through ceding control to a corporate buyer.

5. *The Final Exit: Selling Control.* At this point, the LBO has deleveraged and it has a successful history as a public company. The search begins for a Strategic Buyer or Market Share/Product Line Extender that can afford to pay a substantial premium over the market price for complete control.

A recent example of the successful implementation of these tactics was the Hook-SupeRx buyout, which completed Step 5 in July 1994 by merging with Revco.

The Hook-SupeRx story began in December 1986, when a major portion of the retail drugstore business of The Kroger Company was acquired in a leveraged buyout at a cost of $415 million. Christened Hook-SupeRx, Inc., after the trade names of two major chains involved in the deal, the LBO had a small equity component, reflecting lenders' confidence in the retail drugstore industry's consistent earnings and low-tech attributes. Of this purchase price, less than 10% was put up by the equity investors, which included an investment bank, operating management and various institutional investors. The remaining portion of the purchase price was borrowed, giving Hook-SupeRx a beginning debt/equity ratio of 10:1. After several years of rising EBIT and two add-on acquisitions, the company had substantial operating income, but it was barely breaking into the black after interest charges. Rather than await further debt reduction through internal cash generation, management took advantage of a favorable stock market to increase shareholders' equity and reduce indebtedness. In June 1992, the company sold 7.9 million shares of common stock at $13.00 per share. At this valuation, the LBO investors had a paper profit of 4× their original $3.00 per share investment. Two years later, the entire company was sold to Revco D.S., Inc., a much larger drugstore chain, for $633 million in a classic Market Share Extension deal. In April 1996, Revco was almost swallowed up by Rite Aid, the nation's No. 1 drugstore chain, in a $1.8 billion merger, but the Federal Trade Commission blocked the deal on antitrust grounds.

The leveraged buyout of Welbilt Corporation is another good example of an LBO following the five steps. Kohlberg & Company led a $227 million leveraged buyout (net of cash-on-hand) of Welbilt in August 1988. Welbilt was a well-known manufacturer of commercial food service equipment. Equity in the deal was thin, amounting to only 13% of the purchase price, as shown in Exhibit 18-7.

Three years into the deal, Welbilt's management had made a strategic acquisition, discontinued unprofitable product lines, cut working capital and implemented cost improvement programs, which included a 15% reduction in its salaried workforce. Nevertheless, a crushing interest burden and difficult industry conditions presented the company with problems in paying down its debts. As its industry rebounded and the stock market advanced, Welbilt completed a $87 million initial public offering in November 1993, despite recording losses in two of the prior three years. The proceeds from the successful offering were used to repay borrowings, thus reducing Welbilt's financial risk. At the $18 per share offering price, Kohlberg had an approximate 100% paper return on its investment over its five-year holding period. Twelve months later, the stock market continued to be buoyant and the company's results were promising. After considering a public sale of its shares, Kohlberg cashed out of its investment at $30 per share, as Welbilt was sold in its entirety to Berisford International, PLC, a British conglomerate. The internal rate of return (IRR) on Kohlberg's buyout equity was 23% over its six-year holding period.

EXHIBIT 18-7   Welbilt LBO financing

	Millions	%
Debt	$197	87
Equity	30	13
	$227	100

A recent example of "buying right" and "flipping equity" was the initial public offering of U.S. Office Products Company in February 1995. A collection of six contract stationery businesses formed to create a national chain, U.S. Office Products sold a 46% interest to the public for $32.5 million, placing a value on the total enterprise of $84 million. The total consideration paid by the company to acquire the six stationers was only $56 million, so pre-IPO shareholders enjoyed an immediate $28 million paper gain. Pursuant to this complicated series of transactions, Jonathan Ledecky, Chairman of the newly formed U.S. Office Products, sold General Office Products (GOP), one of the six stationers, to U.S. Office Products for $17.6 million. Only five months earlier, Mr. Ledecky had acquired GOP from Steelcase, Inc. in a leveraged buyout for $4.5 million, investing $1.2 million of his own money. As if to apologize for Mr. Ledecky's windfall profit of more than 10 times his investment in five months, the U.S. Office Products prospectus stated, "The Company (U.S. Office Products) believes that Steelcase was motivated to sell GOP by corporate concerns other than obtaining the highest price . . ."

In the Truck Components leveraged buyout, the sponsors didn't wait even five months. In May 1994, Castle Harlan, a well-known merchant bank, acquired Truck Components, Inc. in concert with its management for $171 million. Only $30 million, or 18%, of the purchase price was financed with equity; the rest came in the form of debt. A short four months later, Truck Components flipped its equity, completing a $35 million initial public stock offering, at $10 per share in a strong equity market. Given that the sponsors had only paid $3 per share for their equity, they were then sitting on a 333% paper gain after a holding period of only four months. With sales and income showing significant gains over the next 11 months, Castle Harlan and management cashed out in July 1995 by selling the entire business to Johnston American Industries for $16 per share. In little more than a year, the Truck Components LBO went through Steps 1 through 5, and enabled its investors to quintuple their original investment.

Not all leveraged buyouts are as successful as Truck Components, GOP, Welbilt, and Hook-SupeRx. Many go bankrupt as reality fails to meet their forecasts, and bankruptcy intervenes. Although their public relations firms downplay this fact, almost every major LBO firm has had a large bankruptcy among its history of transactions. KKR, for example, suffered the bankruptcy of Jim Walter Corporation, which it acquired for over $2 billion, and RJR-Nabisco, the largest KKR LBO on record, has shown marginal returns. Revco, the company which acquired Hook-SupeRx in 1994, went bankrupt in 1988 after it was unable to service its debt from a 1986 LBO. Salomon Brothers, a well-respected investment firm, sponsored the Revco deal. The 1980s saw many failed LBOs, and investors in the 1990s studied the lessons learned. Today's deals, by comparison, tend to have purchase prices with lower EBIT multiples and to use less leverage than the 1980s version.

THE IMPORTANCE OF DEBT FINANCING

LBO activity is directly related to the enthusiasm of banks, insurance companies, pension funds and specialized debt funds toward lending money to highly leveraged businesses. This enthusiasm waxes and wanes with the economy's prospects, acquisition prices, interest rates, and prior LBO performance records. Experienced LBO firms maintain a broad array of lender relationships and a few brief meetings or phone calls with these lenders can provide a good sense of a deal's affordability.

As a general rule, LBO lenders are divided into two camps: senior lenders and subordinated lenders. The senior lender category is relatively risk averse and is composed primarily of large commercial banks and insurance companies. In evaluating a transaction, they need to see a substantial cushion between their loan value and the LBO's purchase price. In an ideal case, the senior lender is fully secured by tangible assets such as accounts receivable, inventories, and real estate. Few deals meet this collateral test and, as a result, most senior lenders are satisfied to look at cash flows as the second layer of protection for their loans. In practice, senior lenders rarely finance more than 50% to 60% of an LBO, so the LBO's value has to decline considerably before their principal is threatened. Subordinated lenders usually fill the 20% to 30% financing gap between the senior debt financing and the promotor's equity. Commonly referred to as "mezzanine lenders," reflecting their position between the senior debt "upper deck" and the equity investor "lower deck," subordinated lenders usually receive a higher interest rate than the senior lenders, and a small equity participation.

EXHIBIT 18-8   LBO financing model

	% of Purchase Price	Prospective Annual IRR	Risk of Loss
Debt Financing			
Senior	50%	LIBOR + 2%	Low
Subordinated	30	12%–15%	Medium
Total debts	80		
Equity Financing	20		
	100%	25%–35%	High

Overall, the prospective subordinated debt return in an LBO is designed to fall between the respective IRRs of the senior lenders and the equity investors. In the 1980s, subordinated LBO debts were referred to as "junk bonds," but the nomenclature changed with the times so we now have mezzanine loans. The 1990s buyout financing model appears in Exhibit 18-8. As illustrated in this exhibit the return of the financing tranche corresponds to its risk; thus, senior lenders incur the lowest risk, but also receive the lowest return.

RISK OF RETURN

LBO firms aim for compound annual returns of 25% to 35% on their equity commitments. This objective is consistent with the academic-oriented Capital Asset Pricing Model, although few LBO sponsors can explain it in such terms. Remember the CAPM as it describes the required rate of return (K) on a company's common stock:

$$K = R_f + \beta\,(E(R)_m - R_f)$$

Where

K = Required rate of return on equity investment

R_f = Risk-free rate, such as the yield on 10-year U.S. Treasury Bonds

β = Beta of company's common equity

$E(R_m)$ = Expected return of broad stock market, usually considered to be 6% to 8% over risk-free rate.

The risk-free rate and expected return are the same for each calculation, but the beta varies significantly among industries and companies. According to the CAPM, the effect of higher leverage changes a company's beta through the next formula:

$$\beta_{\text{Leveraged}} = \beta_{\text{Before Leverage}} \times [1 + (D/S)(1 - T)]$$

Where

$\beta_{\text{leveraged}}$ = Beta of a company with leverage
$\beta_{\text{Before Leverage}}$ = Beta of a company's equity, assuming the company is debt-free
D/S = Company's debts divided by market value of its equity
T = Income tax rate of company

The higher beta associated with leverage implies a higher cost of capital and leverage increases. This makes intuitive sense since higher leverage implies more risk for the equity investor, and more risk-taking should result in higher rewards. A brief example illustrates how expected equity returns should increase under LBO conditions.

Carter-Wallace, Inc. is a debt-free company that manufactures consumer toiletries such as Arid Extra-Dry Deodorant. Its stock trades on the New York Stock Exchange and has a 1.20 beta. According to the CAPM, shareholders expect a 14.4% return on their equity investment, as set forth in Exhibit 18-9.

If Carter-Wallace were to undergo a $600 million leveraged buyout, its beta would increase to 4.08, as shown in the next calculation (Exhibit 18-10).

EXHIBIT 18-9   Carter-Wallace cost of equity[1]

$$K = R_f + \beta (E(R)_m - R_f)$$
$$K = 6\% + 1.2 (13\% - 6\%)$$
$$K = 14.4\%$$

Where

K = Required rate of return for Carter-Wallace shareholder.
R_f = 6% (i.e., yield on 10-year U.S. Treasury Bond).
β = 1.20
$E(R_m)$ = 13% (i.e., R_f + 7%) required rate of return on the broad stock market.

[1]As of November 1995.

EXHIBIT 18-10   Carter-Wallace LBO Beta

$$\beta_{\text{Leveraged}} = \beta_{\text{Before Leverage}} \times [1 + (D/S)(1 - T)]$$
$$\beta_{\text{Leveraged}} = 1.20 \times [1 + (80/20)(1 - .4)]$$
$$\beta_{\text{Leveraged}} = 1.20 \times [1 + 2.4]$$
$$\beta_{\text{Leveraged}} = 4.08$$

The higher beta suggests that an equity investor in the hypothetical buyout, such as an LBO firm, will need a 35% expected rate of return before it considers the deal (Exhibit 18-11).

Most LBO firms publicize the fact that they seek equity returns, on a compound annual basis, of 25% to 35% annually. This goal is consistent with CAPM theory and justifiable in light of alternative investment strategies available in the marketplace.

JUNK BOND FINANCING

During the height of the buyout frenzy, a string of successes led to a rush of lenders into the LBO business. Most had little experience in highly leveraged lending and put their capital to work in poorly structured transactions. In many cases, lenders permitted LBO firms to leverage their equity at unsustainable ratios of indebtedness—typically 10:1 or higher. As the 1990–1991 recession set in and corporate earnings fell, many of the acquired businesses became insolvent. Particularly hard-hit were the subordinated lenders, the "junk bond" buyers, who had no collateral to protect themselves when deals went bad, and limited upside when transactions were wildly successful. In studying 83 large LBOs completed between 1985 and 1989, Steven Kaplan, a

EXHIBIT 18-11   Carter-Wallace LBO cost of equity

$$K = R_f + \beta_{\text{LBO}} (E(R_m) - R_f)$$
$$K_{\text{LBO}} = 6\% + 4.08 \, (13\% - 6\%)$$
$$K_{\text{LBO}} = 35\%$$

University of Chicago professor, found that one-third of the companies defaulted on their debts. Many others had to restructure their obligations to avoid a default.

Now, lenders are more conservative in their buyout lending. Debt-to-equity levels rarely exceed 4 : 1. Watching in the wings to prevent a repeat of the 1980s are bank supervisors, insurance company regulators, and mezzanine fund directors. And while mezzanine financings and junk bonds still represent that critical 20% to 30% junior slice of most deals, the subordinated community is far more professional in its deal evaluation today than it was in the 1980s.

THE PROCESS

LBO firms search for acquisition candidates in much the same way as operating acquirers. In many cases, they search and screen corporate databases, select a few eligible candidates, and approach them directly. At other times, an intermediary such as an investment bank or business broker introduces the buyout firm to the deal. In some cases, the LBO sponsor enters the transaction through a management or owner contact. Since the principal motivation behind an LBO is neither a strategic diversification nor a market share/product line extension, the buyer's due diligence isn't focused on synergies or similar operating benefits. Rather, the investigation centers on two items: one, the ability of management, once it is properly motivated, to improve performance; and two, the probability of the acquisition producing cash from the sale of underutilized assets immediately after the closing. At the start of its due diligence, the LBO firm actively solicits lending sources. It tries to nail down financing commitments early to ensure that the money is available if purchase negotiations are concluded successfully. Unlike many corporate buyers with substantial balance sheets, an LBO firm's ability to close a deal is totally dependent on the willingness of third-party lenders to take risks, and lender behavior is sometimes hard to predict. Getting these lenders in line early reduces the likelihood that the buyout sponsor is spinning its wheels on a deal that can ultimately prove to be unbankable.

The target's owner has a different priority as LBO discussions commence. Sellers need to pressure prospective LBO shoppers to confirm their financing sources before intensive due diligence takes place. While most established LBO firms are very professional, there still remains a fringe group of buyout sponsors who window-shop and repeatedly have problems coming up with their promised financial backing. To limit the Window Shopper problem, sellers can limit their discussion to the 100 or so LBO firms that have set up blind pool funds with sizable coinvestors. The resulting large sums of cash on hand provide the firms with instant financial credibility. One prominent firm, Forstman Little & Company, raised $1.2 billion in 1995 for its latest LBO equity fund, and had $800 million remaining in its own mezzanine fund at year's end.

SUMMARY

Leveraged buyouts have reached a high level of acceptance in corporate America. Over 150 firms specialize in the technique, which has been heavily supported by a variety of banks, insurance companies, pension funds, and debt funds. LBO technology is well known and rests on the basic principle of enhancing equity returns through leverage. The LBO market overheated in the 1980s, and many high-priced deals failed to survive the 1990–1991 recession without a debt restructuring. The lending market now is more circumspect about the pricing and leverage contained in these acquisitions.

19

ASSET DEALS, "BUST-UP" TRANSACTIONS, AND BOTTOM FISHING

Asset deals, "bust-up" transactions, and bottom fishing are acquisitions dominated by financial buyers. These transactions occur when the perceived value of the underlying assets or subsidiaries exceed the company's market value. None of these activities are as glamorous as the LBO business; and consequently; the major players using these techniques have never been accorded the status and respectability of the important LBO firms. In fact, most of the financial buyers in these three deal categories prefer to shun the spotlight, since many of their moneymaking tactics require a great degree of stealth.

Such deals are far more analytically rigorous than the average transaction. Typically, the target is undergoing severe operating, financial, or legal problems, which prove so vexing to the standard panapoly of corporate and LBO buyers that they're not interested. The seller, therefore, must go down the M&A food chain and approach those buyers that specialize in finding value where others can't.

This isn't to say that the majority of asset, bust-up, and bottom-fishing deals are initiated by the seller. Quite the opposite. In many cases, the prospective buyer is an uninvited, and unwanted, guest that has determined the target's value is misunderstood by the corporate marketplace. In the Darwinian world of mergers, it doesn't take long for the wolves to start braying outside the door of an undervalued business having difficulties.

As this chapter illustrates, these acquisition methods frequently involve the dismissal of the candidate's existing management team. For this reason, the would-be buyer can expect little or no cooperation from the target's executives, who actually may be undermining the buyer's efforts to gain access to information. Any circumscribed due diligence effort implies more risk for the purchaser, which is reluctant to buy a pig in a poke. The acquirer discounts its offering price accordingly.

1. *Asset Deals*. The acquirer liquidates the corporation on a piecemeal basis, perhaps retaining a few assets for operating purposes.
2. *Bust-Up Transactions*. The acquirer buys a multidivision company and sells off the divisions.
3. *Bottom Fishing*. The acquirer searches for distressed firms at rock-bottom prices.

ASSET DEALS

In Wall Street parlance, an asset deal is an acquisition transaction whereby the buyer has no intention of continuing to operate the target's business. For the most part, the asset buyer has no use for the acquisition's intangible elements, such as the knowledge and skills of its employees, the lists of its satisfied customers and suppliers, and the goodwill stored in its reputation and history. Rather, the acquirer is making the deal to get its hands on the seller's tangible assets—its receivables, inventories, plant and equipment, and real estate. In certain instances, a select number of valuable intangible assets such as brand names, technology, and patents have cash values. If the buyer is a manufacturer or service business rather than a financial investor, perhaps a few desired assets are retained for use in the buyer's own operations. The rest are sold off piecemeal to a variety of interested parties. If the buyer is a financial investor, all the acquired assets are liquidated and the associated liabilities repaid, with the buyer hoping to turn a short-term profit on its initial purchase investment. As the target's operations are shut down, the liquidator lays off all employees with the exception of a skeleton crew to wind down the business.

Given the human cost of layoffs, the community dislocation in business closings, and the bad publicity of shutdowns, it is not surprising that many asset buyers prefer to remain in the background. Furthermore, this sort of activity is a lightning rod for litigation, which can crop up from disgruntled employees, local governments, and other former constituencies of the acquired business. For these reasons, asset deals remain the province of select number of financial buyers and a few thick-skinned corporations, that don't mind taking the heat for their aggressive tactics in extracting value from a troubled situation.

Two prevalent kinds of asset deals are liquidations and transformations.

Liquidations

A firm facing imminent liquidation has poor future prospects and a history of losses. Would-be purchasers view the business as a collection of assets that are more profitable in the hands of others.

An asset buyer doesn't view the target as a going concern with the potential to generate earnings far into the future. Instead, it examines the worth of each asset category in a quick sell-off, aggregates these liquidation values, and subtracts the estimated cost of closing the business and paying off its liabilities. If this calculation provides a positive number, such as $50 million, the would-be buyer has established its ceiling purchase price. From this $50 million must then be subtracted the buyer's time-adjusted rate of return requirement and the carrying cost of any borrowed funds.

Unless the target business has substantial intangible assets such as well-respected brand names, exclusive patents, or quasi-monopoly operating rights, the analyst's first "back of the envelope" evaluation focuses on historical balance sheet financial data. For each balance sheet item, the analyst determines an estimated range of "liquidated value" percentages, which are based on historical experiences for similar businesses. Later on, after a due diligence investigation, these percentages are adjusted to include the new information. Consider the hypothetical case of Diablo Corporation, a troubled manufacturer of construction materials, which is being reviewed by several asset buyers. Exhibit 19-1 provides the relevant data.

Assuming a 30% annual rate of return requirement, an ability to finance $25 million of the purchase price at 10% and a one-year holding

EXHIBIT 19-1   Diablo Corporation summary liquidation analysis November 1995 (in millions)

	Historical Book Value	Estimated Liquidation Percentages	Estimated Liquidation Values
Assets			
Cash	$ 10	100	$ 10
Accounts receivable	40	70	28
Inventory	40	50	20
	$ 90		$ 58
Plant and equipment	$100	40	$ 40
Goodwill	20	0	0
	$210	Net inflows	$ 98
Liabilities and Equity			
Short-term debt	$ 15	100	$(15)
Other current liabilities	25	100	(25)
	$ 40		$(40)
Stockholders' equity	170	Costs of shutdown	(8)
	$210	Net outflows	$(48)
		Net Liquidation Value (98 − 48)	$ 50

period, the asset buyer is willing to pay $42.5 million for Diablo. The calculation appears in Exhibit 19-2. The reader will note that the $42.5 million affordability price is far below Diablo's stockholders' equity of $170 million as shown in Exhibit 19-1. This significant discount to book value is characteristic of most liquidation analyses and it emphasizes an important point: Most firms realize a better price when they are sold as going concerns, whereby their respective values are based on future earnings power rather than on their tangible asset compositions. To prove this assertion, one can look at the November 1995 pricing for the Dow Jones Industrials, which were then trading at 3.9× historical book value.

By way of illustration, Exhibit 19-3 sets forth a summary liquidation analysis of Cintas Corporation, a leading uniform rental company with a long history of profitability. The $76 million liquidation estimate translated into only a $1.62 per share value, which was a huge discount to historical cost and then existing market indicators. In May 1994, for

EXHIBIT 19-2   Diablo Corporation affordability calculation for one-year holding period (in millions)

Net liquidation value	$50.0
Less: 10% carrying cost on $25 million in borrowed funds	(2.5)
30% IRR on $17.5 million equity investment	(5.0)
Asset buyer affordability price	$42.5

EXHIBIT 19-3   Cintas Corporation hypothetical liquidation analysis May 31, 1994 (in millions)

	Historical Book Value	Estimated Liquidation Percentages	Estimated Liquidation Values
Assets			
Cash and marketable securities	$ 61	100	$ 61
Accounts receivable	56	75	42
Inventories and uniforms in service	103	50	52
Prepaid expenses	1	0	0
	$221		$ 155
Plant and equipment, net	$193	60	$ 116
Goodwill and other assets	88	0	0
	$502	Net inflows	$ 271
Liabilities and Equity			
Stated liabilities	$191	92	$(175)
Shareholders' equity	311	Lease termination payments	(5)
	$502	Cost of shutdown	(15)
		Net outflows	(195)
		Net Liquidation Value (271 − 195)	$ 76

example, Cinta's per share book value was $6.57 and its per share market value as a "going concern" was $31.30 on the NASDAQ. Admittedly, the liquidation analysis ignored some precious intangible assets such as Cintas's trade names in selected markets and a proprietary management information system for the uniform rental business. But these sorts of additions would have to be worth hundreds of millions of dollars before the liquidation value even approached 50% of the going concern value. Unless a company's prospects are hopeless, a seller realizes more value by avoiding an "asset sale" in favor of a "going concern" sale.

Transforming a Corporate Asset

When an operating company pursues an asset deal, it usually covets just a portion of the acquiree's total asset base. The remaining elements of the business are extraneous. In one transaction, for example, Ames Department Stores bought ailing G.C. Murphy & Co. for $205 million. It laid off G.C. Murphy's employees and emptied the stores of all inventory and fixtures. Over the next several months, Ames remodeled 110 of the former G.C. Murphy stores with Ames fixtures and restocked them with fresh inventory. Through this classic asset deal, Ames singled out the most attractive G.C. Murphy store locations. It then transformed them into new Ames stores in a process that went a lot faster than finding 110 new locations separately.

The Ames/G.C. Murphy transaction highlighted real estate, but some corporate asset deals involve intangible assets. In one transaction, a communications firm paid $11 million for an FM radio station with no earnings history, few employees, and practically zero book value. Why? The station owned a license to broadcast its FM signal in a large metropolitan area, and the federal government had stopped issuing new broadcast licenses in that market a long time ago. After the acquisition, the buyer strengthened the station's signal, expanded its marketing budget and changed the music format. The station was later sold to a large media conglomerate for three times the original purchase price.

Key Risks of Asset Deals

In both deals, the buyer transformed the substance of a rundown company's assets. This tactic is far riskier than buying a profitable business and "tweaking" its operations here and there to realize 10% more earnings through synergies. Because of the risk, corporate buyers exercise substantial due diligence before entering into a true asset deal.

Financial investors are active asset buyers, but they have little interest in transforming the acquired assets' characteristics. Rather, the financial player faces other risks. Even after it completes a thorough due diligence, it can't be sure its estimated resale prices are accurate, for appraisals are inherently uncertain. Correct timing is also an issue. If the aforementioned Diablo deal takes two years instead of one year to unwind, the buyer's IRR is halved. And, the uncertainty level goes up as the asset category becomes less common. Specialized machinery and equipment, for example, may require years to unload at a reasonable price.

Financing Asset Deals

Like other corporate acquirers, asset purchasers try to enhance their equity returns through the use of leverage. If the acquirer is a financial buyer without a strong corporate balance sheet, it looks for debt financing by turning to a special class of lender that extends credit primarily on the basis of collateral values, rather than on the basis of past, present, and future operating results. Commercial finance companies represent the bulk of these asset-based lenders, for they have demonstrated the expertise to make such marginal loans without losing their shirts. Commercial finance companies loan against tangible assets such as accounts receivable, inventory, plant and equipment, and real estate. Many make loans collaterized by intangible assets such as patents, brand names, or customer lists. In most cases, however, the borrower has a difficult time justifying to the asset-based lender the value of such intangibles.

As the lender completes its study of the would-be borrower's assets and operations, the various tangible asset categories are allocated specific loan-to-value ratios. The range of ratios varies considerably. With accounts receivables, for example, the lender considers the credit quality of the borrower's customers. If the borrower is selling to the Fortune 500, the loan-to-value ratio is much higher than if its customers are unknown "Mom & Pop" enterprises. Likewise, if the borrower's inventory is a readily salable product such as office supplies,

**EXHIBIT 19-4   Guidelines of asset-based
lenders**

Tangible Asset	Loan-to-Value Ratio
Accounts receivable	50%–80%
Inventory	30%–60%
Plant and equipment	10%–50%
Real estate	30% to over 100%

the loan-to-value ratio is higher than if the inventory is a slow-moving product such as heavy machinery. Typical ranges of loan-to-value ratios for tangible assets are shown in Exhibit 19-4. Note that "value" refers to historical book value, rather than appraised value.

Developing loan-to-value ratios for *intangible* assets requires extra effort. Since the assets are intangible, they usually have little representation on the balance sheet, so the lender begins its analysis by commissioning an appraisal. Most intangible asset appraisals are quite subjective since the assets in question are unique and valuation comparisons are few. Nevertheless, the appraisal is a starting point for lender and borrower alike in constructing loan-to-value ratios for intangible assets such as patents, brand names, or customer lists.

Loaning money to financial buyers for asset deals is a risky business, and commercial financial companies are compensated accordingly. Interest rates on such loans equal or exceed junk bond yields and the financings often include large up-front fees and back-loaded equity participations. Given the 25% to 35% IRR target of financial buyers, the availability of financing is more important than a two or three percentage point premium in interest costs.

Operating companies that intend to transform selected assets borrow off their own balance sheets. A well-capitalized buyer has access to a range of debt sources that is far broader than the commercial finance community.

BUST-UP TRANSACTIONS

A bust-up transaction is a sophisticated asset liquidation. Instead of the would-be buyer evaluating the target's disparate balance sheet categories such as inventories, accounts receivable and real estate, it appraises the target as a collection of separate business units, each of which can be sold off through a distinct auction. Bust-up techniques are thus applied best either to conglomerates with multiple divisions engaged in unrelated businesses or to companies with various complementary businesses that don't fit together well. Because the bust-up buyer is purchasing the target for one price and expecting to sell the pieces for a higher collective amount, a bust-up deal is an example of negative synergy, since more value is created by dismantling the parts than by putting them together.

Bust-up transactions are rare these days. Responding to an upsurge in this activity in the mid 1980s, the government closed loopholes in the tax laws that promoted them. Now, the revised tax burden makes most prospective bust-ups uneconomic. Nevertheless, a bust-up analysis is still a routine part of the valuation of a multiline company, so we will cover the topic here in an abbreviated fashion.

For the most part, bust-up acquirers are financial investors. They have no intention of managing the acquisition's businesses to improve performance. After the target's various component businesses are sold off, its liabilities repaid, and its headquarters staff disbanded, the financial investor moves on to the next deal.

Sample Bust-Up Analysis

As an example of how financial investors approach bust-up analysis, I used information from the 1995 Annual Report of National Service Industries, Inc. (NSI), a diversified manufacturing and service company. At August 1995, NSI comprised three core businesses—lighting equipment, textile rental, and specialty chemicals—which had no operating synergy. Two smaller NSI businesses, insulation service and envelope manufacturing, had no apparent connection either. Despite the varied nature of its operations, NSI's formula seemed to work. Earnings had risen in each of the five previous years and the company maintained a strong balance sheet. Summary operating and market data at August 1995 appeared as shown in Exhibit 19-5.

The company's valuation ratios reflected its solid financial condition. A prospective acquirer would have had to pay a healthy price in a takeover. For the purposes of this illustration, a $42 per share bid (representing a 40% premium to the $30 market price) was necessary to

EXHIBIT 19-5   National Service Industries, Inc., summary of financial and market data (in millions, except per share and ratios)

Income Statement	Year Ended August 31, 1995	1991–1995 Compound Annual Growth Rate[1] (%)
Revenues	$1,990	5.3
EBIT	160	8.8
Net income	94	7.3
Earnings per share	1.93	7.7

Balance Sheet	At August 31, 1995
Cash	$ 82
Net working capital, including cash	438
Fixed assets	350
Total debt	33
Stockholders' equity	744

Market Data	At August 31, 1995
Share price	$30
P/E multiple	15.5 ×
Price/Book value	1.9×
Enterprise value/EBIT	9.4×
Dividend yield	3.7%

[1]Normalized data used for 1991.

purchase NSI. Could an acquirer have made money by buying NSI's shares at this price and then selling off its business divisions on a piecemeal basis?

Business Segment Analysis

The first step in my bust-up evaluation was valuing each of NSI's business segments. Note 8 of the company's 1995 financial statements provided summary information on the segments' respective operating performance. A portion of Note 8 is reproduced as Exhibit 19-6.

The lighting equipment division was the star performer of the group, with a two-year increase in EBIT of 59%. The steady recovery of the construction market contributed to this gain. The other business

**EXHIBIT 19-6   National Service Industries, Inc., business
segment information for the year ended
August 31, 1995 (in millions)**

Business Segment	Revenues	EBIT	EBITDA	Identifiable Assets
Lighting equipment	$ 851	$ 61	$ 76	$ 340
Textile rental	546	51	82	422
Chemical	353	35	42	169
Other	220	14	18	83
	$1,971	$162	$218	$1,015
Corporate[1]		(8)		116
Interest expense		(4)		—
	Pretax Income	$150	Total Assets	$1,131

[1]Corporate operating profit represents corporate overhead less interest income.

lines were consistently profitable, but their growth rates paralleled the growth in the U.S. economy. All three segments held special market niches, carried strong trade names and maintained solid reputations. Individually, each was an attractive acquisition candidate that could have realized a respectable EBIT multiple.

The two smaller lines of business—the insulation service company and the envelope manufacturer—showed favorable operating histories. Each had an estimated value in the 10× to 11× EBIT range.

Estimating a Bust-Up Value

Based on the valuation techniques covered earlier in this book, the business segments had an aggregate value range of $1.7 billion to $1.8 billion. To this aggregate amount were added nonoperating corporate assets of cash, excess pension funds, and headquarters real estate. Subtracted were outstanding corporate debts and stock options. The net "bust-up" value before capital gains taxes was $1.8 billion to $1.9 billion, as illustrated in Exhibit 19-7. In this example, the bust-up value, before taxes, was estimated to be $37.54 to $40.23 per share, which was below the presumed takeover price of $42. Obviously, a "bust-up" deal was inappropriate for NSI.

**EXHIBIT 19-7   National Service Industries, Inc.,
estimated bust-up value before taxes
August 31, 1995**

		Value Range (in millions)
Lighting equipment		$ 560– 600
Textile rental		680– 740
Chemical		330– 350
Other		140– 150
	Subtotal	$1,710–1,840
Add:		
Corporate cash		+82
Excess pension assets @ 50%		+14
Corporate headquarters real estate		+50
Less:		
Corporate debts		−33
Value of management options		−10
Net Bust-Up Value before Taxes		$1,813–$1,943
On a per share basis		$37.54–$40.23

Including capital gains taxes into the analysis lowered NSI's bust-up value substantially. Determining this expected tax liability was problematic for an outsider because the tax basis of NSI in its business segments was (and is) confidential information. If, by way of illustration, the tax basis of the divisions was $500 million, a bust-up acquirer would have had to include a capital gains tax bill of $380 million into the valuation analysis, thereby dropping the estimate by $7.92 per share. The tax-adjusted value of NSI would have been $29.62 to $32.31 per share.

Real-Life Examples

The most profitable bust-up was the Beatrice Company leveraged buyout, completed for $6.2 billion in 1986. Beatrice was a multinational consumer products concern with numerous businesses that held appeal for other acquirers. Immediately following the deal's closing, management began the process of dismembering the company. After two years, the LBO had sold off assets for approximately $7 billion, and retained a storehouse of businesses worth between $3 billion and $4 billion. Total expected sale proceeds: $10 billion to $11 billion. With an initial equity investment of less than $500 million, the bust-up sponsors were looking at a pretax profit of $4 billion to $5 billion over a three-year period. The sponsors eventually sold Beatrice to Conagra in 1990.

Paul Bilzerian's $1.1 billion hostile takeover of Singer Company was the last big bust-up to qualify for favorable tax treatment. Right after the deal's closing, the Congress eliminated the loophole and subjected such transactions to the much higher capital gains taxes mentioned earlier.

Founded as a sewing machine manufacturer, Singer's operations had changed significantly by the time the takeover occurred. It was then a diversified manufacturer of military, industrial, and consumer products with annual sales of $1.7 billion. All of the company's 12 operating units operated independently, which made them easy to divest separately. By August 1988, eight months after the closing, Bilzerian had recouped 85% of his acquisition cost by selling just seven of Singer's 12 main business lines. The remaining corporate assets on the block had a value of at least $742 million. According to the *New York Times,* Mr. Bilzerian and his partners had an estimated profit of 100% on their equity investment in Singer.

Less than 10% of the acquisition's cost came from equity investments by the bust-up's sponsors. Most of the financing came from loans provided by commercial banks and Lehman Brothers. A summary of the deal appears in Exhibit 19-8.

As noted earlier, the likelihood of another bust-up transaction such as Singer is remote. The higher capital gains tax liability is the problem. In the Singer case, these incremental taxes would have cut the value of the deal by about $175 million.

Some conglomerates unlock the value of noncore businesses by spinning them off to shareholders. The parent declares the business's shares as a noncash dividend to the parent's shareholders. Such spin-offs are usually contingent on favorable IRS rulings guaranteeing that the distribution is tax-free to both the conglomerate and its shareholders. Contemplating such spin-offs at the time of this writing were several well-known conglomerates, including AT&T, ITT Corporation, and Premark International.

EXHIBIT 19-8   Singer Company bust-up summary

Acquisition Cost: $1.9 Billion

Purchase of Singer stock and options	$1,060
Repayment of existing Singer debt	660
Financing, investment banking and other fees	103
Carrying cost of buyout debt	100
Severance payments to Singer employees	20
	$1,943

Division Sales through Eight Months: $1.7 Billion

Motor products	$ 325
Career systems development	20
Link Flight Simulation	550
HRB Singer	145
Electronic Systems division	310
Dalmo Victor	175
American Meter	132
	$1,657

Value of Remaining Assets: $0.7 Billion

Five Businesses: Link Miles, Librascope, Kearfott Guidance, Link Industrial, and SimuFlite	$ 660
Interest in SSMC, the former sewing machine unit	42
Joint venture in Mitsubishi Precision	40
	$ 742

Value of Prospective Liabilities: $0.2 Billion

Capital gains taxes	$ 101
Other miscellaneous liabilities	70
Preferred stockholders	43
	$ 214

Source: New York Times: August 28, 1988.

BOTTOM FISHING

Many Bottom Fishers participate in the M&A field. Their fellow practitioners refer to them as "cheapskates." Constantly on the prowl for corporate bargains, the Bottom Fisher prowls the acquisition landscape, searching for value in deals that don't attract the broader corporate and LBO market. Companies falling into the Bottom Fisher's sights are troubled, weak, or financially crippled enterprises. This orientation gives Bottom Fishers another nickname—"Vulture Capitalists."

Acquisition candidates that fit the Bottom Fishing target profile exhibit one of the following characteristics:

- *High Leverage.* The target is operationally profitable before debt service costs, but incurs net losses after interest expense. This situation is unsustainable in the long run. Many LBOs face this problem. In numerous instances, the candidate is in Chapter 11 proceedings and is being reorganized under the jurisdiction of the Bankruptcy Court.

- *Turnaround.* The company's underlying business is in trouble. It is either losing money or is marginally profitable at the operating level. It needs new management, new product lines, or new capital.

- *Out-of-Fashion.* Just as certain industries become Wall Street darlings, like media firms in the 1990s, others lose their luster, like real estate companies in the 1990s. Investing in out-of-fashion businesses is customary for vulture capitalists. This investing style is sometimes called "contrarian investing."

- *End-of-Life-Cycle.* As the demand for an industry's products declines, the participants must either adapt or wither away. Firms adopting the latter course attract the Bottom Fisher because they have cheap prices and draw little corporate interest.

Bottom Fishing for Highly Leveraged Acquisitions

The popularity of leveraged buyouts results in many bankruptcies. In many cases, the ailing LBO has a healthy operating business; it's just the balance sheet that is sickly. Saddled with debts that can never be repaid, the LBO's owners have three options: (1) do nothing and pray for a miraculous recovery; (2) work out a voluntary restructuring plan with the creditors; or (3) play brinkmanship with the creditors and look toward a Chapter 11 filing. Since unpaid creditors lose their patience after a couple of years, Option 1 has a short duration. Options 2 and 3 extend over months and years; they are dubbed "work-outs" because the creditors and company stockholders spend countless hours working out a plan to put the business back on its feet. Work-outs follow two avenues: voluntary restructuring and Chapter 11 reorganization. Both provide Bottom Fishers with multiple opportunities for gaining control over the troubled target as illustrated in Exhibit 19-9.

Once the Bottom Fisher controls the target company, it readies the business for an eventual sale. This preparation could mean new management, a capital infusion, or a strategic realignment.

EXHIBIT 19-9 Work-out company options

Voluntary Restructuring	Bottom Fisher Tactics
Restructuring is a fancy word for paying creditors less than 100 cents on the dollar. In the rare case where the target is sold in one piece to a corporate buyer, creditors split the proceeds according to an agreed-upon formula. In most restructurings, the principal creditors receive a combination of new debt and equity securities, in exchange for their old loans. Even under the most optimistic scenario, the security package is worth less than the loans' face value. Shareholders resist many debt restructurings because the proposed equity issuance dilutes their ownership by 80% to 90%.	The Bottom Fisher anticipates a restructuring and buys corporate obligations at large discounts to face value. Unhappy creditors that need cash incur a loss. By operating as a major creditor, the Bottom Fisher negotiates a restructuring with the target that provides (1) the target with a solid balance sheet and (2) the Bottom Fisher with a controlling equity stake.

Chapter 11 Reorganization	Bottom Fisher Tactics
Unable to reach a compromise with creditors, the target files for Chapter 11, which suspends payment obligations and prevents creditors from filing lawsuits or foreclosing on assets. Unless an asset liquidation provides the highest payout on claims, the target and its creditors pursue a reorganization under the auspices of the Bankruptcy Court. The company survives with a new balance sheet. Dominated by lawyers, the Chapter 11 process is time consuming and very expensive; creditors and debtors alike try to avoid it.	The Bottom Fisher purchases target obligations at large discounts to face value. It becomes a major creditor. It uses this position to influence the reorganization in its favor. The Bottom Fisher proposes to buy the target's operating business for a combination of new cash and securities. Creditors accept or reject the bid. The Bottom Fisher offers to purchase for cash the new equity securities that are contemplated by a reorganization plan. With enough acceptances of its offer, the Bottom Fisher gains a controlling position.

Bottom Fisher Screening Process

Because of the large number of distressed companies, a typical Bottom Fisher monitors dozens of investment situations. Creditors and work-out attorneys supply a constant flow of information, which the Bottom Fisher supplements through its own intelligence network. Distressed investment newsletters, such as the *Daily Bankruptcy Review,* provide up-to-date news on all major bankruptcies, including financial results, court filings, court decisions, reorganization plans, and SEC documents.

Aware of the downside exposure inherent in troubled company investments, the Bottom Fisher tries to manage its risk level by focusing on safe businesses and sensible valuations. Safe businesses are low-tech manufacturers or service providers with the potential to generate operating income from a stable sales base. Sensible valuations start with a low price-to-book-value ratio. "Price" refers to the investor's assumed equity cost after the expected restructuring of the target's balance sheet. "Book value" refers to the restructured corporation's net tangible asset value. A low price-to-book-value ratio acts as an insurance policy for the distressed company investor. If the target's operations fall apart, the buyer always has the option of liquidating the business and receiving a decent recovery of its investment.

Financial Analysis of Company with Leverage Problems

By screening troubled, indebted businesses on industry and asset characteristics, the investor narrows the field substantially. With the remaining candidates, the investor performs a summary financial analysis, concentrating primarily on issues concerning *cash flow, timing,* and *continuing operations.* The analytical emphasis takes on different elements, depending on whether the target company is a restructuring candidate or a bankruptcy (see Exhibit 19-10).

During its initial screen, the Bottom Fisher determines normalized operating results for a leveraged target in an interesting fashion. Most corporate acquirers begin with a bottom-line analysis and attempt to forecast net income and EBIT, but the Bottom Fisher does its analysis backward. It looks at top-line results first (i.e., sales). Over the expected sales data, it superimposes the income statement

EXHIBIT 19-10   Bottom fisher financial analysis of a troubled leveraged business

Critical Issues	Voluntary Restructuring	Chapter 11 Business
Cash	Does the target have sufficient cash to keep creditors at bay until a restructuring is concluded? The investor carefully prepares month-to-month cash flow forecasts.	Does the target need to borrow more money from court-approved debtor-in-possession (DIP) lenders to maintain operations? DIP lenders receive priority claims at a 100% repayment rate, thus reducing reorganization values.
Timing	What is the investor's expected holding period? Restructuring results are uncertain. A long holding period or an unforeseen Chapter 11 filing reduces the investors' rate of return. Postrestructuring, how much time is needed for the business to recover fully? The investor's experience in similar situations provides a guide.	When will the target emerge from bankruptcy? Can the investor's intervention accelerate the process? A long holding period reduces the investor's rate of return. Postreorganization, how much time is needed for the business to recover fully?
Continuing operations	What are the company's normalized operating results?	Same.

template of a successful firm in the target's industry. The investor reasons as follows: If my target wasn't burdened with its leverage problems, it might perform as well as the next company. For example, in considering the normalized results of a processed foods manufacturer in bankruptcy, the Bottom Fisher might construct the template shown in Exhibit 19-11 and conclude that the target's normalized EBIT margin is in the 8% to 10% range.

With its projected margins in hand, the investor forecasts the target's operating income going forward, using sensible sales estimates. In this example, I assumed the target company's sales jumped 10% in the

EXHIBIT 19-11   Bottom fisher financial analysis to normalize the operating results of a bankrupt processed foods company

	Annual Sales ($MM)	Gross Margin	Operating Margin
Target company—actual	$800	42.0%	3.0%
Other Processed Foods			
Flowers Industries	$ 989	46.9%	7.6%
H.J. Heinz	7,103	36.2	12.1
Pet Foods	1,520	50.5	14.9
Sara Lee	14,580	38.0	8.0
Lance Foods	488	51.2	13.1
	Average	44.6%	11.1%
Investor Estimates			
Target company—normalized	$800	44%–46%	8%–10%

first year out of bankruptcy. Sales growth then declined to a constant annual rate of 6%. Operating margins rebounded to 5% in year 1996, increasing steadily to 9% by year 2000 (see Exhibit 19-12). Note how the investment candidate's projected operating income leaps from $24 million in year 1995 to $100 million after five years. This is a Bottom Fisher's ideal situation because there is the possibility of a large increase in value.

The bargain hunter next determines the present value of the target business, on a debt-free basis. The first step is estimating the target's sale price in three to five years, using the techniques described in

EXHIBIT 19-12   Bottom fisher financial analysis of the normalized operating results of a bankrupt processed foods company (in millions)

	Year					
	Actual	Projected				
	1995	1996	1997	1998	1999	2000
Sales	$800	$800	$933	$989	$1,048	$1,110
Operating income	$ 24	$ 44	$ 56	$ 69	$ 84	$ 100
Operating margin (%)	3%	5%	6%	7%	8%	9%

Chapters 9, 10, and 16. This future sale value is discounted to the present at the company's estimated cost of capital, including both debt and equity cost components. To determine this capital cost, the Bottom Fisher makes a lot of assumptions on what the reorganization plan will look like. How much will each class of creditor receive on its claims? How much debt and how much equity will be outstanding after the plan's implementation? Constructing good answers to these questions goes to the heart of the Bottom Fisher's analysis.

Although every distressed situation is unique, the reorganization plan is usually designed to reduce existing debts to an amount that the borrower can reasonably service in the future. Once the composition of the new debt securities is determined, the remaining enterprise value is allocated to newly issued common shares. Both the debt securities and common shares are distributed to creditors on the basis of complicated formulas, which are the product of long and trying negotiations. The company's former shareholders end up with little in this process, and the new majority owners are the former creditors that received the most shares in the distribution.

For our hypothetical food company, a reasonable enterprise value in 2000 is $1 billion (i.e., 10× EBIT). Using a 50%–50% capital structure of debt and equity, the reorganized food company's assumed capital cost is approximately 20% (assume debt costs 10% and equity costs 30%) annually. Given the uncertainties associated with projections in troubled company investments, this high capital cost estimate is justifiable. Discounting the company's $1 billion future value at 20% annually results in the initial "plan capitalization" value of $400 million. As illustrated in Exhibit 19-13, the investor has a reasonable analytical framework that is used to assist in the investment decision.

EXHIBIT 19-13 Bottom fisher cost of capital calculation for a bankrupt processed foods company

Capitalization	After Plan Implementation	Cost of Capital	Rationale
Debt	$200	10%	Equivalent to junk bond yields.
Equity	200	30	Bottom fisher target equity return.
Total	$400	20%	

For example, Carson Pirie Scott, a bankrupt department store chain, had a reorganization plan that was confirmed in 1993; the company discharged $581 million of claims for $369 million, or 64 cents on the dollar. The new debt-to-equity ratio was 60:40. Federated Department Stores, one of the 1980s largest LBO's, was reorganized in 1992. Prebankruptcy claims were paid out 51 cents on the dollar. The revised debt-to-equity ratio was 69:31.

THE INVESTMENT DECISION

Prospective Bottom Fishers participate in an active secondary market for troubled company claims. Buyers and sellers trade all sorts of obligations, ranging from secured loans to trade payables to subordinated debt. The participants set prices for those instruments based on their respective views on time-adjusted returns. In November 1995, for example, the unsecured bank debt of El Paso Electric traded at 64% of face value; the bank loans of London Fog traded at 35% of face value.

For our example, the bankrupt food processing company has $700 million of claims outstanding. For the sake of argument, assume that each claim has the same priority in reorganization. According to our $400 million valuation model, the claims should trade at an average 57% of face value (see Exhibit 19-14).

This example is simplistic. In reality, bankrupt companies have a bewildering variety of claims, most of which are assigned to a specific creditor class. Each creditor class has a priority designation. Those with the highest priorities, such as IRS liens and secured loans, receive the higher percentage payout in the reorganization. The investor faces a difficult task in pricing each claim properly. Also, in seeking

EXHIBIT 19-14 Bottom fisher financial analysis simple pricing calculation bankrupt processed foods company

	($ Millions)
Claims outstanding (1)	$700
Estimated enterprise value (2)	$400
Average claim trading value (1) ÷ (2)	57%

control over the troubled enterprise, it must gauge correctly which class is eligible for the largest proportion of common shares in the eventual reorganization.

In 1993, four large investors purchased many claims from the pre-Chapter 11 secured bank lenders of Carson Pirie Scott. In the subsequent reorganization, these investors obtained significant ownership positions in the company's new equity: FMR Corporation (13.7%), New South Capital Management (10.4%), Dickstein Partners (7.9%), and Intermarket Corporation (7.8%). Since the Carson stock began trading publicly in October 1993, its price has climbed about 50%. In 1991, while bankruptcy proceedings were pending, the Zell/Chilmark Fund acquired $461 million of the $600 million in unsecured claims against Carter Hawley Hale, Inc., a distressed West Coast department store chain. Pursuant to the reorganization plan, these unsecured claims were converted into equity and provided the Fund with a 63% ownership interest. Renamed Broadway Stores, Inc., the company merged into Federated Stores in 1996. The Zell/Chilmark Fund broke even on the deal.

BOTTOM FISHING FOR TURNAROUNDS

While many leveraged companies make money from operations, a turnaround's main problem is losing money from operations. Leverage is a secondary factor. The operating problems stem either from economic conditions beyond the control of management or from conditions that exist inside the firm. If the cause of the failure is external to the company, a takeover is unlikely to reverse the situation. If the reason is found within the business, an outsider can, theoretically, buy the company, replace management, inject new capital, and kickstart the recovery. A firm heading for oblivion can thus be "turned around" into a successful business.

Principal causes for operating problems include:

- Management ineptitude.
- Economic cyclicality.
- Failure to foresee technology, fashion, or competitive challenges.
- Poor cost controls.

- Growing sales without adequate capital.
- Unsound acquisitions.
- Lawsuits.

Companies suffering from these deficiencies survive for years. Operating cash shortfalls are made up through borrowings and asset sales, deferring the day of reckoning.

The management of a turnaround candidate is understandably reluctant to talk to a Bottom Fisher. By helping the Bottom Fisher conduct its due diligence investigation, the candidate's management may be writing its own pink slip. So why talk?

Because the typical financial investor lacks operating expertise, it often joins with a freelance management team in the pursuit of a turnaround. Once control over the target is achieved, the investor fires the existing management group, which is then replaced by the new team.

OTHER BOTTOM-FISHING TECHNIQUES

Entire books cover contrarian investing, and it suffices to say that many stable industries fall in and out-of-fashion. Clever Bottom Fishers acquire companies in these industries at the bottom of the value cycle, hoping to flip them at the top of the cycle. The principal risk for the contrarian buyer is a cycle that never turns up again.

Along the same lines, some Bottom Fishers search for companies participating in declining industries. With a decreasing sales base, these firms have little need for capital expenditures; and as a result, they throw off cash, which can be reinvested elsewhere. The obvious competition for the Bottom Fisher here is another industry player seeking to consummate a Market Share Extension deal.

SUMMARY

Asset deals, bust-up transactions, and bottom fishing are three M&A categories dominated by financial buyers. Each area requires the investor to have a specialized expertise and a thick skin. The high level of risk encountered in these transactions demands that investors pay strict attention to downside asset values.

20

THE POPULAR STRATEGY OF BUYING WHOLESALE AND SELLING RETAIL

Up to now, we have considered how buyers evaluate and close individual transactions, but the M&A process doesn't need to stop at one deal. A popular strategy among experienced players is to acquire multiple small firms operating in the same industry at low P/E multiples (i.e., buying "wholesale"). Once a critical mass is achieved, the acquirer takes the combined group public at a high P/E multiple (i.e., selling "retail"). The securities firm handling the public offering justifies the premium price paid by the new stockholders on the likely synergies achievable through merger-oriented economies of scale.

The process typically unfolds as follows: A sophisticated financial investor such as a venture capitalist identifies a large, fragmented industry that is served primarily by inefficient and undercapitalized mom-and-pop companies. The investor either purchases one of the larger participants or creates a major player by combining a few smaller companies, usually at a cash cost ranging from $15 million to $25 million. Professional management with an equity incentive is installed in the newly acquired business, which serves as the base (or "platform") to which other smaller firms are added. The base company

297

then commences an aggressive acquisition program, buying as many as 15 to 20 mom-and-pops each year at significantly lower prices than the likely price for a large public deal. For example, the acquirer might only pay 10× to 12× earnings for a small private business when larger publicly listed firms in similar industries are trading at 15× to 20× earnings. Few of the sellers receive 100% cash for their businesses because the brand-new acquirer can't raise attractive financing without a track record. Most sellers receive a combination of (1) cash; and (2) shares in the new enterprise. Because the acquirer is privately held and has a limited operating history, the shares received by the sellers are speculative investments, representing at best "hope certificates" that have real value only if and when the acquiring firm goes public at a 20× to 25× earnings multiple. Assuming the acquirer has been buying "right," realizing synergies and showing upward trends in sales and earnings, the initial public offering takes place two to three years after the platform's formation. Following this first offering, the firm has high-priced shares that can be used as an acquisition currency along with a lot of money in the bank. It is thus in a good position to redouble its already intensive acquisition efforts. In practitioner circles, this sequence of actions is called "consolidation," "platform investing," or "leveraged buildup."

Although the acquirers seem to be taking advantage of the mom-and-pops in such schemes, this is not the case. Without a Wall Street-oriented consolidator scooping up these multiple firms, the small business owners would have to turn to a competitor or local investor for liquidity under a sale scenario. Unable to provide meaningful synergies and short on capital, these alternative buyers can't afford to offer more than 6× to 8× earnings. As a result, a 10× to 12× earnings price from an active purchaser looks attractive to many sellers, even if part of this amount is in common shares of uncertain value.

Most of the major successes using this strategy have involved service industries, including garbage collection, security services, and drug distribution. The technique has also been implemented well in some manufacturing sectors. Not all the attempts at consolidation have worked out, and many sophisticated investors engaged in this activity have recorded major losses to show for their failed efforts, notably in consumer sectors such as retailing, dry cleaning, and gas stations.

OPERATING OBJECTIVES OF THE CONSOLIDATION

In integrating a dozen or more acquisitions in a year, the consolidator typically seeks to overlay a standardized business template for each new unit. New management practices (and many times, new managers) and systems are brought in to improve the performance of the acquisition in two important synergies: revenue enhancement and cost reduction.

In the case of a typical mom-and-pop targeted for consolidation, the existing operation doesn't have the capital, know-how, management information system (MIS), or marketing infrastructure to sustain high revenue growth. By combining with a national player, the local unit gains access to better marketing and superior service techniques that can help in retaining existing clients and obtaining new customers. And, as part of a bigger business, the mom-and-pop is often eligible to bid on large regional jobs or national service contracts that would have been too big to handle in its previous stand-alone status.

Cost reductions revolve around the themes that this book covered earlier. The first step for the buyer is to eliminate local facilities and services that are made redundant by the central headquarters. Common redundancies are purchasing, accounting, warehousing, treasury, and personnel departments. Capital is injected into the local unit to upgrade dilapidated facilities and cut operating costs. Since the headquarters has a full complement of senior executives, duplicative personnel at the local level—frequently the former owners—are not brought on board, unless they agree to drastic compensation reductions beforehand. Proper accounts receivable management and inventory supervision are introduced, and working capital investment is decreased accordingly.

The September 12, 1995, prospectus of Corporate Express, Inc., a leading office products supplier that has grown through multiple acquisitions, expressed these operational objectives well:

> Since 1991, the Company has expanded rapidly through acquisitions from a regional operation in Colorado to 131 locations throughout the United States, Canada, and Australia. The Company believes it has developed a substantially different business model from traditional contract stationers, defining itself as a Corporate Supplier. . . . This

business model is based upon the Company's proprietary, full color *In-Stock Catalog*, volume purchasing power, proprietary computer software applications, direct sales force and a centrally managed network of regional warehouses. . . .

The Company operates in a large, fragmented and rapidly consolidating industry. The Company believes that more than one-third of office product purchases are made by its target companies, primarily companies with over 100 office employees (the "Large Corporate Segment"). The Large Corporate Segment is principally served by numerous traditional contract stationers, most of which operate in a single metropolitan area and have annual sales of less than $15 million . . .

When those words were written, the annual sales of Corporate Express were $621 million, representing a 650% increase since 1991, when the Company's annual sales were less than $80 million.

Depending on the industry, the buildup's combination of revenue increases and cost cuts can easily improve the EBIT results of an acquisition by 15% to 20% in the first year. One medical services consolidator I interviewed claimed that on buying a mom-and-pop operation, it routinely increased the target's revenues by 5% to 10%, and reduced expenses by 2% to 5%, during the first year of ownership.

Once a consolidator has solidified its position in a fragmented industry by entering a number of regional markets, it assumes the role of a Market Share Extender. Existing market shares are expanded through "fill-in" acquisitions and new beachheads are established with more stand-alone deals.

The financial mechanics of a consolidation are best illustrated by the following hypothetical case study.

MED SERVICES CASE

On October 1, 1992, four senior executives of National Staffing Inc., a $1 billion temporary office staffing company, rocked their industry when they announced their immediate departure to form a temporary help firm. The new enterprise was going to specialize in staffing health-care providers with needed temporary medical personnel such as nurses, technicians, and doctors. Backing the four executives were two venture capital firms, WiseCorp, Inc., and Hanby Ventures

Corporation, which collectively provided $18 million in equity seed capital. For this cash investment, the two firms received 1,800,000 shares, while the four executives received 200,000 shares without committing cash, as compensation for their "sweat equity." A short three months later, Med Services Corporation, as the new firm was called, announced its first acquisition, the $20 million purchase of Hospital Help, Inc., a Baltimore-based provider of temporary medical service personnel.

In the year before the acquisition, Hospital Help's summary financial results were summarized as shown in Exhibit 20-1. Of the $20 million purchase price, $12 million was in cash and the remaining $8 million was in 400,000 freshly minted shares of Med Services. Only $5 million of the cash requirement had to come from Med Services' internal resources because a commercial bank loaned the company $7 million to fund the rest of the $12 million cash need. Thus, Med Services had $13 million of cash left over from its initial $18 million venture investment. With this cash hoard and their newly acquired "platform," the four executives spread the word—Med Services intended to be in the acquisition business in a big way.

EXHIBIT 20-1   Hospital Help, Inc., summary financial data (in millions)

	Year Ending December 31, 1992
Income Statement	
Service sales	$50.0
Cost of services sold	35.0
Gross profit	15.0
Selling, general, and administrative expenses	10.5
Depreciation and amortization	0.5
EBIT	$ 4.0
Balance Sheet	
Assets	$10.0
Liabilities	4.0
Stockholder's equity	6.0

The price of the Hospital Help deal served management as a good guide for future acquisitions. The cash portion of the transaction, $12 million, represented 3× Hospital Help's EBIT, while the equity "paper payment" covered another 2× EBIT, bringing the transaction's total cost to 5× EBIT. In contrast, their former employer, National Staffing, which was a major participant in a related business, traded on the New York Stock Exchange at an implied value of 12× EBIT. The Med Services executives knew there was plenty of money to be made if they could construct an attractive group of businesses at around 5× EBIT.

EXHIBIT 20-2 Med Services Corp. summary of financial data (in millions, except per share data)

| | | Med Services Year Ended December 31, 1993 | | |
Income Statement	Predecessor[1] Year Ended December 31, 1992	(1) Original Platform Acquisition	(2) Ten New Acquisitions Combined	(1+2) 1993 Consolidated
Service sales	$50.0	$52.0	$50.0	$102.0
Cost of services	35.0	36.0	35.0	71.0
Gross profit	15.0	16.0	15.0	31.0
Selling, general, and admin. expenses	10.5	9.5	10.0	19.5
Depreciation and amortization	0.5	0.8	0.8	1.6
EBIT	4.0	5.7	4.2	9.9
Interest, net	—	0.2	0.8	1.0
Pretax income	4.0	5.5	3.4	8.9
Income taxes	1.6	2.2	1.4	3.6
Net income	$ 2.4	$ 3.3	$ 2.0	$ 5.3
Net income per share	—	$1.38	—	$ 1.96
Shares outstanding				
Before 10 acquisitions in 1993	—	2.4		
Newly issued for acquisitions			0.5	
Average shares outstanding during 1993				2.7

EXHIBIT 20-2 *(Continued)*

Balance Sheet	At December 31, 1993
Cash	$ 4.0
Tangible assets	30.0
Goodwill	42.0
Total assets	$76.0
Current liabilities	$12.0
Bank debt	22.0
Stockholders' equity	42.0
Total liabilities and stockholder's equity	$76.0

Where

- All purchase accounting adjustments are included.
- Debt bears interest at a 10% annual rate.
- Synergies accounted for a 2% margin improvement in platform's results over 1993 and a 1% margin improvement in 10 acquisitions' results over the average six-month holding period.

[1]Predecessor was Hospital Help, Inc., purchased on January 1, 1993.

Over the 1993 fiscal year, Med Services bought 10 more companies for an aggregate purchase price of $40 million, equivalent to 5× EBIT. The structure of the consideration remained 60% cash and 40% equity, but the equity portion was costing Med Services less. As the company's results improved, the executives convinced the sellers to value Med Services stock at up to $40 per share, which was a lot higher than the $20 per share value assigned in the earlier Hospital Help deal and the $10 per share price paid by the founders.

Again, the banks assisted with the cash needs of the company by approving more loans, and at year's end, Med Services had $22 million in outstanding debts. Nevertheless, on an accounting basis, the company's balance sheet appeared strong and debt service coverage was solid. Revenues and earnings were increasing quickly and Med Services was starting to look like a real growth company. With the average holding period of the acquisitions being only six months, Med Services' 1993 income statement showed just $50 million of the new purchases' $100 million in annual revenues, but combined with the improving results of the original platform transaction, the infant company was demonstrating substantial progress. Summary results are shown in Exhibit 20-2.

As the financial results showed, management had increased the company's sales by over 100% in the first 12 months through acquisitions. Earnings had more than doubled and interest costs were covered well. $36 million in cash had been spent on takeovers, and $22 million had been borrowed from banks, leaving Med Services with $3 million in cash from its original equity investment and $1 million in cash from operations. Management believed the company had enough financial firepower to complete another $20 million of acquisitions before it sought more equity financing.

Med Services' Goodwill Concerns

One troubling aspect of the company's financial situation was the sizable amount of goodwill on its balance sheet. Because temporary help service businesses had few fixed assets relative to their EBIT-derived purchase prices, Med Services paid the owners substantial premiums over book value, resulting in significant additions to its own goodwill account. By December 31, 1993, goodwill represented over 50% of total assets. Most banks preferred to lend against hard collateral for new ventures such as Med Services, so management knew long-term growth would eventually rely on equity-oriented investors who focused on net earnings performance rather than a good balance sheet. Goodwill didn't play a large role in the company's calculation of net income gains because Med Services amortized the $42 million in 1993 goodwill over a 40-year period. This long amortization schedule minimized amortization costs, although the Securities and Exchange Commission (SEC), which regulated the public securities markets, frowned on a 40-year duration. In the opinion of the SEC's economists, 40 years overstated the economic life of most corporate assets. Nevertheless, the SEC took little enforcement action against service sector consolidators which sold shares publicly, and Med Services, as a result, continued the practice. A shorter goodwill life would drastically cut reported earnings. The use of a 20-year amortization period, for example, would boost amortization expenses by $1 million annually. A 10-year horizon, which fit the temporary help industry's actual economics, would eliminate entirely Med Services' ability to show earnings growth under its current business model.

THE INITIAL PUBLIC OFFERING FOR MED SERVICES

As Med Services' business plan continued on course, the treasurer realized that the company would run out of acquisition cash by July 1994, only six months away. Working with WiseCorp and Hanby Ventures the firm's management recruited several venture capital firms that invested $15 million into the business in exchange for 500,000 new shares priced at $30 per share. This was simply a stopgap measure, however, and the company made plans to go public in early 1995.

The year ending December 31, 1994, was a success (see Exhibit 20-3). Fifteen more businesses had been acquired, representing six new markets and nine fill-in acquisitions. Med Services then participated in eight of the country's 20 largest metropolitan markets and was the second leading provider of temporary health care personnel. Annual sales exceeded $230 million and net earnings rose 126% in 1994, compared with 1993's results. Earnings per share increased 76%, even after taking into account the 500,000 and 600,000 new shares issued to the venture capitalists and business sellers, respectively.

In January 1995, Med Services met with three investment banks to discuss their sponsorship of an initial public offering of common stock. In reviewing the company's historical results, business plans, and future prospects, all three banks were enthusiastic about the prospective offering, indicating that Med Services was a true "growth

EXHIBIT 20-3 Med Services Corp. summary income statement data for years ending December 31 (in millions, except per share data)

	Predecessor	Med Services	
	1992	1993	1994
Service sales	$50.0	$102.0	$233.1
EBIT	4.0	9.9	24.7
Net income	2.4	5.3	12.0
Net income per share	—	$ 1.96	$ 3.45
Average shares outstanding	—	2.7	3.5
Total shares outstanding	2.4	2.9	4.0

company" leading the trend toward consolidation in its industry. Based on their respective analyses of comparable stocks and recent IPOs, the banks suggested a target P/E range of 20×–25× for the company's shares. This range valued the entire business at $240 million to $300 million, and provided the founders with the possibility of a 500% capital gain in just over two years. The estimated per share value ranged from $69 to $86, compared with the founders' original buy-in price of $10 per share.

Management selected a lead underwriter for the offering and work proceeded expeditiously. To lower the prospective price on its shares into the $20 to $30 range preferred by individual investors, Med Services split its stock on a 3:1 basis in February, and total shares outstanding equaled 12 million. The company's outside counsel finished the draft prospectus by March 1 and the SEC completed its review of the document by April 8. Two weeks later, the company sold three million shares for $25.30 each, netting, after commissions and expenses, approximately $70 million. As stated in the prospectus, the company's use of proceeds was "for general corporate purposes, including acquisitions and the repayment of borrowings."

REAL-LIFE CONSOLIDATORS

In the hypothetical MedServices case, the public paid a hefty premium to participate in the company's growth. Including the initial platform, the founders had spent only $120 million in building up the business. In the offering, these same acquisitions were assigned an implied enterprise value of $280 million (assuming all bank debts were repaid with the offering proceeds). The $160 million difference between the "wholesale cost" and the "retail price" was a function of both the investors' views on the additional value contributed by synergies and the underwriters' skills in selling securities for an relatively untested business.

Three recent stock offerings provided real-life evidence of the continuing success of this acquisition strategy. The three issuers operated in different business sectors, but each followed the tactics of consolidation described in this chapter. A brief summary of the companies and their respective financings follows:

American Medical Response, Inc.

4.25 million common shares
$108 million
September 1995

> American Medical Response Inc. (AMR) is the leading provider of ambulance services in the United States. The company has acquired more than 30 ambulance service providers since its formation in August 1992.
>
> Including capital expenditures of $29 million, AMR invested approximately $211 million in its acquisitions. The September 1995 offering valued these businesses at approximately $440 million.

Corporate Express, Inc.

16 million common shares
$384 million
September 1995

> "Corporate Express is a leading supplier of office products to large corporations. Since 1991, the Company has expanded rapidly through acquisitions from a regional operation in Colorado to 131 locations throughout the United States, Canada, and Australia." (from Prospectus, September 12, 1995)
>
> Including capital expenditures of $17 million, Corporate Express invested approximately $462 million in its acquisitions. The September 1995 offering valued these businesses at approximately $1.3 billion.

Mail-Well, Inc.

5 million common shares
$90 million
September 1995

> Mail-Well is the largest manufacturer of envelopes in the United States and Canada. Founded only 18 months before its initial public offering, the company had achieved annualized sales of $653 million through multiple leveraged acquisitions.
>
> Including capital expenditures of $8 million, Mail-Well invested approximately $446 million in its acquisitions. The September 1995 offering valued these businesses at approximately $481 million.

In each of these three transactions, the "buy wholesale" and "sell retail" strategy was very profitable for the founding shareholders. Even the Mail-Well deal, which had the smallest markup over original cost, made its original owners over three times their initial investment. All of Mail-Well's acquisitions were financed through the use of high leverage, so the equity portion of the wholesale cost was quite small.

SUMMARY

A popular strategy in the acquisition business is buying into a fragmented, low-EBIT multiple industry by using high-multiple stock and borrowed funds. As this process continues, earnings per share increase rapidly and the consolidation acquirer goes public at a premium price, applying the offering proceeds to more acquisitions and debt repayments. Implemented properly, this acquisition technique can bring recently formed enterprises the same P/E multiples of strong, established firms with demonstrated track records.

21

WHEN TO SELL A COMPANY OR A DIVISION

So far, this book has examined the buyer's role in the acquisition process. On the opposite side of every transaction is the seller. Indeed, most buyers become sellers at one time or another. The next two chapters concentrate on key seller issues. This chapter explores the proper moment for business owners to sell out. The next chapter reviews the tactics needed to carry out a successful sale.

SELLER CATEGORIES

Sellers fall into four categories: a family business; an entrepreneurial enterprise; a large corporation implementing a divestiture; and a large corporation selling control. These four sellers share a basic need for liquidity—either because they must access more capital to support their respective businesses or because they choose to disinvest from their ownership positions and spend their money elsewhere. Causes linked to liquidity are many and varied, but the following themes appear repeatedly.

Retirement Planning

Whether driven by an estate tax issue, a lack of management succession, or a wish to "smell the roses," the impending retirement of a company's owners/executives is a common time to consider a sale. Family businesses and entrepreneurial enterprises are most often prompted by these concerns.

The Target's Capital Needs

If the target business is prosperous and growing rapidly, it may require capital that is simply unavailable to the owners at a reasonable cost. An alliance with a bigger, capital-rich concern is appropriate in this instance. Entrepreneurial firms frequently merge with larger companies for this reason. Witness the 1995 sale of Ivax, a small biotech concern, to Johnson Products, the large personal care company.

The Seller's Capital Needs

Alternatively, the owner may need cash to reinvest in another line of business. The sale of one business is therefore used to finance another. This rationale is common among larger, publicly traded companies that view themselves as a portfolio of operating assets rather than as an integrated whole. In 1995, Philip Morris, for example, sold its baking division to CPC for $865 million in order to concentrate resources on its Kraft packaged foods business.

Strategic Association

In today's rapidly changing marketplace, sustainable growth for a business is dependent on obtaining access to proprietary technologies, distribution outlets, and production strengths.

For some companies, the availability of such resources can be more important than fresh capital in ensuring future success, but the price is often steep: the loss of total control through a full or partial sale of the business to a strategic partner that can provide these items.

Performance Problem

At times, the sale candidate suffers from operating problems that the present owners either can't fix, or don't want to fix, because of the time and effort involved. A new owner may be ready to tackle the challenge of turning the target business around. In other cases, the nonperformance issue is centered on the candidate's inability to service its debts, perhaps accentuated by the use of high leverage. A fresh face is needed to restructure the company's debts with its creditor group, which may have grown weary of the existing owners' failed promises.

Lack of Strategic Fit

From time to time, a large company changes its strategic orientation. As yesterday's priorities become today's divestitures, certain business lines don't fit into the owner's new plans. Alternatively, the stock market is giving the parent company little credit for a small division's contribution, so its hidden value is "unlocked" through a sale. Raytheon Corp. demonstrated this motivation when it sold its D.C. Heath textbook publishing unit to Houghton Mifflin Co. for $455 million in October 1995. While a sizable publishing business on a stand alone basis, D.C. Heath never quite fit in with the three larger core businesses of Raytheon—defense electronics, engineering, and avionics.

Opportunism

Industries go in and out of fashion. Prices for TV stations, for example, have exhibited a broad range in the past dozen years. From a typical price of 10× to 12× cash flow in the mid-1980s, valuations declined 30% to 7× to 9× cash flow in the late-1980s, only to climb back to 10× to 12× cash flow in the mid-1990s. Opportunistic owners take advantage of peak valuation cycles to "cash out" of their in-fashion businesses at premium prices.

Opportunism is part of a broader theme—when is the right time to sell?

TIMING CONSIDERATIONS

The best time to sell a company is when the owner doesn't have to sell. This means neither the sale candidate nor the owner is under financial pressure to repay creditors or to raise new money.

The sell decision should also reflect the broader financial environment. Businesses fetch higher prices when economic confidence is high, the stock market is up, and interest rates are low. This combination of positive macroeconomic indicators usually occurs every few years, so owners have to be ready.

If the candidate operates in a cyclical business such as home construction or metal mining, the sale needs to be timed for the company's "peak earnings" year. Most buyers are unduly optimistic with respect to the inevitable downside results, so the purchase price is inflated. Similarly, a fashion-timer must act quickly when its industry's popularity heats up. The market can be fickle in anointing an industry, and then quick in discarding it. In 1980, the oil-drilling business was booming; by 1983 it was moribund; it's now "hot" again. Likewise, mom-and-pops participating in a consolidating industry have to choose their timing carefully. The "buildup party" only lasts so long, and the small business owner wants to be invited at the same high multiple as everyone else.

MAKING THE DECISION

After making the sale decision, most sellers have a straightforward objective—achieving the maximum price. This being said, entrepreneurs and family business owners usually display strong secondary concerns. The former often want to see the merged business carry on successfully after the sale, which means an effort is made to point the deal to a Strategic Buyer or a Market Share/Product Line Extender. Family owners share this sentiment, but they also focus on maintaining relatives in executive positions postmerger.

The emotional attachment of an owner to a business can make the sale decision a difficult undertaking, but once the decision is made, it should be implemented properly. Done right, initiating the sales process costs time and money, and reluctant sellers should think twice before starting down this road.

CONFRONTING REALITY

Before putting a business up for sale, the forward-thinking owner conducts some research on valuation. Knowing the approximate worth of one's business is advisable before discussing the sale decision with potential advisers. Business brokers and investment bankers who handle many medium- to large-size deals, are a good source of information, but in presenting their credentials to an owner, they have a tendency to wax optimistic about the target's likely sale price. To avoid disappointment later on, an intelligent owner gathers information independently. Some data are available through newspapers and financial publications, and other facts are found in conversations with industry contacts who have experienced the process firsthand.

For most medium- to large-size sellers—particularly unsophisticated owners entering the market for the first time—I recommend commissioning a business appraisal from an independent valuation firm. This is another means of collecting information. (To avoid a conflict-of-interest, this firm should not engage in representation work on behalf of either buyers or sellers.) While lacking part of the deal flow information known to the larger intermediaries, such an appraisal delivers a decent ballpark estimate that doesn't incorporate the typical intermediary's upward bias. Furthermore, the appraisal only costs from $20,000 to $30,000 for most midsize to large businesses, and it can be completed without an involved due diligence effort.

For smaller companies with less than $2 million to $3 million in annual EBIT, the appraisal route is inadvisable. Sufficient details on comparable transactions are simply unavailable and the appraiser, as a result, will only provide general ranges on valuation, such as "3× to 5× EBIT" or "50% to 100% of sales." Such conclusions are of little use to the prospective seller.

If the owner's research indicates that his company can realize an acceptable price, the time is ripe for beginning the sale process.

22 GOING THROUGH THE SALE PROCESS

A prospective seller operates far differently than a would-be buyer. Before making a commitment, a buyer conducts an exhaustive analysis of the seller's business from a number of viewpoints—financial, operational, and legal among others. At the same time, a buyer looks at the deal's likely impact on its future operations and stock market values. In contrast, the seller's principal concern is much narrower—price. It needn't worry about its operating results postclosing, and its analysis of the prospective buyer is limited, in most cases, to whether the buyer has (or can raise) the money required to purchase its business. Despite the seller's singular orientation, there are numerous steps between the seller entering the M&A market and the seller receiving the sale proceeds. Chapter 22 reviews these steps, presents observations on tactics, and suggests ways of avoiding common pitfalls.

Key Seller Steps

1. Retaining a financial adviser.
2. Setting the stage.
3. The buyer list.
4. Approach tactics.

5. Coming up with a bid.

6. Final steps.

RETAINING A FINANCIAL ADVISER

Once the business owner has made the sale decision described in the previous chapter, the search begins for a competent financial adviser. A financial adviser, such as an investment bank, commercial bank, or business broker, is critical to the sale process because it occupies the best position for conducting an orderly auction. Why use an auction? Because the competition fostered by an auction is the best means for the seller to achieve an optimal price. Unless the seller is an experienced M&A tactician, it can't realize the same results as a knowledgeable adviser. Only an intermediary can inject into the process the proper amount of cajoling, tension, and spirited competition that advances the desired price objective. If the seller itself tries to orchestrate these same dynamics, it comes off looking desperate and unprofessional, two qualities that don't go very far in the M&A business.

Large corporations with extensive Wall Street contacts know well the capabilities of the firms offering merger advisory services. For these big companies, the selection of an intermediary is a straightforward action. Either a trusted adviser is rewarded for some ancillary work, such as recommending the parent company's shares, or a specific firm is matched to the particular needs of the transaction. The latter happens frequently with specialized industry deals. The biotech industry is a prime example. An adviser with technical skills and good industry contacts is almost mandatory for solid deal execution. On the other end of the corporate spectrum are middle-market companies, which make the advisory choice in a haphazard fashion. Typically, they enlist an intermediary on the basis of a friend's referral or the strength of a lawyer's recommendation. Retaining an intermediary in this way is a mistake. All business owners should select a financial adviser rationally. Three criteria are critical:

1. *Experience.* It goes without saying that the advisory firm—and the specific executive handling the deal—should have extensive experience in closing a variety of M&A transactions. With the

increasing globalization of the economy, an adviser with an international background is helpful if the deal exceeds $50 million. This size attracts multinational players.

2. *Industry Expertise.* Although most advisers can muddle their way through any sort of deal (i.e., "learning by doing"), they enhance results when they have a track record in closing transactions in the seller's industry. The same due diligence questions, valuation issues, and closing problems arise in related-industry deals, so there's little point in the intermediary reinventing the wheel for the seller's benefit in one transaction. The primary pitfall for the seller comes with choosing an adviser that is *too* close to that small group of industry participants representing the logical buyers. The adviser may figure its most dependable income is with these repeat customers, and accordingly, it may not bend over backward to achieve the highest possible price for a one-time client. A secondary concern for the seller is whether the executives comprising the adviser's "industry experience" still work there. When I worked at Lehman Brothers, the firm routinely showed potential retailing clients a marketing presentation with a laundry list of retailing deals that Lehman had closed, thus demonstrating its expertise. The trouble was, however, that most of the bankers who had executed the transactions had long since moved to competing investment banks. Few prospective clients thought to ask this question.

3. *Commitment.* In most transactions, the optimization of the sale price depends on the dedicated commitment of the adviser's senior personnel. Too many intermediaries, feeling the pressure to generate fees, use the venerable "bait and switch" tactic to attract new clients. A senior executive wines and dines the owners, but he disappears after his firm receives the assignment and the real work commences. The seller's transaction is then consummated by junior personnel who are "learning by doing." A careful seller demands senior executive commitment of its transaction. If assurances are made and then not followed, the smart seller cancels the arrangement immediately.

As a means of ensuring senior-level commitment, a seller should try and match its deal to the intermediary's interests and capabilities. Exhibit 22-1 is a good guide. Some sellers are tempted to select the intermediary promising the highest price. While enthusiasm for a

EXHIBIT 22-1   Guidelines on selecting an intermediary

Deal Description	Appropriate Intermediary
Small business, $1–$20 million value.	Reputable business broker or regional investment bank.
Medium-size company, $20–$100 million value.	Regional investment bank, medium-size New York investment bank, or New York commercial bank.
Large company, $100 million value and up.	New York investment bank.
Exceptions: specialized industries, $20–$200 million value.	M&A boutiques such as Financo (specialty retailing) and Vector Securities (life sciences).

transaction is important, a banker's wishful thinking is no substitute for hard experience. Likewise, shopping for the cheapest adviser ultimately can be counterproductive. If the intermediary's fee schedule appears expensive, negotiate an incentive that guarantees a big fee only if the seller receives a high price. As a final note to the selection process, the careful seller makes a reference check, verifying the would-be adviser's claims regarding experience, industry expertise, and commitment.

SETTING THE STAGE FOR THE SALE

Retaining an intermediary is only the first step in readying the target business for an orderly auction. Subsequent preparation work costs money and consumes time. The retainer fee of a financial intermediary ranges from $0 for a freelance business broker to $100,000 for a prestigious New York investment bank. Follow-up costs include accountants, legal counsel, and consultants, who usually charge by the hour. Depending on the amount and complexity of the work involved, "prepping" a business for sale requires anywhere from a few weeks to several months.

In larger transactions, the investment banker acts as the coordinator of the sale process, including the prep work. Following the signing of a retainer letter, the bank conducts a two- or three-day field visit, inspecting facilities, interviewing management, and "getting a feel" for the business. With the result of this due diligence and similar information gathering, the adviser commences three premarketing tasks: (1) "dressing up" the candidate, (2) confirming a value range for the business, and (3) writing the information memorandum (including financial projections) which is later provided to would-be buyers.

Dressing Up the Sale Candidate

Big corporations that pay premium prices prefer "clean" businesses with readily understandable products, demonstrable operating histories and minimal extraneous issues. To have its client fit this criteria, the banker many recommend that the candidate take remedial action. For example, if the target's earnings are derived 80% from life insurance operations and 20% from theme restaurants, the banker may suggest spinning off the restaurant business. Why complicate discussions with large insurance buyers by diverting them with the tangential restaurant operation? If the client's financial statements are unaudited, the banker may suggest an independent audit to verify the historical income statement and balance sheet results. Many a deal has been derailed when the seller's results failed the *buyer's final audit*. If the seller has a problem that appears open-ended to the casual observer, such as an environmental cleanup or a continuing lawsuit, the banker may recommend solving the problem in advance. Why force potential buyers to spend time on extraneous matters, when they need to hone in on the target's core business?

Confirming a Valuation Range

The investment banker's due diligence permits a refinement of its preliminary valuation. The banker also gains a further opportunity to polish its "sales pitch" explaining why the property is worth $10\times$ EBIT, $3\times$ book value, and so forth.

Writing the Information Memorandum

Public companies issue annual reports and financing prospectuses that provide detailed business and financial summaries publicly. Private businesses don't publish these documents. In the sale of a privately owned company, the information memorandum describing the business is the prospective buyer's first real introduction to the company. The memorandum must be written with care, outlining the basic facts while emphasizing the target's positive attributes. Any financial projections should err on the side of optimism, without succumbing to wildly exaggerated claims of future performance.

THE BUYER LIST

Assuming the information memorandum is near completion, the seller and its financial adviser agree on a list of prospective buyers to contact. The length and composition of this list is dependent on many different factors. In my experience, it usually breaks down into 50 to 100 contacts. Exhibit 22-2 illustrates a buyer list for a U.S. pillow manufacturer.

Each contact has to have the financial wherewithal to acquire the target. Providing that this requirement is met, the seller and its adviser winnow out companies that are unsuitable to the owner. At times, these

EXHIBIT 22-2   Sample prospective buyer list for a pillow manufacturer

Buyer Categories	Description
Market Share Extenders 1	Other U.S. pillow manufacturers.
Market Share Extenders 2	Foreign pillow manufacturers.
Product Line Extenders	Producers of related soft lines such as blankets, sheets, curtains, and towels.
Strategic Buyers 1	Producers of related hard lines, such as furniture and home accessories.
Strategic Buyers 2	Any conglomerate business interested in diversifying into home furnishings.
LBO Firms	Firms that consider almost any profitable manufacturer.
Other Financial Buyers	Specialized investment firms with a reason for entering the industry.

rejects are direct competitors that the owner believes are not real buyers. At other times, eliminations result from unsavory reputations, window shopping inclinations, or bottom fishing tendencies. The end result depends on the seller's individual situation. Some companies, such as high-tech firms, don't appeal to LBO investors, so there's no point in contacting the LBO community. Others offer a unique product or service that doesn't have direct competition, so the search focuses on Strategic Buyers and Product Line Extenders.

APPROACH TACTICS

After the adviser draws up the list, it considers the various ways to approach the market, ranging from calling a handful of likely buyers to contacting every name on the list. The various tactics have nicknames and are summarized in Exhibit 22-3.

With the sales tactic established and the prospect list set, the seller's agent calls a senior executive at each of the would-be buyers. Following a brief description of the seller, the intermediary asks if the executive's company has an interest in pursuing the matter. If the answer is yes, the executive receives an information memorandum, along with a confidentiality letter requiring an authorized signatory.

Confidentiality, Operational, and Personnel Issues

If the seller is a publicly traded company, the start of an auction is a reportable event under SEC regulations and employees, suppliers, and customers learn right away of the company's intentions. If the seller is privately owned, or a small division of a publicly held business, it doesn't publicize the beginning of a sale process. Nevertheless, rumors inevitably reach the rank and file, building anxiety. Private company owners maintain secrecy as long as practicable, disguising due diligence visits as supplier calls, for example. The top executives at the public corporation inform the affected division managers beforehand, asking their cooperation during the division's sale and motivating them with "stay bonuses" that aren't paid unless they remain until closing. Such division managers cope with the worries of the larger employee

EXHIBIT 22-3 Primary marketing tactics

Description	Comments
"Rifle Shot"	
The banker contacts 3 to 5 very likely acquirers, which have independently contacted the target earlier. Usually, these companies are Market Share/Product Line Extenders.	Sellers find it difficult to obtain top dollar via the rifle shot route. There isn't enough competition, although this method is the best for preserving secrecy.
"Shotgun" Approach	
The banker contacts 100–150 names, encompassing any business that might have a remote interest in the client.	This approach is difficult to administer smoothly. It is most appropriate for sizable targets (+$50 million) with solid operating histories because they have wide appeal. It is almost mandatory for publicly traded companies.
Full-Blown Auction	
This is a derivative of the Shotgun Approach. The added twist is that potential buyers meet a strict deadline for responding with an offer, including their comments on the prepackaged legal documentation.	This technique instills speed and tension into the process, but many large corporations refuse to participate in full-blown auctions. Thus, the client loses potential buyers with the aggressive approach. Full-blown auctions work best with extremely attractive companies that are sure to attract multiple bidders.
Modified Auction	
The financial adviser groups would-be buyers according to their perceived level of interest (e.g., Very High, High, Medium, and Low). Each group contains 30 to 40 names. Beginning with the Very High category, the banker contacts each group sequentially, stopping when three or four real bidders surface. The banker then sets a definite deadline for negotiating final deal terms.	The modified auction is appropriate for most transactions. It doesn't turn off buyers and it keeps the process manageable by limiting the number of interested parties at any one time.

group and assure customers to adopt a "wait and see" attitude regarding the possibility of new owners. If a few months pass without a transaction, the continued uncertainty affects operations, so many investment bankers advise sellers to complete the process within six months.

Maintaining confidentiality with direct competitors is important. While competitors may know a lot of the material in the seller's offering memorandum, they present obvious problems in the due diligence investigation. Some bankers suggest a signed letter of intent before recommending that their clients open their books to a competitor.

Due Diligence Visits

The intermediary coordinates the buyers' visits to the seller and manages the buyers' data requests. Faced with a buyer visit, a smart seller begins the on-site meeting with a formal presentation that complements the information memorandum. For each buyer, the seller then arranges meetings with senior executives in key functional areas such as finance, marketing, and operations. To assist the buyer's analysis, the seller's operational data are readily available in a recognizable form. Under the full-blown auction format, this information occupies a separate room equipped with phones, fax machines, and copiers for the prospective buyers' convenience.

COMING UP WITH A BID

In a typical modified auction, sending out information memoranda, conducting due diligence trips, and fulfilling information requests requires a minimum of two to three months. Alternative tactics have different durations, with the full-blown auction covering the shortest period, perhaps as short as 45 to 60 days. In the face of a hostile takeover offer of a publicly traded company, the intermediary can insist on answers in 30 days or less.

The adviser's primary challenge during this time is obtaining a bankable bid that falls within the expected valuation range. Note the adjective "bankable" before the word "bid." Offers from prospective acquirers that can't raise the purchase money aren't worth much. Once the banker has the first bankable bid in hand, he is free to pressure the remaining would-be acquirers to accelerate their respective evaluations. Recognizing the likelihood of its offer being shopped, the initial bidder sets a time limit for acceptance so as to upset the seller's shopping plans. Understandably, the adviser stalls negotiations on the first proposal to permit more time for recruiting competing offers. In an ideal situation, two or three bidders operate on parallel tracks and the banker realizes the opportunity to pit one prospective buyer against another, thus achieving a good price.

In the common situation where the bid(s) come in lower than expected, the seller can choose to (1) expand the contact list to find a higher bidder, (2) try and negotiate the existing bids higher, or (3) withdraw the target business from the market. Most choose alternative 1. This is a wise course of action if the contact group has been limited to 100 calls or less. If the seller has no luck after 100+ calls, it needs to consider lowering its price expectations or withdrawing the deal. Alternative 2 works well when the bids are only 10% to 20% below the valuation range, since bidders typically leave 10% to 15% of "room" in their offers. The intermediary's experience is particularly useful in making these decisions correctly.

At times, a buyer asks the seller to take the buyer's securities in lieu of cash. The value of such securities, particularly common shares, is intertwined with the buyer's future results and the stock market's fluctuations. Complicating the decision is the buyer's typical request that the securities be held for a minimum period, such as two to three years. This restriction limits the downward pressure on the buyer's stock, but it places market risk on the seller. Because few corporate shareholdings can be effectively hedged against price declines, the seller must then balance the risks and rewards of owning the buyer's securities for an extended period.

FINAL DUE DILIGENCE AND LEGAL DOCUMENTATION

As noted in Chapter 17, the negotiating leverage in a transaction shifts from seller to buyer after the letter of intent (LOI) is signed. This change usually results in the buyer gaining small reductions in the purchase price as its due diligence process unfolds. Most sellers exhaust the positive attributes of their businesses during the solicitation phase, so the buyer is left ferreting out whatever minor negatives arise from its investigations. Prices reductions of 3% to 5% are not unusual.

During the documentation drafting, the buyer tries to limit its exposure to possible problems that weren't discovered or anticipated through the due diligence process. While the unknown problem may never crop up, the buyer likes to be protected if, and when, the problem arises. Unless the target itself is a publicly traded company, the owners of the seller usually provide some comfort to the buyer through an escrow account or warranty. The latter gives the buyer a strong legal recourse against the owners in certain instances. Negotiations in these areas focus on arcane points of law, and a rational seller acts in partnership with its practitioner team—financial adviser, counsel, and accountant—before reaching an agreement.

Finally, to further protect its interests going forward, the buyer may demand that the owners promise not to participate in the seller's business for a fixed period, usually three to five years. Large corporations divesting a division don't mind entering into noncompete arrangements. Entrepreneurs and family business owners reluctantly sign these provisions.

SUMMARY

A seller's main concern is maximizing price. Usually the objective is best achieved through a modified auction conducted by an experienced intermediary.

23 FINAL THOUGHTS ON DOING DEALS

Over the past 20 years, merger and acquisition activity has accelerated at a rapid pace. Large and small companies alike have recognized the importance of "buying" versus "building" in the attainment of corporate growth objectives. As operating firms have built up their businesses through acquisitions, they have competed increasingly with an expanding number of professional financial buyers that have brought substantial innovation to the merger field. Leveraged buyouts, consolidation transactions and vulture deals have risen to positions of prominence and their promoters have obtained access to tens of billions of investment dollars. From this changing environment has evolved a virtual army of intermediaries, lawyers, accountants, and consultants, all available to service the ever larger group of corporate buyers and sellers.

This book has presented a succinct guide to mergers and acquisitions. It has followed the acquisition process sequentially and offered a balanced assessment of the risks and rewards. For the average executive who has read the book, I hope it is now clear that the business of mergers and acquisitions is not "rocket science." An intelligent businessperson can easily discern the fundamental principles underlying a deal, given sufficient time to conduct a proper analysis.

The basic thrust behind most acquisitions is boosting the acquirer's shareholder value, but there are no guarantees that a specific transaction will make a positive contribution. Like any other corporate investment, an acquisition's potential benefits are tempered by its possible problems. Many transactions have failed while others have been fantastically successful. So who is to decide? The very popularity of acquisitions—thousands are completed every year—indicates that the M&A business is here to stay.

This book doesn't give acquirers a magic formula for success, but it demonstrates that sensible strategies can produce substantial rewards and keep risks at a tolerable level for each of the five categories of buyers:

1. Window Shopper.
2. Bottom Fisher.
3. Market Share/Product Line Extender.
4. Strategic Buyer.
5. Leveraged Buyout.

The key to success is a disciplined purchase plan.

In constructing this plan, the prospective acquirer's key managers and stockholders make a self-assessment by answering the following questions:

- Which buyer category is appropriate for us?
- Can we commit executive time for a long search?
- What is the our tolerance for risk?
- How much can we afford?

The responses to these questions form the foundation of the would-be acquirer's strategy for reviewing investment opportunities. Before putting this strategy to work, however, the potential buyer needs to complete the preparations for its plan. Such tasks include:

- Assigning an executive to be in charge of the acquisition search.
- Completing target industry research to cover in-house knowledge gaps.
- Understanding target industry valuations.

- Establishing the buyer's Deal Killer criteria to speed the decision process.
- Deciding on the aggressiveness of its proactive tactics.

There is no substitute for this amount of preparation, coupled with a disciplined approach. The M&A market is a perilous place filled with unrealistic sellers, rosy projections, and thick-skinned practitioners. The principle of caveat emptor reigns supreme and the prospective buyer must do its homework in order to prosper.

Overpayment remains the buyer's number one risk. Comparable transactions provide a guide to value but each sale candidate is unique. Furthermore, every deal takes place under conditions unique to the market, the buyer, and the seller at the time of negotiations. To guard against paying too much, a careful buyer runs a series of pro forma combined financial projections that show both the *upside* and the *downside* of any deal. Growth of future earnings per share is an important yardstick. The in-house development executive then consults with operating personnel who provide a "reality check" on this data, which is subsequently confirmed by a thorough due diligence process. Aware of the psychological elements embedded in stock prices, the disciplined buyer withdraws from expensive auctions rather than compromise on its rationally crafted synergy and price expectations.

Smart acquirers know what they don't know, and they aren't shy about hiring expert advisers. If they need to learn more about target industry valuations after finishing their research, they retain a financial adviser experienced in that industry. If a deal has a thorny environmental issue, they employ the proper consultant. Forming the right team is essential to closing deals successfully. Many companies can't afford to maintain this kind of talent in-house so they contract for it on the outside.

This book has taken a hard look at mergers and acquisitions. It's an exciting field that attracts some of the brightest minds in business, and it combines vision, glamour, and big money. Its scope is exceptionally broad, encompassing almost every industry and manner of company. This wide playing field results in substantial profit opportunities for participants, who can either wait for deals to show themselves or make the first move without an invitation. Initiative and creativity are rewarded handsomely in this business, and if a buyer's persistent search program doesn't pay off, its strategy can be easily shifted to respond to market constraints. If the market is still uncooperative, the buyer can innovate, perhaps by creating a national firm through consolidating dozens of small companies in the same industry. The main problem with the M&A business is that it takes a lot of hard work. For each purchase, dozens of candidates have to be run through the painstaking due diligence process. Another problem with acquisitions, as many investors have discovered, is that no deal comes with a profit guarantee. In fact, poor investment returns are commonplace. On balance, however, the rewards outweigh the risks, particularly if the buyer follows the disciplined approach outlined in this book.

Buying remains an attractive alternative to building, and the modern corporation stays alert for the next deal. Firms that ignore this message are reminded of an obvious risk: They may *be* the next deal. One investment banker's comment summarizes the situation clearly: "There are two kinds of companies: *clients* and *targets.*" The facts bear out the implications of this remark. Of the companies appearing on the original Fortune 500 list in 1955, only 116 are operating independently today. Most have been merged out of existence. Thus, this book closes with a piece of advice. If you don't want your company to be a takeover target, plan its growth strategy well. Include potential acquisitions as part of the tactical mix, and keep this book in a convenient place—desk, office, or home. You never know when you may need it.

INDEX